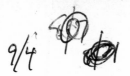

9/4

SKOKIE PUBLIC LIBRARY

W9-CFZ-781

The Billy Goat Curse

JUN   2009

ALSO BY GIL BOGEN
AND FROM MCFARLAND

Johnny Kling: A Baseball Biography (2006)

Tinker, Evers, and Chance: A Triple Biography (2003)

The Billy Goat Curse

Losing and Superstition in Cubs Baseball Since World War II

GIL BOGEN

Foreword by Ernie Banks

McFarland & Company, Inc., Publishers
Jefferson, North Carolina, and London

SKOKIE PUBLIC LIBRARY

LIBRARY OF CONGRESS ONLINE CATALOG

Bogen, Gil, 1925–
    The billy goat curse : losing and superstition in Cubs baseball
since World War II / Gil Bogen ; foreword by Ernie Banks.
        p.   cm.
    Includes bibliographical references and index.

    ISBN 978-0-7864-3354-4
    softcover : 50# alkaline paper ∞

    1. Chicago Cubs (Baseball team)—History.   2. Baseball—
Illinois—Chicago—History.   3. Superstition—Illinois—Chicago.
GV875.C6B64   2009
796.357'640977311—dc22   2008049010

British Library cataloguing data are available

©2009 Gil Bogen. All rights reserved

*No part of this book may be reproduced or transmitted in any form
or by any means, electronic or mechanical, including photocopying
or recording, or by any information storage and retrieval system,
without permission in writing from the publisher.*

Cover image ©2008 Shutterstock

Manufactured in the United States of America

McFarland & Company, Inc., Publishers
  Box 611, Jefferson, North Carolina 28640
  www.mcfarlandpub.com

To the fans who have remained loyal to the Chicago Cubs
for well over 60 years in spite of disappointment,
and who still voice the familiar mantra:
"Wait till next year."

Acknowledgments

It was an honor and privilege to interview Andy Pafko and Lenny Murello, two former Cubs who played at Wrigley Field on October 6, 1945, as the Cubs battled it out with Detroit in the World Series, the year the Curse of the Goat was thrust upon them. Their views on the curse are greatly appreciated.

A huge debt of gratitude is owed to Bill Cliff of the Harold Washington Library in Chicago. He helped me find microfilm for old issues of the *Chicago Tribune*, from which a great deal of information was obtained. Thanks for your invaluable assistance.

A very special thank you to Randall Weissman, deputy managing director of the *Chicago Tribune*. He gave permission to publish information that Bill Cliff helped me find, information still under copyright.

Another special thank you to Jack Heffron, editorial director for Emmis Books. For a token fee, he gave me permission to use quotes and information from the *Cubs Journal*, a book published by Emmis.

I want to tip my hat to a wonderful group of Cub fans in Wrigleyville who gave me their views about the Curse of the Goat: Kathie Clifford, Karen Kasparaitis, Brian Gallivan, Julie Jensen, Ryan Harpold, Kasey Harpold, John Willhite, Mike Solbing and Ryan Rushing.

Thank you, thank you, thank you to Rick Kogan, a Chicago newspaperman who has written extensively about the Chicago Cubs. In regard to one of his latest books, *A Chicago Tavern: A Goat, a Curse, and the American Dream*, his comment to me was, "you can use anything of mine with proper credit." I will remember his generosity with fondness.

A very special thank you to Bob and Judy Rosencranz, two lifelong friends living in Highland Park. They saved and gave me the *Chicago Tribune* sports pages for 2007, allowing me to obtain information for the Conclusion of the book.

Acknowledgments

I am deeply indebted to Daniel Socek, a Ph.D. in computer science, and his wife, Sandy. They came to my aid when I had a major problem with my computer, and rescued me. Words alone cannot express my gratitude for what they did.

I am also deeply indebted to my son, Dr. Steve Bogen, and my grandson, Michael Bogen. They were always there with answers to questions about the computer.

A hearty thanks to a young lady, Bukala (Buki), an employee at the Old Orchard Hampton Inn in Skokie. She spoke freely about curses and the breaking of a curse from her own personal experience in Nigeria.

I must give Ali Adabieh, a sales and leasing consultant at JM Lexus in Margate, Florida, and a die-hard Cubs fan, a hearty pat on the back for introducing a new and novel way of thinking about the Curse. Thanks much, Ali.

A thank you also goes out to Tim Adams, manager of a tavern, and to Marcia Kamstock, a tavern patron. Both of them reviewed the practical jokes that William Sianis played on his customers, and both of them were candid in expressing opinions about the propriety of such jokes.

From the depths of my soul, I want to thank two wonderful men of the cloth who gave freely of their time and wisdom regarding the use of exorcism to break the Curse at Wrigley Field, Father Michael at St. Mark's Church in Boynton Beach, Florida, and the Rev. Herman Jayachandra, a pastor of St. Martin de Porres, a parish in Boulder, Colorado. Father Herman is also an exorcist from India. Gentlemen, again I thank you.

I am also indebted to Teresa Casselman, an authority on goats who owns the Six Point Goat Farm in Bloomington, Illinois. She gave me a real education on goats, and her information added flavor to this book.

What can I say about my son Mark and my daughter-in-law Kathleen, who gave me two rooms of working space in their home when they moved from Las Vegas to Florida? Imagine! Two rooms that provided the space, the serenity and the silence needed to dwell upon the chapters in this book. Mark and Kathleen, thank you. I want you to know I will always love you.

An expression of love also goes out to my daughters Lynn and Marla, who were always there to rejuvenate my spirit when at times it needed a lift.

And most of all, I will always be eternally grateful to Eunice Insel for the endless hours she devoted to the editing of this book.

I am and always will be indebted to all of you.

Table of Contents

Contents

Foreword

by Ernie Banks

I welcomed the opportunity to do the foreword for this book that talks about the Curse of the Goat and about breaking it.

The book goes into the 1969 season when it looked as if we were finally going to win the pennant and maybe go on to win the World Series. We had Leo Durocher, Glenn Beckert, Don Kessinger, Ron Santo, Billy Williams, Randy Hundley, Fergie, Bill Hands, Ken Holtzman and other great players. We had a great team. We had talent! I always wanted to help the Cubs make it to the top. My motto was: "The Cubs Will Shine In '69."

But in early September, the Mets drew close, then passed us and took the flag. Many fans blamed it on the Curse of the Goat. Sportswriters wrote about it. We all felt bad. And although my playing days ended in 1971, talk about the Curse continued.

This book reminds us all about those years when it looked as if the Cubs would surely capture the flag, only to lose it at the very end by an unlucky break. Each time fans blamed it on the Curse.

I remember 1994 when Tom Trebelhorn desperately wanted to break the Curse. The team had lost the first 12 games at Wrigley, and I was asked to walk around the field with Sam Sianis, his goat, and a robed group of chanting monks in order to break the curse. Well, we won the game that day, 5–2, and it felt good.

It would have felt so much better if we could have taken the flag that year. This book points out that a priest had offered to come to Wrigley to perform an exorcism in 1994, and for whatever reason, the exorcism never came about.

Foreword by Ernie Banks

Anyhow, I believe the Curse of the Goat will be broken. And I predict the Cubs will be great in 2009. All the way to the World Series.

—⁓—

Hall of Famer Ernie Banks spent his entire Major League career (1953–1971) as a Chicago Cub.

Introduction

The Chicago Cubs have been referred to as "Lovable Losers."[1] It's easy to see why. The stretch of postseason futility is by now familiar to even casual fans; the last pennant was won in 1945, the last Series title in 1908. But it hasn't always been this way. In fact, at its inception, the Chicago National League ball club was a power in the world of baseball.

In 1871, entrepreneurs, intent on making money, organized the National Association of Professional Baseball Players of America. The White Stockings, as the Cubs were then known, represented Chicago. The Association was not well organized. Teams came and went at an alarming rate, sometimes throwing the league standings into disorder; players jumped contracts with near-impunity; and game-fixing, or at least the suspicion of it, was widespread. By 1876, William Hulbert, president of the White Stockings, was fed up with the unrelenting problems, and with the East Coast sympathies of the Association's leadership.

Using his influence, Hulbert formed the eight-club National League. The White Stockings represented Chicago and the league had a regular schedule. In 1876, new league's first year, the White Stockings went on to win the championship with a 52–14 record.

It was a great team. They had pitcher Al Spalding, who won forty-seven games in that first year. They also had Ross Barnes, who had a sizzling .404 average. But best of all, they had Adrian "Cap" Anson, who became player-manager in 1879. His batting average of .343 the first season, batting averages of .350 or higher four times after that, and his three league batting championships made him a superstar.

Although the team had dropped down in the standings in 1877, '78 and '79, the White Stockings, with Anson leading the way, bounded back with a fury in 1880 and dominated the National League, winning 67 of 84 games and capturing the NL pennant by 15 games. The White Stockings repeated this performance the following year with a 56–28 record, winning comfortably by nine games. And in 1882, those remarkable players became the first team to win three straight National League Championships with a record of 55–29, holding off the Providence Grays by four games.

Anson's feats as a skipper were as impressive as his accomplishments as a player, as he led the White Stockings in 1885 to their fifth NL pennant in the 10-year history of the National League, holding off the New York Giants by two games with an 87–25 record. The team went on to play in an early version of the World Series against the rival American Association's St. Louis Brown Stockings; the two teams splitting six games and tying another.[2]

The Chicago White Stockings were near the top of the standings in most seasons. In 1888-89, the team, under the presidency of Al Spalding, became one of two clubs to go on a world tour. Morale amongst the players must have been extraordinary. When the players arrived in towns, they rode in parades, attended parties and were introduced to local officials and dignitaries. But the 1890 establishment of the Players' League weakened the team. And by the early 1890s some of their top players were older and the competition was getting tougher. This resulted in the team having a poor record in 1894. It was then that they changed their name to "Colts."

Three years later, Anson, who was regarded as the greatest player of the nineteenth century, was fired at age 45. Without "Cap" to guide them, the team was dubbed the "Orphans" by Chicago papers.[3]

The "Orphans" started the new century on the wrong foot, finishing fifth with a 65–75 record. After the rival American League rose to major-league status in 1901, and players jumped leagues, further decimating the team, the Colts dropped to sixth place with a miserable 53–86 record.

The Colts began to acquire many young players and, the *Chicago Daily News* became the first known entity to call the team "the Cubs."[4] With the team playing at the West Side Grounds, a number of sportswriters began referring to the team as the Cubs.

In 1902, Frank Selee was brought aboard as the new manager. He had been a long-time skipper of the Boston Braves who had won five pennants in the 1890s while finishing only once below .500. He knew talent.

He also had a keen sense of knowing what position a player should play and why. To play for Selee, a player had to be not only aggressive and high spirited, but he had to be bold and smart as well.[5]

So in 1903, as had happened in the past, the young team began to show promise as they were in the race all season before finishing eight games out of first, finishing third with a record of 82–56.

In 1904, the team continued to improve, finishing second with a record of 93–60. Selee was satisfied with the results; satisfied with his double-play combination as the team scrambled, schemed, slid, clawed and connived their way to victory; and satisfied with his catcher who knew the strengths and weaknesses of every player on every team and brought out the best in every pitcher on his own team.

In 1905, Selee was forced to quit the game because of tuberculosis, but his husky first baseman Frank Chance took over. Between then and 1945, the Cubs, like every other team, had their ups and downs. When it looked as if 1945 would be a fantastic year for the Chicago team, an unusual incident occurred.

With Charlie Grimm at the helm in '45, fighting it out with St. Louis for the top spot, the Chicago Cubs beat the Pittsburgh Pirates 5–3 on September 30 in the final game of the season, thereby capturing the National League flag. Phil Cavarretta had led the way, his .355 average making him the first Cub to win the National League batting championship since 1912.

The team was hailed as favorites to win the 1945 World Series. Their season record was 96–56, compared to Detroit's 88–65.[6] On October 1, the Cubs boarded a train for Detroit to engage the Tigers at Briggs Stadium in baseball's classic showdown.

October 3 brought out 54,637 fans who watched the Cubs devastate the Tigers 9–0 in Game 1. The Cubs scored four runs in the first inning and Detroit's Hal Newhauser, the only 25-game winner in the majors, was routed in the third. The Cubs had turned loose a barrage of hitting power. Phil Cavarretta had three hits, including a homer, in four at bats. Andy Pafko collected two singles and a double, while Bill Nicholson slammed a triple. The team was out to convince everyone that they were going to be the 1945 World Champions, a feat the Cubs had not achieved since 1908.

On the following day, the Tigers evened the Series with a 4–1 win in Game 2. The Cubs led 1–0 before the Tigers scored four runs in the fifth, three of them on a homer by Hammerin' Hank Greenberg off Hank Wyse. But Claude Passeau took the mound on October 5 and stunned the Tigers with a 3–0 shutout, allowing just one hit. The series then moved to Wrigley Field.

The dawn of October 6 saw fans who had kept a vigil all night, waiting to buy the remaining 5,000 bleacher seats and 2,500 standing room admissions.[7] They knew the Cubs were leading 2 games to 1. They also knew that their team needed only to win two of the next four games to become World Champions.

William Sianis, a longtime Cubs fan and owner of the Billy Goat Inn, lived close to Wrigley Field. He bought two tickets to Game 4, one for himself and one for his goat. But Cubs owner Phil Wrigley refused to allow the goat into the park. When asked why, Sianis was told "the goat smells."[8]

Outraged, Sianis put a curse on the Cubs, saying they'd never again play in a World Series. This meant they'd never again win a pennant.[9]

The fortunes of the Chicago team immediately began to spiral downward as 49,923 fans watched Paul Trout beat the Cubs 4–1 in Game 4. His 5-hit pitching performance squared the Series at two games each.

Irving Vaughan, sportswriter for the *Chicago Tribune*, came out with an article on October 7. "The Tigers, who before the series generally were doped for the losers' role, and who at various times have looked the part 100 percent," he wrote, "now appear to have the upper hand in pitchers, the always important factor in a short series."[10]

And so it was. Detroit took Game 5 to move into a 3–2 Series lead, and called on Virgil Trucks to end the Series in six games. Chicago again called upon Claude Passeau, who was in control of his pitches until the sixth inning when Jimmy Outlaw's line drive split the nail of the third finger on his right hand. He could no longer pitch, and it looked as if the Tigers might take the game as they tied the score in the ninth. But the Cubs prevailed and won it 8–7 in twelve innings.

The Cubs' celebration was short-lived. On October 10, the Tigers captured the World Championship by winning the seventh and deciding game, routing the Cubs 9–3 before 41,590 fans at Wrigley Field.

Charlie Grimm had gambled by bringing Hank Borowy back as the starting pitcher, despite his five innings as a starter in Game 5 and a four-inning relief stint in Game 6 two days earlier. Borowy failed to retire a single batter as the Tigers scored five runs in the first inning. In his October 11 *Trib* article, "In the Wake of the News," Arch Ward wrote, "The Detroit Tigers may be one of the weakest clubs that ever has won a World Series, but they convinced 41,590 spectators at Wrigley Field yesterday they are the best team in 1945 baseball."

On October 12, Irving Vaughan's *Trib* article said, "Nobody will deny that the Tigers make up just about the weakest team the American league has entered in a series in many years. When you say weakness you mean fielding, running, throwing, hitting, etc., as a whole."

Nevertheless, the Tigers were the 1945 World Champions. And Cub fans had to be glum and downcast. All, that is, except one — William "Billy Goat" Sianis. After the Cubs lost the Series, he reportedly sent Wrigley a telegram saying, "Who smells now?"[11]

In the ensuing years, when it looked as if the Cubs were going to make it to the top, something unexpected happened, and the team did not prevail. As amazing as it may seem, many people blamed this on the Billy Goat Curse. You, the reader, will have an opportunity to meet the managers and the players, and read about the Cubs playing ball from 1905 through 1945 and beyond. You decide.

CHAPTER 1

The Glory Years

After Frank Chance took charge of the Cubs in 1905, he began to make his opinions known and never backed down from an argument. The team learned from the outset that their new skipper was a stern disciplinarian and a firm believer in fines whenever anything was done that was detrimental to the winning of a game. He ran the club with a clenched fist and came down hard on any player who gave less than 100 percent. "Play it my way or meet me after the game," was his motto.[1]

The team did not resent the way he chose to manage because they knew he was sincere. Some may not have liked him, but they respected him. He was pugnacious and he was the boss, and he insisted his players give the best that was in them.

In a game at the Polo Grounds, when Chance was playing first base against the Giants, he chased after a foul ball, crashed into the stands while making the catch and was knocked senseless. When the players dashed over and picked up his limp body, the ball was still tightly clutched in his hands.[2]

Throughout the month of August and early September 1905, the team fought for third in the standings. Spurred on by Chance's leadership, they won 40 of their last 63 games to finish a strong third at 92–61.

That winter, seeing that attendance had climbed to 509,900, Charles Webb Murphy jumped at the chance to purchase the Chicago National League franchise and the West Side Grounds. He appointed Chance as manager for the coming year.

1906

Although the nucleus for a great team was there when he took over, Chance had to fill some very big holes. He concocted a scheme that parted the Brooklyn club from Jimmy Sheckard, a star left fielder. Chance got Orval Overall, a fantastic pitcher, and Harry Steinfeldt, third baseman, from Cincinnati; negotiated to get Jack Taylor from St. Louis; and insisted on having another catcher to back up Kling, and dealt with Boston for Pat Moran. And it was Chance who sent a baseball scout on a hunt for a twenty-game-winning pitcher, finally signing Jack Pfiester for $2,500.[3]

In 1906, Frank Chance knew his team was ready. All they needed was a winning attitude. After a talk with his men, they knew that every opposing team was the enemy. And you don't fraternize with the enemy. Every time they played, they were at war, not at a "pink tea."[4] If a player shook the hand of a member of the opposing team, it would cost him $10. From now on, Cubs players either followed the rules or paid up.[5]

When the 1906 opening series with Cincinnati started, the opposing team knew that the Cubs would let nothing go unnoticed even if it meant throwing a few punches, and this established the tone for the remainder of the season.

On April 16, in a game with the Reds, Chicago was leading 2–0 going into the last half of the eighth. Carl Lundgren was pitching a great game. He looked like a sure winner. Suddenly, he disconnected, losing control. He hit a batter with a wide curve, issued a walk and then a few hits changed the tally. This electrified the shivering fans. It was a mad bunch of Cubbies that came in off the field, especially the manager and Evers whose sharp tongue bedeviled umpire Jim Johnstone nonstop. Things had not been going smoothly between Johnstone and the visitors earlier in the fray and now they reached a climax. Walking over toward the Chicago bench, Johnstone waved Chance and Evers off the field.

The final score of 3–2 was in favor of Cincinnati but further excitement was yet to come, as reported by the press:

> Manager Chance and shortstop Tinker, of the Chicago team, were beaten up somewhat in a fight with spectators shortly after the game today, and had not the police interfered, both players would have received a severe drubbing. During the game it was noted that several of the spectators seated in the pavilion opposite to first base were continu-

ally hurling insults at Tinker, Evers and Chance. The players answered them on numerous occasions but nothing serious was thought of it.

After the game however, these spectators found their way to the Chicago bus and proceeded to abuse Tinker in very vile terms. Tinker lost his temper, jumped from the bus and attacked one of the men. The man was too much for the shortstop however, and Tinker would have sustained a severe beating had not Manager Chance come to his rescue. Chance threw the man off Tinker. By that time, he himself was almost surrounded. He wielded his arms right and left and made his way to the bus. But by that time a great crowd had gathered. Luckily, the police got wind of the affair and three of them came running up. They soon put a stop to hostilities and the Chicago team was allowed to drive out of the grounds.

Tinker was to blame to a certain extent for losing his temper. The spectators were blamed in general for following a conversation that started as a jest. Chance was to be congratulated, as his intervention probably saved Tinker from serious injury. It also helped stop what appeared to be a general fight among the spectators and other players that came running. Luckily, the affair happened after the majority of the crowd had left the grounds, or it might have turned into something serious.[6]

This entire affair followed a series in which the Cubs had trounced the Reds in most of the games. Charles Murphy, owner of the Chicago team, hurried home and made no mention of the fisticuffs as he issued a press release to the *Chicago Daily News:* "Frank Chance says the team is getting better every minute. I really think we have a great club there. We would have won every game from Cincinnati if Seymour's hit had not become lost in the sun. Schulte is playing grand ball and he is the fastest young man I've seen in a long while. He stole two bases yesterday. I am going crazy over Steinfeldt at third. He is hitting and fielding fast. He is a big, rangy fellow to throw at and altogether helps out a lot."[7]

Charles Murphy had rushed home not just to issue a press release but also to arrange for the homecoming of the team on the following day. He wanted publicity for the Chicago club. He wanted the attendance at the West Side Grounds to keep going up. What better way to do it than to have the world see his team.

The opening day at the West Side Grounds found splendid weather, though a bit on the cool side. The ceremony attending the flag-raising was simple. The Cardinals and the Cubs marched around the field to the music of a brass band and then stopped long enough to pull up the flag at the clubhouse while the crowd cheered the pennant as it swung in the breeze.

It was nip and tuck for most of the game. The Cubs took a slight lead and tried to hold it as the Cardinals threatened. The *Chicago Daily News* told it best when on the following day it reported: "John Evers was the hero for the Cubs of yesterday's game. Frank Schulte was a close second to the second baseman, for he pulled off a fielding trick that brought the crowd to its feet and saved the day for the locals when he made a brilliant running catch of a hard line drive to right field by Wagner. Evers contributed two timely hits and helped put the score out of danger. The score was 3–1 in favor of the Cubs."

So it went. The Cubs were winning close ones. On April 27, it was the Cubs playing the Reds at the West Side Grounds. In their half of the eighth, when the Cubs tied the score, Sheckard singled to right. Schulte hit a little fly to left that Hinchman never saw because of the sun. The ball struck the ground a yard in front of him. There was a delay while Manager Hanlon searched their baggage for smoked glasses but none were found. A pass to Chance filled the bases with none out. Then Steinfeldt hit to Delahanty who forced Sheckard at the plate and a double play was in sight. But Livingstone threw wildly to first letting Schulte score. Chance rounded third and stopped halfway home. Barry, who had retrieved the ball, hesitated, wondering where to throw it. Suddenly, Chance made a dash for the plate and scored the tying run. The next two batters were retired.

After nine, ten and eleven the score was still tied. Seymour opened the twelfth with a clean hit. Delahanty fanned and the next two were retired easily. The end of the game came quickly. Schulte opened Chicago's half with a single but was forced on Chance's effort to bunt. Chance attempted to steal second and it looked as if he was out, but he knocked little Miller Huggins senseless, dislodging the ball from his glove before he could make the tag. Then Steinfeldt slammed a single, sending the manager home with the winning tally. Final score: 7–6.

The following day found the Cubs again playing the Reds, a duel between "Three Finger" Brown and Jake Weimer. For eight and a half innings both teams found the going slow because of a heavy shower that preceded the game. Neither team had found a way to score. It was getting late. Because of the delayed start there was danger of darkness bringing about a draw.

Five times, Chicago had been denied scores when hopes were high for a tally but the fans were still confidently rooting. They cheered Chance when he stepped to the plate to open Chicago's last half of the ninth. They stood and roared jubilantly when the manager lined one straight to left, his second hit off Weimer. The thunderous noise grew as Steinfeldt laid down a perfect sacrifice putting Chance in scoring position.

Then began a duel between Weimer and Tinker. Jake wouldn't give Joe anything he liked, and Joe wouldn't hit anything he didn't like. After a dozen fouls, Tinker finally walked. Evers started for the plate. Chance sent him back to substitute a right-handed batter, choosing Moran for the pinch hitter. Morgan rapped a hot one to Delahanty and a double play seemed certain to retire the side. Delahanty shot the ball to Huggins, forcing Tinker at second, but Tinker blocked the play, preventing a throw to first. Huggins protested and began dancing around Umpire Bill Klem, demanding an out on Moran at first base on the grounds of interference. Chance had rounded third and seeing the opening, dashed for the plate while Huggins was off guard. A yell from the Reds alerted the second baseman. Huggins's hurried heave to the plate went high, and Chance slid under it safely with the winning run.

In early June, Manager Chance and his men headed for New York for a series with John McGraw's 1905 World Champions. Chicago was leading the pack and extending their lead with every game.

After the second game of the series on June 6, the *Chicago Tribune* proudly announced, "Nationals Trim Champions 11 to 3." Chance's men couldn't stop hitting, as they collected 18 safeties off Dummy Taylor, driving the Giants back into third place.

The third game of the series was even more of a rout. After it was over the fans had every reason to be proud as they read the bold headline of the *Chicago Daily News*: "Chance's Men Get Awful Revenge." The *Daily News* reported: "Not content with the humiliation of the Giants on two previous days, Chicago's Nationals, remembering what McGraw did to them in Chicago, set out to annihilate the world champions today in the third game and succeeded. A score of 19–0: 11 runs in the first inning, 22 base hits and the scalps of McGraw's two crack pitchers, Mathewson and McGinnity, was the harvest for the Cubs."

Whitewashed and disgraced again, the World Champions were hooted and jeered by their fans, who for three years had hooted and jeered all visiting teams alike at the Polo Grounds. They never dreamed of seeing McGraw at the head of such a dilapidated and lifeless band as the Giants seemed that day. At least half of the 8000 spectators left long before the farce ended. Chance's men had to allow themselves to be put out on the bases after getting hits in order to get the game over.

In 1906, the Cubs under Frank Chance had put together a juggernaut that even McGraw's once mighty New Yorkers could not stop. The lean and hungry team rang up a record 116 wins, against 36 losses, for a still unsurpassed .763 winning percentage, leaving the Giants 20 games behind in second place. Having led his team to such heights, Chance was named player-manager of the year and became known as the "Peerless Leader."

By comparison, the best the Tigers could do with Ty Cobb and Sam Crawford in 1909 was 96–54 for a winning percentage of .645. The best the mighty Yankees could do with Ruth and Gehrig in 1927 was 110–44 for .714. In 1939 with Red Rolfe, Charlie Keller and Joe DiMaggio, the Yankees were 106–45 for a .702 percentage and in 1998 the Yanks, playing 162 games, went 114–48 for a .704 percentage. The 2001 Seattle Mariners tied the Cubs' 116 wins but they lost 46 games, for a winning percentage of .716, not even close to the Cubs' .763.

But that great team was about to be tested by the "Hitless Wonders"— the name given to the Chicago White Sox that year because they were seen as a fluke winner of the American League pennant with a flimsy team batting average of .230.

In contrast to the mighty Cubs, the Sox were a so-so team that should never have won a pennant. For most of the season they seemed doomed to stay in the second division but with a sudden run of superb pitching they won 19 consecutive games in August and rose to the top. The national debate favored the Cubs to win the World Series.

It wasn't to be. The Sox exploded. They astonished the baseball world by cranking up their hitting while the Cubs' pitching staff slumped. Those marvelous pitchers who had recorded an incredible staff ERA of 1.76 during the regular season allowed the Sox 22 runs in six games, thereby losing a world championship. The Cubs themselves scored just two runs on nine hits in four games.

1907

When the season started in 1907, Frank Chance had already reminded his players that he expected them to be tough and smart. That was the recipe for winning ball games. As the season moved forward, the Cubs were hard to beat because Chance insisted that the team talk baseball at all times: new strategies, new plays, anything that would help win games. They did this on the bus, at breakfast, in the clubhouse, everywhere. When Joe Tinker came to Chance and talked about his difficulty in handling a ball on a wet and muddy field, they devised a new play. It was just too great a risk for Joe to throw the ball straight across the diamond. "Bounce the ball to me," Chance said. "I'll throw it so it will hit about ten feet in front of first base and you can take it on the bounce," Tinker replied.[8]

During one of their games, when there was enough rain to make the ball wet and slippery, they tried it, and it turned out to be a perfect play. The first baseman and the shortstop had to be in perfect accord. It was up to both players to know when the play was going to be made. The signals were very subtle.

Chance became quite proficient with a ball thrown into the dirt. He would either step back with one foot on the sack and take the throw waist high, or step forward and snatch it out of the dirt. It was great defense.

On offense, Chance and his players talked about getting that one run to win a ball game. That meant getting a man on base. Once on base he had to be moved along either by a hit, a steal or a sacrifice. The Cubs became masters in using the bunt. Instead of allowing the ball to hit the bat and drop in front of the plate, the ball was pushed. It became a slow roller, giving the batter more time to get on base. Once on base, it was commonplace to steal.

The season was going well. The team had become accustomed to talking strategy and they became adept in devising new plays to defeat the enemy.[9] That was what Chance expected from his men. He didn't demand perfection. He did demand that a player try. As long as a player gave it his best shot, he was in. To do otherwise meant goodbye.

With Chance setting the example, the season ended with Chicago holding a 107–45 record, a .704 winning percentage, 17 games ahead of Pittsburgh.

Chance did not forget the World Series of the previous year when the "Hitless Wonders" defeated his team. He was not going to allow it to happen again. With time to spare before squaring off with Detroit, Chance allowed himself to be interviewed by a *Chicago Daily News* reporter. On the following day, Chicago fans read: "Tomorrow is an open date for the champions, no game is scheduled. However, Manager Chance will not permit his players to spend it in idleness. He plans two sessions of hard practice at the West Side Grounds, one in the morning and another in the afternoon. This work will be given to keep the men keyed up to the highest pitch for the coming struggle in the World Series."[10]

The 1907 World Series between Chicago and Detroit got underway on October 8 and the game ended in a 3–3 tie, called because of darkness. But the Cubs then ran away with the Series. Jack Pfiester made short shrift of Detroit, 3–1 in Game 2. The Tigers' attempt to switch to a new catcher, Freddie Payne, didn't help. He couldn't stop the Cubs from stealing five bases during the victory.

Fans whooped it up one day later as they watched their team maul Detroit 5–1. Two scratchy hits were all the Tigers got off Reulbach in five innings. And when the Detroit squad started what seemed to be a rally in the sixth, the Cubs broke it all up with a fast double play. The Series now moved to Detroit.

Critics pointed out that the Cubs were not better hitters. They pointed to the fleetness of the team in stealing bases. They pointed to the daring, when with two men on base, Chance signaled for a double steal. That's why they were winning ball games.

The "Peerless Leader" did not like the critics' point of view. On October 11, the *Chicago Daily News* carried a story titled, "Cubs Quit Base Stealing Under Chance's Orders to Prove Hitting Superiority." It went on to say, "In order to convince baseball critics, he has told his club to abandon efforts to steal bases and concentrate its energy with the stick."

The team followed his order and beat the Tigers easier than before, 6–1. Chance knew that the way his team was playing, he'd win four straight with "Three Finger" Brown at the helm on the following day. His expectation was correct as the Cubs took the last game of the series, 2–0. Frank Chance had his first World Series victory.

Opinions of the best-informed baseball experts were that the Chicago National League team stood alone above every other organization the baseball world had ever known. Yet, they didn't know why.

It was several ingredients that Chance had instilled into the team. The first was an attitude: team harmony. This meant that even if players hated one another, they loved the Cubs. Although they wouldn't fight for each other, they'd do anything for the team. The entire team felt this way and it was one of the reasons for the Cubs' success.[11]

Another reason for the Cubs' success was the almost mystical way the infield played together. It was as if they could read each other's mind by the mere shrug of a shoulder, turn of a head or subtle look. Whatever the situation, they seemed instinctively to know where to move and *how* to move to get opposing players out. They did it with style and class, without a moment of hesitation. It was this infield that made the club what it was.[12]

During the 1907 World Series, Ty Cobb took a lead off second base. Kling, one of the first Jewish players in the majors, was catching. Tinker said to Cobb, "Don't get too far away from that bag or the Jew will nip you off." With that, he gave Evers a signal to take the throw. Tinker knew that Kling had also received the message. As Cobb turned to sneer at Tinker, Evers rushed to cover, took the throw and tagged Cobb out before he could get back to the bag. This one play helped to win the game and the Series.[13]

A third reason for Chicago's success, was the excellent pitching staff Selee and Chance had put together, in addition to the one catcher, Johnny Kling, who could bring out the best in all of them.

In addition, Kling knew the tricks and habits of every batter, knew their weaknesses and strengths, knew which men would steal and on what ball. He had a keen, analytical mind that, having made an observation, knew exactly what to do to get a batter out. When Boston brought a young outfielder to Chicago, with a reputation for being able to hit, Kling and Brown watched him closely during batting practice. "He'll fish," remarked Brown. "Anything low — in or outside," whispered Kling.

During the game, Brown pitched low curves outside the plate and low fastballs inside, and the new man fished, swung at balls he could not reach. Brown, when asked to explain how he knew this, said: "He showed nervousness and pulled his left foot. I knew he would swing at anything that broke quickly."

"He held his hands with the wrists turned too high," added Kling, "and fully an inch too far apart to get a good swing at a low ball inside."[14]

Kling's powers of observation and judgment were superb. He looked closely every time a batter came to the plate — the kind of bat he carried, the position of his feet and body, and how he gripped the bat. All of this told him of the batter's intentions and how to prevent him from tearing into a pitch. He was also a master at working umpires on balls and strikes and winning their friendship — no small matter when it came to getting close calls that could win ballgames. Kling's method was to be friendly with all umpires, siding with them, telling them they were right and frequently whispering to them to be on guard for a certain pitch that was coming.

An intricate part of Kling's work, and most important for the Cubs' success, was throwing to catch runners, not only when they were stealing, but also while they were taking a lead off a base. The number of runners caught didn't matter as much as the throwing, which had the effect of keeping runners close to their bases and preventing them from trying to steal.[15]

Kling called the shots for such famous pitchers as "Three Finger" Brown, Big Ed Reulbach, Orval Overall and left-handed Jack Pfiester. At one time or another all were 20-game winners, and there was no doubt about Kling's role in the success that those record-setting pitchers achieved on the mound.

Brown once said, "I'm not ashamed to admit that I was just a so-so pitcher before I teamed up with Kling. A pitcher can always tell you how good a catcher is, and take my word, Johnny Kling was the best."[16] Cubs pitcher Ed Reulbach called Kling one of the greatest catchers to ever wear a mask. And Brown, Reulbach, Overall and Pfiester all gave Kling much of the credit for their success.[17]

Chance knew it. He knew his pitchers and catcher would be around for the 1908 season. With them and his other men he knew he had a winning combination. Chance knew he could win it all over again.

1908

And so they did. But it took a remarkable turn of fate in what became perhaps the most controversial game ever played.[18]

The Cubs opened the season defeating the Reds in Cincinnati 6–5, Heine Zimmerman winning the game with a pinch single in the ninth, driving in Johnny Evers with the winning run. It was a three-team race and by September 22, with the Cubs winning a doubleheader against the Giants, they were only six percentage points behind the Giants. New York had a record of 87–50, the Cubs 90–53, and the Pirates were 88–54, 1½ games behind.

On September 23, the race was close. In the final game of a Giants-Cubs series, Jack Pfiester started for the Cubs against Christy Mathewson. A crowd of 20,000 filed in, knowing the importance of the game. It became a pitching duel between Mathewson and Pfiester, a scoreless tie going into the fifth. Joe Tinker, facing his favorite pitcher, hit an inside-the-park homer, taking advantage of the long center-field power alleys at the Polo Grounds to leg out his sixth homer of the year, tops on the team.

With one man on in the last of the sixth, Turkey Mike Donlin singled over Evers's head to tie the score 1–1. Three New York rallies threatened to take the lead but were stopped by double plays from Tinker to Evers to Chance.

In the last of the ninth, the score was still knotted 1–1. There was one out and the tension was rising. Art Devlin singled to center to get the Giants going. The winning run was on first. Moose McCormick hit a slow grounder to Evers who relayed it to Tinker in time to get Devlin at second but the throw to first was too late for the double play that would have retired the side. Up to bat with two out and McCormick on first came a nineteen-year-old rookie first baseman, Fred Merkle. Pfiester studied the young right-handed hitter and delivered. Base hit to right field. McCormick raced to third.

Al Bridwell, the next batter, took Pfiester's first pitch and lined it to center for the game-winning single. McCormick raced home with the winning run and fans poured onto the field yelling with elation at the Giants' 2–1 triumph. Merkle, seeing crazed New Yorkers heading his way, stopped running the bases and made a beeline for the clubhouse beyond right field.

Evers, known for having one of baseball's most agile minds, began screaming for center fielder Solly Hofman to throw him the ball. Hofman's throw went over Tinker's head and rolled to where Joe McGinnity, the Giants pitcher, was standing. Tinker raced for the ball. Joe McGinnity realized what was happening, outwrestled the Cubs shortstop for the ball, and with Tinker on his back, he heaved the ball into the crowd.

Rube Kroh, a second-line Cubs pitcher who was not even in the game, saw who caught the ball, a tall, stringy, middle-aged gent with a brown bowler hat. Rube demanded the ball. When he wouldn't cough it up, Kroh hit the fan on top of that stiff hat, drove it down over his eyes and as the gent folded up, the ball fell free. Kroh grabbed it and tossed it to Tinker. Evers was yelling and waving his hands out by second base. Tinker fired the ball to him. Evers stepped on the base and made sure umpire Hank O'Day saw him.

When the hit was made and the crowd swarmed onto the field, O'Day, remembering a Pittsburgh game several weeks earlier where the same situation had come up, raced toward second base. He saw Merkle turn and go to the clubhouse, waited until Evers received the ball, then saw the second baseman touch second base.

"The run does not count," O'Day said, as the crowd swarmed over him. Fans shrieked, struck at him, pulled him and threatened his life. He made no attempt to continue the game because of the confusion. It was a tie game. The next day, Manager John McGraw filed a protest, asking National League President Harry C. Pulliam to award the game to the Giants. The world waited for a decision.[19]

Regular-season play continued, and on October 2, Pulliam said he was upholding the umpire's decision, ruling that the game had ended in a 1–1 tie and that the contest would have to be continued. The Giants appealed Pulliam's decision to the NL Board of Directors.

When it looked as if the decision might be rendered in favor of the Giants, Jack Ryder of the *Cincinnati Enquirer* broke into the meeting. He delivered a tremendous speech in favor of the Cubs, claiming that there was no choice but to play the game over, saying that the league would make itself a laughingstock if it let the Giants get away with the pennant on a bonehead play.

The board met again on Tuesday, October 6. A decision was not released. On that day the Giants beat Boston, 4–1. With the Cubs' season over, the Giants still had one game remaining against the Boston Braves. If the Braves won, the entire matter would be moot.

In Chicago, the *Tribune* was offering prayers that the next day's Giants-Boston game be rained out, preventing the Giants from finishing in a tie with the Cubs. Such was not to be. The season ended with the Giants and Cubs in a tie, with identical 98–55 records. The Board decided to replay the disputed game.

1. The Glory Years

There were choices to be made. They could play a single game or the best out of five. Charles Murphy liked the idea of five games because of the extra money a series would bring. He didn't want to risk everything on a single game against Christy Mathewson, the best pitcher in baseball. McGraw didn't give a hoot about money. He cared only about winning. He had Mathewson and would be happy to play just one game. Ultimately, the decision fell to National League president Harry C. Pulliam: one game it would be.

On October 7, the *New York Herald* wrote: "The coming showdown is going to be a war. Never before have two teams been tied at the end of a season. Never before has the race been so close. Never has it been necessary to play off the tie of six months' baseball in a single gigantic battle. That the game will be a struggle to the death is certain."[20]

When Frank Chance led the Cubs into New York the morning of October 8 to meet the Giants that afternoon, Mordecai Brown had a half dozen letters in his coat pocket. "We'll kill you," these letters said, "if you pitch and beat the Giants."[21]

The match-up, was one of the most fiercely fought in the history of baseball, featured Mathewson versus Pfiester, the same pitchers who dueled it out during the 1–1 tie in the Merkle game.

The Cubs started with their first three men making easy outs. In the Giants half of the first, the first ball pitched by Pfiester was a sign of disaster. Tenney was hit on the arm. With two strikes on Herzog, Pfiester lost control and passed him, putting Tenney on second. Bresnahan struck out, but Kling dropped the third strike. Bresnahan was out anyway because first base was occupied. Seeing Herzog taking a long lead, Kling fired a throw to Chance, nailing Herzog for a double play.

Despite Kling's play, the Giants scored the game's first run. Donlin pulled a liner over first base close to the foul line scoring Tenney. Chance argued the ball was foul. The crowd hooted and the tensions rose to such a high pitch that a fireman out beyond center field fell off a telegraph pole and broke his neck.

After Seymour was given a base on balls, Chance removed Pfiester from the slab, replacing him with Brown. Brown's first act was to strike out Devlin, leaving two men on base.

Chance came to bat in the top of the second. The fans met him with a storm of hisses; he responded with a single. The ball came back to Math-

October 8, 1907: Frank Chance swings away at a curveball (National Baseball Hall of Fame Library, Cooperstown, N.Y.).

ewson. He looked at Bresnahan behind the plate, then wheeled and threw to first, catching Chance off guard. Chance slid. Tenney came down with the ball. Umpire Bill Klem threw up his arm.

Called out on the pickoff, Chance ripped and raved, protesting. Most of the Cubs rushed out of the dugout. Solly Hofman called Klem so many names that he was ejected. The stands went into an uproar, and the noise became even wilder when Matty went on to strike out Steinfeldt and Howard.

After a scoreless bottom of the second, Tinker led off the Cubs third with a long ball to center over Cy Seymour's head. Kling then singled on a line to left center, scoring Tinker. Brown bunted toward first for a sacrifice and was retired by Tenney unassisted, putting Kling on second. Johnny Evers came to bat and Mathewson deliberately pitched four wide balls, sending Evers growling on his way to first. Frank Schulte, the next batter, hit a liner over third base into the crowd in left field, giving him a ground-rule double, scoring Kling with the go-ahead run, and moving Evers to third.

It was now Chance's turn. With the crowd howling, he swung with a vengeance and met a curve squarely in the middle of its break, driving the ball far out of reach of Mike Donlin. With that, two more runs crossed the plate, borne by Evers and Schulte. Chance made it to second with a slide that beat a great throw by Donlin, and the Cubs were ahead 4–1.

Back in Chicago, the *Tribune* showed the game's progress on the Electrical Baseball Board at Orchestra Hall. A howling, shrieking, ball-mad crowd, wild in its enthusiasm, sat through it all. When the Giants were retired at the close of the ninth, with the Cubs winning 4–2, the cheering reached a fever pitch.[22]

Praise for the Cubs poured in from the baseball world. But these praises were soon replaced by World Series news.

October 10 brought out a Detroit crowd to root for the home team in Game 1. For eight innings they had something to scream about. The Tigers were ahead 6–5, going into the ninth. Three more outs and Ed Summers, a rookie knuckleball pitcher would have put one away for Detroit.

With Evers out, Schulte sped down the path, beating out a hard drive to deep short. Then came Chance with a vicious single to center, putting Schulte on second. Steinfeldt came to the plate and lined a single to McIntyre in left. So quickly did he field the hit, the fleet footed Schulte had to hold third. Then Solly Hofman, a great utility man, came to the plate. After taking two strikes and waiting out three balls, Hofman smashed a fastball into left, scoring Schulte and Chance, with Steinfeldt taking third on the throw home.

Next, Joe Tinker bunted on a squeeze play. And it worked: Steinfeldt scored, Tinker got to first, and Hofman went to second. Then Tinker and Hofman worked a double steal. Now the Cubs were playing rings around the discomfited Tigers. There seemed no way of stopping them. Kling delivered a single to center to score Hofman and Tinker. Finally, Brown sacrificed and then Sheckard, who got hits his first three times up, flied to Sam Crawford.

The agony was over. With a scoreless bottom of the ninth, the Tigers were subdued 10–6.

The remainder of the Series was brilliantly played, full of pretty fielding and timely hitting on the part of the Cubs. They took Game 2 handily, 6–1, but Hughie Jennings, the Detroit manager, vowed that the Tigers would come from behind and take the lead as they had done in the past. This seemed plausible after Game 3 which Detroit won 8–3. But the Cubs came right back with "Three Finger" Brown who shut out the Tigers in Game 4, 3–0. Overall then took the mound for the Cubs and proceeded to toss another shutout over the American League champions, the Cubs winning this one 2–0 — and capturing the Series.

On October 15, the *Chicago Tribune* said it all, "Cubs Supreme in Baseball World." Decades later, some believed that the Cubs' subsequent misfortunes over the years were not due to the Curse of the Goat, but to the "Curse of Merkle," the Giants player who made a "bonehead" play, allowing the Cubs to win the 1908 pennant.[23]

Fred Merkle of the New York Giants, who made the infamous "bonehead" play on September 23, 1908, at the West Side Grounds (Chicago History Museum. *Chicago Daily News*, 1908. SDN-054363).

1909

In 1909, before the season started, it wasn't a curse that destroyed team harmony, that removed an ingredient that contributed to the team's success. It was Frank Chance who did it.

On January 24 Chance paid $46,500 cash for a California home and orange groves for himself and family. He expected to realize $10,000 yearly from the property. Now, he declared positively that he would stay in California unless Murphy, the owner of the Cubs, gave in to his demand for a raise. Although the details were not released, Murphy caved in and gave Chance what he wanted.[24]

When Joe Tinker reported that he had a contract to perform on the vaudeville stage, earning $3,000 a week, and could not report on time for spring training, no fuss was made. Chance allowed him to fulfill his contract before reporting to Shreveport for spring training.[25]

Then there was Johnny Evers. He notified the club that he was going to take the year off and rest up, but then changed his mind and told Chance and Murphy that he would report around the middle of June, long after the season started. The bosses had no problems with this, either.[26]

But when Johnny Kling announced the opening of a billiard hall in Kansas City, a venture that required an investment of $75,000, and asked that he be allowed to report to the team on April 10, Chance put his foot down. Chicago fans learned that Chance had been agitated about this since the end of February and that on March 20 he'd ordered Kling to report immediately to the club.[27]

Chance would not back down. So Kling didn't report, and his loss was a devastating blow. A premier catcher, he had played in 765 games, an average of 109 games a season. "The classy catcher is a rare breed," the *Kansas City Star* said.

> He is the mainspring of the baseball machine. Being stationed behind the batsman, he has greater opportunities than the pitcher for observing what a batter can and cannot hit. Knowing the man with whom he works, he can tell if his curves are breaking right, can make him work slowly when inclined to hurry and can make him hustle when he inclines to slowness.
>
> The catcher is the chief watcher of the bases when occupied, passes the signals for the pitcher, throwing to catch runners too far from the bags and signals the proper time for delivering the ball to the bat. He

must have a keen eye and a strong, accurate arm to keep opponents from stealing bases.

Aside from all this mental effort, he must snatch any sort of curve the pitcher lets loose, must dig wild pitches that go into the ground and must chase the elusive foul fly. He must block runners who slide into the plate and must take his turn at bat. These few things are calculated to keep a man of average intellect and physical ability quite busy. Catching is a difficult and thankless job, and good catchers are scarce.

How often has it been observed that many young pitchers go along as only ordinary performers until some smooth, heady catcher commences to work with them, and then suddenly they blossom out as stars.

If you offer John Kling and Mordecai Brown for sale, clubs would go for the catcher, for he could take a lot of ordinary pitchers and get good work out of them.[28]

The players had reason for gloom. They knew that without Kling, the Cubs would not be as strong, and their advantage over the other national league contenders was just about nullified.[29]

Without Kling, the Cubs finished second that year with a win-loss of 104–49, six and one-half games behind the Pirates. Had Kling played, there is every reason to believe that the Cubs would have won their fourth straight pennant. Compare the stats of the Cubs' three catchers in 1909 with those of Kling for 1908.

	G	R	H	2B	3B	HR	RBI	SB	BA	SA
Archer	80	31	60	9	2	1	30	5	.230	.291
Moran	77	18	54	11	1	1	23	2	.220	.285
Needham	7	3	4	0	0	0	0	0	.143	.143
Kling (1908)	**126**	**51**	**117**	**23**	**5**	**4**	**65**	**16**	**.276**	**.382**

When Kling made what seemed to be a reasonable request, Chance failed to act in accordance with the best interests of the team.

1910

On April 14 an umpire stood behind the plate at the West Side Grounds and shouted, "Play ball!" Manager Frank Chance was delighted to see that Johnny Kling was back. As he thought about the team, he was satisfied with his outfield. He had a solid infield, men who could play every day. And his pitching staff was superb.

The Cubs started slowly, while the Giants and Pirates started with a bang. By mid–May, the Cubs were fifth place. Then the team began to play smart baseball and they inched their way into first place by May 25. The momentum continued, and the Cubs pulled away by winning the close ones.

A cork-center ball had been introduced and it began to pay off with four-baggers, Wildfire Schulte pacing the way. The Cubs had a commanding lead in July when the team walloped McGraw's Giants, the team they hated most. But the lead dwindled and a race developed between the Cubs, Giants and Pirates. The race was still in doubt on October 1, the Cubs needing a win against Cincinnati to clinch a tie for the pennant.

The Cubs won that game, 9–6, but Johnny Evers left the line-up for the rest of the season because of a serious injury. In the two weeks of regular-season play left, Chicago then romped home with the pennant, 13 games ahead of the second-place Giants. It was Chicago's fourth championship in five seasons and the first time a major-league club, after winning three times in a row and then losing, regained the title within a year. It was an excellent show of strength.

The World Series was another matter. For the fourth time in five years, the Chicago team charged into the Series as heavy favorites. On the other side of the diamond were the Philadelphia A's, featuring the "$100,000 infield" and four pitchers who'd each won more than 15 games that season. It turned out that the A's needed only two pitchers, Jack Coombs and Charles "Chief" Bender, to dispose of the Cubs in five games.

The Chicago team avoided a sweep by pulling out a tight win in Game 4. Trailing 3–2 going into the bottom of the ninth, they knotted the score on a triple by Chance before winning with a two-out single by Jimmy Sheckard. The team batted .222 for the Series compared to Philadelphia's .316.

So went the Chicago Cubs glory years, winning four pennants (1906, '07, '08 and '10) and two World Series championships (1907 and 1908) in five years. Besides holding the single season win-loss record of 116–36, that team also had the best-ever win-loss record for two seasons in a row, and for three, four, five, six, seven and eight seasons in a row. Without question, those Cubs were great.

CHAPTER 2

"Billy Goat" Sianis

In 1911, as happens to all great teams, the Cubs began to fall apart. Harry Steinfeldt was sold to the Braves. Kling, Kaiser and Weaver were traded to the Braves for Curtis, Good and Collins. And Chance collapsed on the field in Cincinnati because of a blood clot in his brain.

His injury was caused by the numerous beanings he'd suffered during his career, and he was no longer able to play as he had in the past. Evers, too, declined, and one of the great pitchers, Orval Overall, quit because of the way owner Murphy treated him. The club slipped to second place that year.[1]

While this was going on, a young man, William Sianis, made arrangements to come to America from Paleopyrgos, Greece, where he had been born and had lived since 1894.[2] Sianis wanted an education, but his family couldn't afford it so he borrowed money to travel to the United States. Reportedly, he was on the ship for 55 days before arriving in the United States on January 1, 1912.[3]

The 55 days at sea must be questioned because the passenger vessel HMS *Sirius* made the North Atlantic crossing in April 1838 in 18 days, 14 hours and 22 minutes.[4] In our times, a solo rower, Rob Munslow, went from St. Johns in Canada to the Isles of Scilly in 64 days, 10 hours and 48 minutes, landing in August of 2006, despite capsizing twice, losing his water maker and surviving on rain water for more than half the journey.[5]

In addition, it seems reasonable to question whether Sianis landed in New York. A search of immigration records on www.ancestry.com for New York arrivals at Ellis Island between 1910–14, failed to reveal Sianis's name on a passenger list. It is possible that his name was spelled differently at the time of his arrival, and thus could not be found.

2. "Billy Goat" Sianis

I sent a letter of inquiry to the District Counsel, Municipality of Ano Pogoni, Paleopyrgos, on April 16, 2007, which was referred to Speros A. Coutsoubinas in New York for a reply.

Mr. Coutsoubinas wrote, "Insofar as they know and according to their records, there is and there was not any William Sianis as a member of their municipality mentioned in your letter, nor does he appear to have been buried there. In my opinion, perhaps he came from a small nearby village and used the name of Paleopyrgos as a better and wider known town."[6]

In pursuit of the facts, I wrote to Sam Sianis at the Billy Goat Tavern in Chicago, then called him after receiving no reply. I told him I would soon be in Chicago, and would call for an interview. He seemed receptive to the idea. But all my further attempts at interviewing Sianis were rebuffed. It is reported that Sianis made his way to Chicago via freight train.[7]

He was soon selling newspapers on Chicago's near south side. When you consider all the other young men on the street, peddling newspapers, trying to make a buck, one can easily imagine that this kind of life made William into a shrewd, resilient businessman.[8]

In 1916, he became a U.S. citizen and later worked as a copy boy for a Chicago newspaper. After many years he had enough money to buy a small building not far from Lake Michigan. There he opened a small diner, and scrimped and saved as much as he could before losing everything in the 1929 stock-market crash.

Then Sianis was forced to go back to hawking papers on the near south side.[9] In addition, he was a waiter in a restaurant, according to a 1930 U.S. census. Sianis can easily be seen as an individual with a great deal of grit and determination, someone with the drive to carve out a future in the land of opportunity.

Sianis's determination and entrepreneurial spirit paid off when in early 1934 he bought the Lincoln Tavern for $205. He paid with a check that bounced, but made enough money during his first weekend to repay the debt.[10] He now was working behind a long, horizontal bar, a shot-and-beer joint at 1855 West Madison, across the street from Chicago Stadium, which had opened on March 28, 1929, with a prizefight, between light heavyweight champion Tommy Loughran and Mickey Walker.

The Blackhawks played their first hockey game at Chicago Stadium on December 16, 1929. It was then the largest indoor arena in the world.

Top: Exterior view of Chicago Stadium, seen from across the street (Chicago History Museum. *Chicago Daily News,* 1930. DN-0090384). *Bottom:* Light heavyweight champion Tommy Loughran (with arm lifted) before his bout with Mickey Walker. Their fight on March 28, 1929, was the inaugural event at the new Chicago Stadium (Chicago History Museum. SDN-068024).

2. "Billy Goat" Sianis

After Prohibition ended in 1933, these kind of events were good for the shot-and-beer-joint business. While Sianis was on his way to becoming an entrepreneur between 1912 and 1933, the Chicago Cubs had been having their ups and downs.

In 1912, the Cubs came in third, 11½ games behind the New York Giants. Chance was fired, Johnny Evers took over in 1913, and the team again came in third. The Cubs continued to go downhill, finishing fourth in 1914 and '15. By the end of the 1915 season, William Sianis probably had been hearing Cub fans talking about baseball.

Some of the talk may have been about Charles Weeghman who broke ground March 4, 1914, at Clark and Addison for Weeghman Park, a new baseball field with a seating capacity of 14,000. Other talk would have been about the first National League game at the ballpark April 20, 1916, and the Cubs taking that game from the Reds 7–6.

Excitement would have been high in 1918 when Manager Fred Mitchell, with veteran players not accepted for military service, and with a sprinkling of newly acquired youngsters and some minor leaguers, carried the Cubs to the top with a record of 84–45, ending the season a month early because of World War I.

Sianis would certainly have heard talk about the federal government's edict that major leaguers either had to enlist or take war-related jobs. But the war ended in November and the edict fell by the wayside. Talk of baseball quickly replaced that of war.

By the twenties Sianis was probably following the baseball sections in the *Chicago Tribune*. Here he would have read about new Cubs owner William Wrigley Jr. and seen that the firing of Cubs managers had become common — seven were fired before Joe McCarthy came aboard in 1926.

McCarthy's arrival might have strengthened Sianis's interest in the Cubs and given him something new to talk about with die-hard Cub fans. He would have heard the excitement that Cub fans expressed as they saw the starting lineup and names of pitchers listed in the newspaper: Charlie Grimm —1B, Sparky Adams — 2B, Jimmy Cooney — SS, Howard Freigau — 3B, Cliff Heathcote — RF, Hack Wilson — CF, Riggs Stephenson — LF, Gabby Hartnett — C; Charlie Root, Tony Kaufmann, Sheriff Blake, Percy Jones, Guy Bush and Bob Osborn — pitchers.

McCarthy began building a winner, signing on fine pitchers and power hitters and took the team to within seven games of the pennant his

Joe McCarthy going into the Cubs' office to sign a contract (Chicago History Museum. SDN-065698).

first year on the job. The Cubs finished fourth in the league in 1927 and climbed to third in 1928, with Hack Wilson's 34 homers and a .313 batting average. With Rogers Hornsby, Hack Wilson, Charlie Grimm, Riggs Stephenson, Woody English, catching stalwart Gabby Hartnett, and Guy Bush, Charlie Root and Pat Malone on the mound, the Cubs roared out of the gate in 1929. They were beating everybody, and by the end of the season, close to 1.5 million people had come to stomp their feet, cheer, take off their straw hats and sail them onto the field. Sianis may have been one of them, these fans who watched the Cubs win the pennant with a record of 98–54, 10½ games ahead of Pittsburgh.

Joe McCarthy after signing a contract to manage the Cubs in 1926 (Chicago History Museum. *Chicago Daily News*. SDN-065699).

In spite of the Cubs' menacing lineup, they lost a hard-fought World Series to Connie Mack's Philadelphia A's. Then, on October 24, 1929, the stock market crashed.

William Sianis was back selling newspapers, along with cigars, candy and magazines. Relatives pitched in and helped. The 1930 U.S. Federal Census tells us that Sianis moved in with his cousin, Peter Sianis, at 2058 Clark Street, not far from Wrigley Field, as Weeghman Park had come to be known.

During the 1930 season, Cub fans saw Hack Wilson turn his body into the ball and watched it soaring high and out of the park. They watched English, Cuyler, Stephenson, Hartnett and Showboat Fisher, all with batting averages well above .300. They roared as Pat Malone won his twentieth game and as Root won his sixteenth. But these performances could not get the team in first place. They finished second to St. Louis, even

New manager Joe McCarthy watches his Cubs from the dugout (National Baseball Hall of Fame Library, Cooperstown, N.Y.).

though Hack Wilson had put together one of the greatest hitting seasons in baseball history, pounding 56 homers and driving in a single-season record of 191 runs.

What made matters worse was Wrigley's firing of Joe McCarthy with a week left in the season. His being let go would come back to haunt

Wrigley in 1932 and in 1938. Hornsby took over as skipper and the Cubs came in third in 1931. While the Cubs were in first place by mid 1932, Hornsby was fired when he had severe disagreements with Bill Veeck Sr., the new club president. Wrigley then retired and turned the team over to his son, Philip.

Phil Wrigley was as determined to win as his father. He spotted first baseman Charlie Grimm, nicknamed "Jolly Cholly," getting along well with other players, and made him manager. The new skipper led the team to a 37–20 record and they went on to win the pennant. The players expressed their attitude about their former manager, Hornsby, by voting not to give him one cent of the World Series money. Though the 1932 team appeared to be unbeatable, with four .300 hitters and four pitchers who had won fifteen games or more, the Cubs were up against the Yankees, with Ruth and Gehrig and the Yank's skipper — Joe McCarthy, who was thirsting for revenge.

The Yankees won the first two games in New York and the series moved to Chicago. With the score 4–4 in the fifth, Ruth came to bat. The Cubs taunted him as he took a first strike. He then pointed a finger toward the center-field bleachers. Cub players hooted and fans booed as he took strike two. But Charlie Root threw the next pitch and it reportedly sailed into the exact spot where he had pointed (the historic "called shot"). The Cubs then fell apart, losing that game, the next one, and the Series.

If William Sianis was a Cubs fan then, he must have been unhappy, but this wouldn't have kept him from rooting for his team, working, and saving his money. In February 1934, just two months after Prohibition ended, Sianis opened the Lincoln Tavern.

CHAPTER 3

Enter the Goat

Legend has it that in 1934 an injured baby goat found its way into the Lincoln Tavern located on Madison Street.[1] But how do you explain two goats at Wrigley Field in 1933?

Babe Herman and Pat Malone, with goats, at Wrigley Field, 1933 (National Baseball Hall of Fame Library, Cooperstown, N.Y.).

3. Enter the Goat

My search of baseball literature on the Chicago Cubs failed to reveal any information about goats, other than that related to the Lincoln Tavern and "Billy Goat" Sianis.

Sianis is said to have treated the Lincoln Tavern goat like a baby, feeding it with a baby bottle, and deciding to file adoption papers as he would for a child, knowing he would get a great deal of publicity.[2]

Phil Wrigley and Charlie Grimm at Wrigley Field, 1934 (National Baseball Hall of Fame Library, Cooperstown, N.Y.).

If the legend is correct, could the goat have grown into adulthood with full-sized horns before the '34 season ended, as seen in the photograph of Charlie Grimm and Phil Wrigley?

Remember that Sianis lived with his cousin Peter on Clark Street, not far from Wrigley Field. It isn't unreasonable to speculate that Sianis may have kept goats long before 1934 when reportedly a baby goat found its way into his tavern.

Teresa Casselman, an authority on goats who looked at the 1934 photo of Charlie Grimm astride a goat, said, "I would guess that goat to be 1 to 1½ or possibly 2 years old." If the photo *was* taken during the 1934 season, it would be unlikely that it was a baby goat that had found its way into the Lincoln Tavern earlier that year.[3] (According to the National Baseball Hall of Fame, the photo of Grimm, Wrigley and the goat *was* taken in 1934.)

William Sianis reportedly had his attorney tend to all of the legal requirements as he would have done for adopting a child, thereby making Sianis the proud father of a goat. He changed the name of the Lincoln Tavern to Billy Goat Inn and grew a short, pointed beard, giving him an image that went along with his being the father of a goat.[4]

It seems fair to say that William Sianis was not only a master showman, but also an expert at marketing techniques. When the 1944 Republican National Convention opened, Sianis was not at all happy with having taken in a few measly dollars. So, being smart and bold, he posted a sign outside of his tavern that told conventioneers that they would not be served.

The Republican delegates were abuzz about this, and it didn't take long for them to storm into the Billy Goat, shouting their outrage, ordering and guzzling beer. When they eventually staggered back to the convention floor, somewhat tipsy, they reportedly bragged about their accomplishment and urged other delegates to do likewise.[5]

Sianis must have been overjoyed. The cash register was packed solid with greenbacks, well over $2,000.[6]

Some of his favorite customers were from shows taking place across the street at the Stadium, including circus performers. And along with these troupers were the audiences and fans following the show people.[7]

Because of this success, William "Billy Goat" Sianis became a well-respected businessman.

1944 Republican Convention at the Chicago Stadium (Americana Resources).

As Sianis followed the Cubs, he may have had in mind the belief that all good things come in threes. And, having seen the Cubs take the flag in 1929, '32, and '35, he would have been full of anticipation in 1938. He also would have been completely surprised when the Cubs traded to the Cardinals for Dizzy Dean three days before the season opened. With ol' Diz aboard, it was going to be an interesting season.

And so it was. The Cubs took off with a winning frenzy, and on April 24, Dean faced his former teammates and pitched a complete-game shutout, beating the Cardinals 5–0 at Wrigley before 34,520 fans.

As the season moved forward, Sianis would certainly have had a radio behind the bar, where he and his patrons could listen to Cubs games. And imagine how noisy they must have been on May 5 when the Cubs annihilated the Phillies 21–2 at Wrigley. And the next day, when the Cubs beat the Braves 13–9.

When the Cubs were hitting, they continued to win big, like on May 20 when they collected 22 hits, clobbering the Phillies 16–7 in Philadelphia. When the pitchers were putting the ball where they wanted it, they too won big, like on June 3 when Bill Lee pitched his third consecutive shutout, and his fourth in five starts, winning 4–0 over the Braves in Boston.

As the games continued to be exciting, the Billy Goat Inn was probably filled to capacity with all of its patrons drinking cold beer and all of them urging the Cubs on.

Such a game took place on July 14 when Clay Bryant retired 23 batters in a row, from the first inning to the eighth against the Phillies in the first game of a double-header. Going for a no-hitter, Bryant settled for a three-hitter and a 3–0 win. The Cubs also won the second game 4–1.

"Jolly Cholly" Grimm was back for the 1945 season (National Baseball Hall of Fame Library, Cooperstown, N.Y.).

At mid-season, July 20, patrons sitting in the bar would have been abuzz with conversation, and possibly outrage, at the sudden firing of Charlie Grimm as manager, and his replacement Gabby Hartnett. After all, the Cubs were 45–36. Why fire him? At the time, P. K. Wrigley believed that Grimm was too easy on his players, and wanted the tougher and gruffer Hartnett in charge.[8]

The club didn't catch fire immediately under Hartnett. In his first 45 games, the Cubs went 23–22. Nevertheless, the team battled on. Their hopes for a pennant took a jolt on September 3 with a double-header loss to the Reds, 6–0 and 7–5, in Cincinnati. The Cubs were now in third with a 68–61 record, seven games behind the Pirates.

All of a sudden, the Cubs caught fire. Beginning September 4, led by Stan Hack (who'd bat .320 that year) and Bill Lee (who'd win 22 games) they won 20 of 23 games to once again take the National League flag.

The Cubs were now up against Joe McCarthy and his Yankees. But again McCarthy had his revenge and the Yanks swept the Series.

The team floundered in 1939, finishing fourth, and fell apart in 1940, finishing fifth, both years under Gabby Hartnett. In 1941, Jimmie Wilson took the helm, and the Cubs finished sixth that year, sixth again in '42, fifth in '43 and fourth in 1944.

In 1945 "Jolly Cholly" Grimm was back. He'd led the Cubs to the flag in '32, and '35. Could he do it again?

CHAPTER 4

Curse of the Goat

Although Grimm was back, World War II was raging, and many good players were wearing military uniforms, not baseball gear. Prospects for a good team were dim. But there were players who had been fortunate in finding off-season jobs that carried military exemptions. They were now looking forward to playing ball.

On March 21, Paul McNutt of the War Manpower Commission helped the game by ruling that individuals could leave their military-exempt jobs and play ball without fear of being drafted into the military.[1]

The Cubs set up preseason camp in the resort town of French Lick, Indiana, and the war's effects were such that only nine players reported for spring training. By the second week, Grimm was so desperate for players that he welcomed two semi-pros from Pennsylvania, had one of his catchers at shortstop, and relied on a 53-year-old coach at third. If that wasn't bad enough, a creek overflowed, forcing the team to practice indoors and at times in the meeting hall of their hotel.[2]

Jolly Cholly was then notified that Dom Dallessandro, the second best hitter at .305 on the 1944 team, had been called into service by his draft board. General Manager Jim Gallagher finally admitted that he had not heard from 11 players on the active roster in more than two months.[3]

This put a damper on spring training, but things became more encouraging when All-Star second baseman Don Johnson and first-string catcher Dewey Williams arrived for the Cubs' first outdoor workout. But when the team held its first three-hour drill on March 10, Charlie Grimm learned that John Ostrowski was going for a pre-induction physical in spite of ear problems and a missing kidney for which he had been given a 4-F rating.[4]

This must have caused concern amongst the team and management. If Ostrowski could be called in, who would be next? Players who had not yet reported might never give up their draft-exempt civilian jobs.

With all the ups and downs, spring training really got underway on March 13 when A and B teams were organized and games were played. Games were also played against the Reds, Pirates, Cardinals and other teams. And on April 11, the Cubs settled into Chicago for the start of the season that was scheduled to begin after the weekend's annual exhibition series with the White Sox.

April 17 saw the season opener against the Cardinals before 11,785 fans at Wrigley. William "Billy Goat" Sianis may have been one of these fans. If he was there, he would have yelled with the rest of the crowd when Bill Nicholson homered in the second inning to give the Cubs a 1–0 lead. And he would have gone home a happy man when the scoreboard showed a final score of 3–2 Cubs.

Chicago was soon on the road, heading toward Cincinnati. On April 25, with Claude Passeau on the mound, they took a game from the Reds 4–0. Besides pitching a shutout, Passeau helped his own cause by hitting a homer.

Three days later, April 28, Hank Wyse pitched a one-hitter to defeat the Pirates 6–0 at Wrigley. The only Pittsburgh hit was a lined single to right field by Bill Salkeld with one out in the eighth.

The Cubs continued to do well. On May 12, five days after Germany's surrender closed the European phase of World War II, the Cubs battled back to defeat the Braves 13–12 in Boston after trailing 10–3 in the fourth inning. The Cubs scored six runs in the seventh, the last four on a grand slam by Phil Cavaretta that tied the score 12–12. All six runs in the inning were scored after two were out. Bill Nicholson's homer in the ninth broke the tie. But after the victory, the Cubs lost six in a row to drop their season record to 10–13, nine games behind the first-place Giants. This certainly would have caused frustration and gloom in the Billy Goat Inn, especially after the team had been coming from behind to win close ones.

Nevertheless, the Cubs did not fall apart. June 3 saw Passeau pitch a two-hitter, defeating the Braves 3–1 in the second game of a double-header at Wrigley. Things really perked up on July 3 when the team collected 28 hits, burying the Braves 24–2 in Boston. Cavaretta, Don Johnson and

Stan Hack each scored five runs. Cavarretta had five hits, including a double, in seven at-bats. Johnson also had five hits, with two doubles, in seven at-bats.

Five days later the Cubs moved into first with a 12–6 and 9–2 double-header sweep of the Phillies in Philadelphia. The victories were the team's ninth and tenth in a row.

While the Cubs enjoyed their league lead, "Billy Goat" Sianis was happy too, not only because his team was in first, but also because he was doing so well. He enjoyed being behind a bar where he would talk with people, get to know them, joke with them, and they with him. In a restaurant, people would eat and run. At a bar, they could relax behind a cold beer and stay a while.

He wanted his tavern to be a fun place. So he had his goat standing inside the front door where it would attract the attention of customers and entertain them. The goat became a celebrity. People would feed him, and he would eat whatever was put into his mouth. They gave him beer, he drank beer. They gave him chips, he ate chips. They gave him money, he ate money.[5]

It was also fun to have headliners from the Chicago Stadium drop in, as well as sports celebrities, politicians, city officials, the press and notables such as Irv Kupcinet, who was the master of ceremonies for The Festival, an annual amateur dance concert in the 1940s. And along with Kup, came his pals, like Bing and Frank and Liz. Another notable was Pee Jay Ringers, an Australian circus daredevil of the day whose specialty was "The Ride of Death." He would ride a bike down a ramp from the Stadium ceiling and then drop 60 feet straight down into a small tank filled with water. But the most famous circus star had to be Gunther Gebel-Williams, the celebrated Ringling Bros. animal trainer who could command 24 white horses to dance on their hind legs.[6] William Sianis and his Billy Goat Inn became known to important people in Chicago.

In the summer of '45, many of them were talking about the Cubs who, by July 12, ran their winning streak to 11 games, defeating the Braves 6–1 in the first game of a double-header at Wrigley. The streak was stopped with a 3–1 loss in game two, but the Cubs won the next five games, giving them 16 wins in 17 games.

They kept on winning. August 3 saw the Cubs clobber the Reds 11–5 and 9–1 in a double-header in Cincinnati. Phil Cavaretta paved the way with six hits, including a homer and four doubles, in eight at-bats, scoring five runs, and collecting eight runs batted in.

August 11 saw the Cubs wallop the Dodgers 20–6 in Brooklyn, and they increased their lead to 7½ games, sweeping the Giants 3–1 and 8–0 in New York. But a week later, the lead had dwindled to 2½ games, after a three-game sweep by the Cardinals.

It was a nail-biter season. William Sianis and his beer-guzzling patrons must have had a lot to talk about. Stan Hack's 2000th career hit, a single off Preacher Roe on August 30, might not have created much of a stir, though. "So what," one fan might have said, "the Cubs lost anyhow."

On September 3, the goat standing near the front door might have heard loud shouts when the Cubs took two from the Reds by scores of 7–2 and 7–1 at Wrigley. The sweep was set in motion by Andy Pafko who hit a grand slam in the first inning of the first game.

On September 23, Pafko hit another grand slam, this one off Preacher Roe of the Pirates, giving the Cubs a 7–3 win. With only a week left in the season, the Cubs were leading the Cardinals by only 1½ games.

On the 25th the Cubs beat the Cards 6–5 behind Hank Borowy's 20th win of the season. But the next day the Cards beat the Cubs 11–6. On September 27, with five games left for Chicago and four left for St. Louis, the Cubs defeated the Reds in a doubleheader 3–1 and 7–4, clinching a tie for the pennant.

September 29 saw the Cubs sew it up with a 4–3 win over the Pirates at Wrigley. William Sianis and even his goat may have been at that crucial game; regardless, the occasion may have resulted in a boisterous celebration at the Billy Goat Inn.

The baseball world now readied itself for the World Series. Most believed that Chicago would capture the title in six games. After all, the *Chicago Daily News* hired Rogers Hornsby to analyze the match-up before the series started and he would know.[7]

Hornsby thought the Cubs had better balance and a deeper pitching staff. They had a bench that proved itself all season long, both in the field and at the plate, and that helped the team win many crucial games. He also pointed out that Chicago held onto first place in spite of the end-of-season charge by the team that many considered to be stronger, the Cardinals.

Hornsby also saw the Cubs as having a stronger infield, and he pointed

The 1945 Chicago Cubs. *Top row:* Ed Sauer, Don Johnson, Frank Secory, Heinz Becker, Paul Derringer, Hy Vandenberg, Ed Hanyzewski, Paul Gillespie, Ray Starr, Bob Chipman, Hank Wyse, trainer Andy Lotshaw. *Middle:* Len Merullo, Jorge Comellas, Johnny Ostrowski, Andy Pafko, Dewey Williams, Mickey Livingston, Peanuts Lowrey, Len Rice, Ray Prim, Mack Stewart. *First row:* Bill Schuster, Stan Hack, Roy Hughes, coach Roy Johnson, manager Charlie Grimm, coach Red Smith, coach Milt Stock, Bill Nicholson, Claude Passeau, Phil Cavarretta (photograph by George Brace).

to Andy Pafko's abilities on offense and defense, as being superior to that of Doc Cramer. But he had to admit that the right-field spot was a toss up between Bill Nicholson and Roy Cullenbine, especially because Nicholson had not been swinging the bat too well. Hornsby also had to admit that Peanuts Lowrey could not be considered better than Hammerin' Hank Greenberg, but he gave the catching nod to Chicago.

On Monday, October 3, the Chicago team headed for the LaSalle Street Station, and hopped aboard the New York Central Limited for Detroit to open the World Series.[8]

Detroit, managed by Del Baker, had an 88–65 record, nosing out the Washington Senators for the AL pennant by 1½ games. With many wartime fill-ins on both rosters, the 1945 Cubs and Tigers were probably the two least-talented teams ever to reach the World Series. "I don't think either one of them can win," said Chicago sportswriter Warren Brown.[9]

Game 1: October 3

In a poll of 80 writers covering the game, 45 picked Detroit, 35 picked Chicago.[10] The nod to the Tigers was probably based on Newhouser's record. He had outshone all American League hurlers in 1945 and had been named MVP in '44 when he posted a 29–9 record. He was scheduled to start two games in the '45 showdown classic.

Hal Newhouser warming up for the 1945 World Series (National Baseball Hall of Fame Library)

In Game 1, Grimm shuffled his lineup around. Stan Hack, .323 for the year, would lead off. Johnson (.302) would bat second, Lowrey (.283) third, and the cleanup man was Cavarretta whose .355 was the team's highest batting average for the year.

Baseball Commissioner Happy Chandler threw out the ceremonial first pitch on a cold day, but Chicago began playing as if the weather was perfect for the national pastime.

Hack led off by bouncing out. Johnson followed with a single, then stole second. Lowrey flied out to center. Cavarretta then hit a slow roller to Mayo at second, beating the throw, then made it to second when there was a play on Johnson at third.

The Cubs had two men in scoring position and two outs when Tigers catcher Paul Richards allowed a passed ball, Johnson scoring and Cavarretta going to third. Newhouser then issued an intentional walk to Pafko, knowing that Nicholson's batting had been on the decline. But the big right fielder slammed a pitch off the right-field wall for a triple, scoring Cavarretta and Pafko. Mickey Livingston then drove in Nicholson with a single but was thrown out by Richards when he tried to steal.

In one-half inning of play, the dominant pitcher of the American League found himself on the short end of a 4–0 Cubs' lead.

Hank Borowy had a rough bottom of the first, allowing baserunners, but was saved when Cramer bounced into a double play and York popped up to Cavarretta.

The Cubs scored again in the third when Johnson got a double to center. Lowrey moved him to third with a sacrifice bunt, and Cavarretta singled him home. Pafko slammed a double to left, scoring Cavarretta, and Livingston followed with his second hit, sending Pafko home — and Newhouser to the showers.

As the game moved on, the Tigers had every reason to lose hope. The Cubs continued to hit, showed off superior fielding, and frosted the cake in the seventh when Cavarretta drove the ball deep into the right-field bleachers, the first homer of the 1945 World Series.

Borowy went all the way, winning a six-hit shutout 7–0, for his tenth career win against the Tigers in 13 starts, this time with 54,637 fans looking on.

Cubs trainer Andy Lotshaw claimed some credit for Borowy's success, telling the press that he found two huge paving bricks that he steamed and then submerged in scalding water when the Cubs were on the field. But when that half of the inning was over, and Borowy left the mound and came into the dugout, Lotshaw put one brick under Borowy's feet and wedged the other behind Borowy's right arm to keep him warm and limber.[11]

The Tigers offered no excuses. Hammerin' Hank merely said that they played a bad game. And Newhouser promised to show the baseball world what he could do the next chance he got.[12]

While Detroit fans were crying, Cubs fans in the Billy Goat Inn were whooping it up.

Game 2: October 4

The lineups were the same except for the pitchers and one other change. Grimm started Gillespie as catcher instead of Livingston. Livingston had 2-for-4 in game 1 and it seemed reasonable to leave him in the lineup.

Hal Newhouser warming up for the 1945 World Series (National Baseball Hall of Fame Library, Cooperstown, N.Y.).

Hack led off against Virgil Trucks with a slow roller to short, beating it out. Johnson bunted him to second. Lowrey came up and proceeded to slam the first pitch to left for a single. Hack rounded third and kept going as Grimm waved him on. But Hammerin' Hank threw a perfect strike to cut down the fleet-footed Hack. Cavarretta then grounded out.

With Wyse on the mound for the Cubs, the Tigers could do nothing for the first three innings and neither side had scored a run. In the fourth, things began moving when Cavarretta powered a double into right-center. After Pafko grounded out to short, Cavarretta holding at second, Nicholson came through, lining a single over second, driving in Cavarretta with the first run of the game. The score remained 1–0 until the Tigers' half of the fifth. With two out, the Tigers started to connect.

Webb singled to left and Wyse walked Mayo. Cramer then singled to left, scoring Webb and tying the game 1–1. Then Greenberg slammed a curveball into the left-field stands for a three-run homer, and the Tigers took the lead 4–1.

The game was scoreless the rest of the way, and the Tigers evened the Series before a crowd of 53,838. Trucks, who had been out of the Navy for only a week, was the winning pitcher.

The Tigers' clubhouse rocked with noisy celebrations. Greenberg and Trucks hugged one another, each crediting the other for the victory. Both of them reminded the press that it would now be a competitive series and said they were looking forward to another victory on the following day.[13]

Game 3: October 5

It was Claude Passeau for the Cubs and "Stubby" Overmire for the Tigers on a mild Friday afternoon, with eager eyes following every pitch. For the first three innings, the fans saw each pitcher give up only one hit.

In the fourth, Lowrey hit a long drive off the left-field fence for a double. Cavarretta pushed him to third with a sacrifice. Pafko walked. Then Nicholson came through with a clutch single, driving in Lowrey and sending Pafko to second. Livingston flied out, but Pafko then scored on a hit by Hughes. The Cubs now led 2–0.

That score held until the seventh when Overmire was sent to the showers and replaced by Benton who gave up a double to Livingston. Liv-

"Hammerin' Hank" Greenberg slamming a home run (National Baseball Hall of Fame Library, Cooperstown, N.Y.).

ingston was brought around and managed to score, the Cubs were ahead 3–0, and that was more than sufficient.

Passeau, the tough right-hander, had pitched what was then the best game in the history of the World Series, a one-hit, 3–0 shutout, giving the Cubs a 2–1 game lead. Passeau gave credit to his outfielders, who had made nine putouts. The Tigers had little to say and issued no excuses. O'Neill simply praised Passeau who threw perfect sliders throughout the game. Catcher Richards said that Passeau's sliders were the best he had ever seen.[14]

The Series now moved to Wrigley Field, and that night, at about 10:00 P.M. Chicago time, the Cubs pulled into Union Station, where dozens upon dozens of Cubs fans were waiting to greet them and cheer them.

It's impossible to know if William Sianis and his goat were at the station to greet the team, but he must have known about the problem Wrigley was having with the ticket situation for the coming games.

51

Fans had begun queuing up for the 5,000 bleacher and 2,500 stand-ing-room-only tickets for Game Four earlier that evening. Bleacher seats were $1.20, and standing-room-only tickets were $3.60, but none of the latter were to be offered until all of the bleacher seats were sold. Within two hours, the crowd swelled to 5,000, and 60 police officers were called to supervise them, and to prepare for an all-night vigil because the box office would not open until 8:00 A.M. When the police were not looking, some youngsters in line were selling their place to latecomers for as much as $15, twice the cost of a box seat ticket.[15]

Phil Wrigley had a problem in knowing how to sell the tickets fairly. He had become angry at the widespread practice of scalping, ticket-hold-ers selling tickets at inflated prices, legal at the time. He tried to answer letters of complaint but there were just too many. On Thursday, October 4, he addressed a letter to Cubs fans and paid the Chicago papers to guar-antee that it would be published.[16] The letter, titled "We're Burned Up, Too," read as follows:

> The Cubs went to a lot of trouble and extra expense to engage outside office space and a large force of bank tellers and clerks to try and do an extra good job of distributing evenly and fairly the comparatively lim-ited supply of World Series tickets, the sale of which, because the pro-ceeds go into a special account of the Commissioner of Baseball, have to balance out to the penny, to say nothing of settling up with Uncle Sam for the exact tax on the printed price of each ticket. However, once the tickets are in the hands of the public, there is nothing to prevent individuals from selling their seats at a neat profit through scalpers. Unfortunately, there are always a few people who prefer a quick profit to anything else. We all know this to be true, but as we said to start with — we still do not like it.
> — The Chicago National League Ball Club

William Sianis, although he may have known about the ticket crisis, didn't care much because he had purchased two tickets at the regular price of $7.20 each, one for himself and the other for his goat.[17]

Game 4: October 6

William "Billy Goat" Sianis stood in line outside Wrigley Field, his left hand holding his goat close beside him. As he edged his way toward the gate, he and the goat were a center of attraction. Always the showman, William was dressed as if he were going to a cocktail party: suit, white shirt, bow tie, topcoat and hat. His goatee was neatly trimmed. The goat too was smartly attired. Fans smiled and a few petted the goat. Sianis could see Andy Frain's usher ready to collect his tickets as he held them in his right hand, ready to hand them over.

One source says an usher, dressed in a blue and gold trimmed uniform, politely refused to allow Sianis entry as long as he had his pet goat, because the animal smelled. When Philip Wrigley supported the usher's decision, the indignant Sianis declared the Cubs would never again win a World Series.[18]

Another source, Gene Kessler, sports editor for the *Chicago Times*, claimed the goat was allowed in and reportedly published a photograph of Sianis waving his hat at the crowd while he and the goat sat in their box seats. Reportedly the goat wore a sign that read "We got Detroit's goat," and when it was brought onto the field, "Billy Goat" Sianis and the goat were ejected and once outside, Sianis threw down his curse on the team.[19]

As for Game 4, 49,923 excited fans watched 39-year-old Ray Prim on the mound, warming up for his battle with 30-year-old Dizzy Trout, an 18-game winner who was one of the toughest pitchers to hit when he was on his game.[20] The fans knew that Chicago needed only two of the remaining four games to take the series.

Neither team had a hit until the third when Cubs catcher Livingston singled to left, but the inning ended quietly.

The Tigers began their work on Prim in the fourth. After Hack threw out Webb, Mayo walked and Cramer singled to right. Greenberg then singled to left, driving in Mayo and sending Cramer to second. Cullenbine followed with a double down the left-field line, scoring Cramer and sending Greenberg to third.

Prim had retired the first ten Detroit hitters, but suddenly he had fallen apart.

Grimm had seen enough. He went to the mound, took the ball from Prim, called in Derringer from the bullpen, and gave him instructions to walk York to set up for a double play.

Then the right-hander delivered to Outlaw who hit a grounder to second, but a force at second was all the Cubs could get, as Greenberg

William "Billy Goat" Sianis holding his goat and two tickets to Wrigley Field, October 6, 1945 (*Chicago Tribune* file photograph. All rights reserved. Used with permission).

scored and Cullenbine made it to third. Catcher Richards, not known for his hitting prowess, then singled to center scoring Cullenbine. Trout made an out to end the inning, but the Tigers now led 4–0.

During the rest of the game, the Cubs made a little noise but nothing came of it. Nicholson popped out to catcher Richards in the end of the ninth, making the final score 4–1, and the Series was tied two games apiece.

The Cubs were very quiet after the game. All they could point to was the difficulty they'd had picking up Trout's fastball throughout the game.

But Billy Sianis had something to say, as reported by the October 9, 1945, *Chicago Times* columnist Irv Kupcinet. Reportedly, Sianis had sent Phil Wrigley a wire saying, "Who smells now?"[21]

Game 5: October 7

Before the game, Cubs shortstop Roy Hughes was hit in the left ankle by a line drive off the bat of Detroit's Rudy York during batting practice, putting Hughes out of the game.[22]

A crowd of 43,463 had come to watch Borowy battle it out with Newhouser on a nice Sunday afternoon, but it wasn't much of a battle. After the game, an upset Cubs manager proclaimed that his team "just got the hell kicked out of them." He attributed the 8–4 outcome to Newhouser's changeup, calling it the best he had ever seen. Cavarretta, on the other hand, claimed that the only difference between Newhouser's pitches that day and those of his Game 1 outing was that he had them all in the strike zone that day.

Borowy couldn't explain anything, claiming his pitches were no different than they were when he dominated the Tigers in the first game. Regardless, the Cubs were behind 3–2 and one more loss would give the Tigers the Series.[23]

Game 6: October 8

Grimm called upon Passeau who had pitched the 1-hit shutout in Game 3, and O'Neill called upon Trucks, who'd won Game 2. With the Tigers ahead 1–0, the Cubs made their fans happy when they put it all together in the bottom of the fifth.

Livingston singled. Hughes beat out a bunt. Passeau weakly grounded to Trucks, who threw too late to third to force Livingston, and the Cubs had the bases loaded and no outs. Hack's clutch single drove in Livingston and Hughes, and Hack made it to second after the relay went home, trying to catch Hughes who slid under the throw. Trucks was allowed to stay in, even though Chicago had two on, none out and were now ahead 2–1.

Johnson then grounded out, both runners holding. Lowrey walked, loading the bases. Then up came Cavarretta, the National League batting champion. The crowd went wild, knowing what Phil could do. They were not disappointed when they saw a clean single to center, driving in Passeau and Hack and sending Lowrey to second.

Manager O'Neill came to the mound and took the ball. George Caster was called to stop the Cubs. And he succeeded. Pafko popped out and Nicholson struck out. But things were looking good for Chicago. They were ahead 4–1, and had knocked fireball Trucks out of the game.

In the top of the sixth, Passeau was doing well, having just struck out York. Up came Outlaw who hit a smash back to the mound. Passeau deflected it with his bare hand, picked it up and threw him out. But the fingernail on his middle finger had been partially torn off. Time was called, and his hand treated. Then Passeau faced pinch hitter Bob Maier.

Again there was a hard smash to Passeau, who again deflected the ball with his bare hand. His throw was too late to catch the fleet-footed Maier. McHale came to pinch-hit for Caster, and Passeau — although in obvious pain — struck him out.

After the Cubs scored again in the bottom of the sixth, Passeau allowed base runners and signaled to the Chicago dugout. Grimm came out, looked at Passeau's hand, then called in Wyse to finish up Game 6. But it wasn't a mop-up.

Detroit scored two runs that inning, but Chicago still led, 5–3. With two in the bottom of the seventh, the Cubs went ahead, 7–3 and were six outs away from forcing a seventh game.

But the Tigers went to work against Wyse in the eighth, and scored three runs, forcing Grimm to bring in Prim to face Greenberg. Hammerin' Hank was ready, and hit a long fly to left for a game-tying homer. It was a new game.[24]

Dizzy Trout came on in relief for the Tigers, and Hank Borowy for the Cubs. No runs were scored and the game went into extra innings. Three hours and 28 minutes after the first pitch, the Cubs finally prevailed in the twelfth, wining 8–7. The crowd went delirious. It had been the longest World Series game ever played. A seventh game would now be held on October 10. Both teams welcomed a day of rest.[25]

Game 7: October 10

The evening of October 9 saw the temperature drop to the low 40s in Chicago, but fans began to line up at 28 ticket windows, hoping to be one of the lucky ones to see the last game of the series. A full complement of Andy Frain ushers and dozens of Chicago police officers were on hand to maintain order. And when fans lit fires in a number of metal trash cans to keep warm, police looked the other way.[26]

Grimm had difficulty in deciding upon a starting pitcher. Passeau's injury had forced him to go into his starting rotation, and he found himself changing his mind several times. He finally settled on Borowy, even though Game 7 would be his third start in the Series, and the third game

Detroit Tigers (left to right) Harold Newhouser, manager Steve O'Neill, and Hank Greenberg celebrate the team's 1945 World Series championship (National Baseball Hall of Fame Library, Cooperstown, N.Y.).

in a row in which he'd pitched, this time with less than two days' rest. Nevertheless, the right-hander assured Grimm that he felt up to the task.

But the Tigers hit him soundly. The first three batters got hits, and the Tigers had scored a run and had two on, when Grimm hurried to the mound, and without a word, took the ball and called in Derringer.

Up came Greenberg, who sacrificed the runners to second and third. After Derringer intentionally walked Cullenbine, the pressure seemed to ease a bit when York popped up to Hack for an easy second out. But Derringer walked Outlaw on four pitches, forcing Mayo home. Then Richards cleared the bases with a double down the left-field line and the Tigers led 5–0. Newhouser made the final out but Detroit had batted around in the first inning, and the Series was effectively over.

The Cubs had no success against Newhouser. Their pinch hitters, so effective throughout the season and in several appearances in the World Series, had as much trouble with the tall left-hander as the regulars did.

The final score was 9–3 really, but the game had ended in the first. And Chicago fans had every reason to be disappointed with Grimm's decision to pull Borowy and put Derringer in. All the fans, that is, except one, William "Billy Goat" Sianis who reportedly had put a curse on the team.

Opinions differ as to whether or not "Billy Goat" Sianis really did this. Nevertheless, the Tigers took the World Championship and once again the Cubs would have to wait till next year.

CHAPTER 5

Disasters ad Infinitum

According to Rick Kogan's, *A Chicago Tavern: A Goat, a Curse, and the American Dream*, William Sianis did not put a curse on the Cubs on October 6, the day of Game 4. But reportedly he did arrive at Wrigley Field with two tickets, one for himself and one for his goat. And he did ask an Andy Frain usher to ask Phil Wrigley for permission to bring the goat into the ballpark. And Wrigley said no.

Sianis told his story to the newspapers. Years later, because of the Cubs' losing ways, Sianis's friends would sit at the bar and jokingly accuse him of jinxing his favorite team. Sianis loved the story and ran with it.[1]

Steve Gatto's *Da Curse of the Billy Goat* says otherwise, that William Sianis and his goat were admitted and then removed from Wrigley Field before the end of the game. Gatto quotes Arch Ward of the *Tribune* to support his contention that the goat was not only admitted, but was paraded in front of box-seat fans. Gatto also claims that when ejected from the park, Sianis put a curse on the team.

The Cubs Journal, by John Snyder, claims that Sianis was denied admission to Wrigley Field, and — because of this — put a curse on the team.

I think that columnist Irv Kupcinet reported events in a forthright and factual manner. Here is what *Chicago Times* "Kup's Column" reported on October 9, 1945:

> William (Billy Goat) Sianis, the W. Madison St. tavern owner, created a stir at Wrigley field Sunday when he led his pet goat into the ball park and then insisted on having the animal occupy the seat next to him. He pleaded to no avail that he spent $7.20 for a box seat for his pet goat.... Ushers finally evicted the goat, over Sianis' strong protests. After

Detroit defeated the Cubs, 8–4, Sianis sent P. K. Wrigley this wire: "Who smells now?"

Regardless of what you think of the Billy Goat Curse, the Cubs' downhill slide in '46, '47, and '48 was remarkable. They went from first in 1945 to second in '46 (14½ games behind), sixth in '47 (25 games behind), and eighth and last in 1948 (27½ games behind). P. K. Wrigley issued a public apology in September 1948 when the Cubs collapsed into last place.[2]

But the Cubs did it again in 1949. Not only did they finish last, but they set a club record for the most defeats in a season for the second year in a row, with records of 64–90 in '48 and 61–93 in '49.

While the Cubs hit bottom in '49, "Billy Goat" Sianis and his tavern thrived, was mainly due to its location.

When Frank Sinatra played the Stadium on June 12, 1946, as a Knights of Columbus benefit show for the Catholic Archdiocese of Chicago's "underprivileged youth" fund, the arena was packed solid. When the Harlem Globetrotters moved in, some 22,000 came to check out what they had heard was a rare type of basketball. They saw the Globetrotters play a-mile-a-minute sort of game, twice as fast, twice as thrilling and three times as tricky as that displayed by ordinary clubs. They saw Globetrotter Sonny Boswell hit a shot from midcourt at the buzzer to push the game into overtime.[3] In the fifties Meadowlark Lemon joined the team and would later toss buckets of water on fans (actually it was silver confetti) and throw basketballs into the crowd only to have them return on rubberbands.[4]

After these events, the Billy Goat Inn would be packed. Sianis did a landslide business. Many people who performed at the Stadium dropped in for a drink at the Billy Goat afterward, including the likes of Sonja Henie, Peggy Fleming, Bobby Riggs, Don Budge, Dorothy Hamill, Sugar Ray Robinson, Rocky Graziano, Jerry Lewis, and Bob Hope.[5]

In contrast, the 1950s were the worst decade in Cubs history. None of the teams fielded by the club posted a winning record. The 1952 club was the only one that didn't finish below .500, coming in fifth with a record of 77–77. Overall, the Cubs were 672–866, with a winning percentage of .437, seventh among the eight teams in the National League that decade.

There are many who justifiably argue that the Cubs' losing record had nothing to do with a curse. Instead of blaming a goat, Royko placed the blame on a multimillionaire. P. K. Wrigley, that is, a nice man, shy, modest and very good at selling chewing gum. P. K. was a lucky man, inheriting a thriving company and a fine baseball team from his more aggressive father.

Royko pointed out that in baseball, what P. K. Wrigley was best known for was preserving day baseball long after all other franchises were playing most of their games at night. A myth grew that Wrigley believed baseball was meant to be played in sunshine and, as a matter of principle, kept lights out of his park.

Royko went on to say that the only other baseball feat P. K. was known for was running the worst franchise in baseball. And he blamed it on racism, if not Wrigley's, then that of those he hired to run his organization.

After World War II ended, players were discharged from the military and they returned to teams they had starred for a few years earlier. There were outstanding players in the old Negro leagues who could field a team and beat the white all-star teams.

By 1947, the year Branch Rickey signed Jackie Robinson to a contract with the Brooklyn Dodgers, the Cubs were already pathetic doormats, so said Mike Royko.

Had Wrigley followed Rickey's lead, he could instantly have had a competitive team. Had he signed many black players, he may have had a *great* team. But the Cubs front office would not listen to those who urged them to sign Negro League players. It wasn't until 1953 that Wrigley signed two black athletes. By then, the Dodgers — with Robinson, Campanella, Junior Gilliam, Don Newcombe and Joe Black — and the New York Giants, with the amazing Willie Mays and clutch-hitting Monte Irvin, had become dominant teams.

Who did Wrigley *not* sign to a contract? Besides those already mentioned, there was Larry Doby, who became an American League home-run leader, slugger Luke Easter, the great Satchel Paige and Hank Aaron, who broke Babe Ruth's lifetime home-run record.

By the time Cubs management got over their racial fears, the Negro leagues were getting ready to fold. Fewer players were available by then.

The Cubs' record of failure had nothing to do with the Curse of the Goat, Royko pointed out, unless the goat wore a pin-striped suit and sat behind a desk in an executive suite.[6]

Maybe the Cubs' losing record was equally due to another factor.

On June 15, 1951, the Cubs traded Andy Pafko, Johnny Schmitz, Rube Walker, and Wayne Terwilliger to the Dodgers for Joe Hatten, Bruce Edwards, Gene Hermanski, and Eddie Miksis. Andy Pafko was arguably the best player on the team, having batted .304 in 1950. Trading him and the other three for four Dodger players who had been sitting on the bench must have been the work of someone under a voodoo spell.

One of the Dodger players, Edwards, reported with a sore arm and was virtually useless. But Cubs general manager Wid Matthews (from 1946 to 1949 scouting director for the Dodgers) thought that Miksis would save the day for the ailing Cubs. The only thing Mixsis did that the other three didn't do was get into the starting line-up, but he was a light-hitting second baseman whose .266 batting average that year was as good as he'd ever do again. As one Chicago sportswriter put it, "this was a bad deal all around."[7]

There were more such deals. On October 4, 1954, the Cubs traded Smoky Burgess and Bob Borkowski to the Reds for Johnny Pramesa and Bob Usher. Burgess went on to play another 16 seasons in the majors, appearing in 1,578 games, while Pramesa and Usher combined played in only 23 games with the Cubs. Burgess ended his career with a batting average of .295 and was the all-time leader in career pinch-hits with 145. If he had not been traded, he would have been the starting catcher for Chicago at least through 1963.

In 1960, the Cubs' struggles continued into the new decade as they finished in seventh with a miserable record of 60–94. The next year, desperate for a winning team, Phil Wrigley tried something new. He announced in December 1960 that the Cubs would use eight coaches as managers. He argued, "Managers are expendable. I believe there should be relief managers just like relief pitchers." The Cubs front office argued that under this system, players would be exposed to the wisdom and experience of eight coaches instead of just one field manager. Four would serve in the minors, while four would serve with the Cubs. Each member would serve as "head coach" before rotating back to the minors.

It may have sounded good, but it was a disaster. It was not always clear which coach would be in charge for a given game, and occasionally the various coaches were at odds with each other. Each coach brought a different playing style and a different lineup.[8]

It all ended without success after two seasons with a horrible 59–103, ninth-place finish in 1962. The only bright spot for the team in '62 was the Rookie of the Year Award for second baseman Ken Hubbs. (The Cubs' Billy Williams won the same award in '61.)

In 1963, with Bob Kennedy as the single new manager, the team showed promise, and finished 82–80, a 23-game improvement over the previous season. But in 1964, tragedy struck before the start of the season when Ken Hubbs was killed as his plane slammed into a mountain in Utah. And the Cubs took a step backward that year, finishing 76–86.

Besides the loss of Hubbs, 1964 also marked the death of the Billy Goat Inn on Madison Street. Sporting events were no longer being held at the Stadium because the neighborhood had been going downhill, with stick-ups and other criminal behavior taking place regularly. The neighborhood had become dangerous.[9]

Sianis chose to reopen the Billy Goat on Hubbard Street, below 430 North Michigan Avenue, a dark and dismal location in the belly of the Loop, a place that would forever hide the tavern from sunlight. The move was made at the end of the season, in October.[10]

The location may have seemed gloomy to some, but the employees of Chicago's major newspapers were overjoyed to find themselves so close to the Billy Goat.[11] Working for the papers, they probably talked at length about the latest goings-on at Wrigley. "Wait till next year" was still the mantra for Chicago fans. And wait they did.

In 1965, the team spiraled downward to an eighth-place finish with a 72–90 record. Sitting in his spacious office at the Wrigley Building, agonizing over his team, Phil Wrigley

Leo "The Lip" Durocher (National Baseball Hall of Fame Library, Cooperstown, N.Y.).

1968 CHICAGO CUBS

turned to Leo "The Lip" Durocher in 1966. Durocher had gained fame as manager of the Dodgers and Giants after leading them both to pennants in the 1940s and 1950s. On arrival, he said, "The Cubs are not an eighth-place team."[12]

He was right. In 1966 the team dived to the National League cellar with a pathetic 59–103 record. The following year, Leo must have sprinkled a bit of magic dust over the Cubs as they finished the 1967 season with 87–74, an impressive 28-game improvement, moving up to third place, 3½ games behind second-place San Francisco and 14 games behind first-place St. Louis.

That was quite an improvement when you consider the history of the team. With eight teams in the league prior to 1945, the Cubs finished in the upper half 32 times. From 1946 through 1961, and still eight teams, the club finished in the top half three times and the bottom half 18 times. In 1962, two teams were added to the league, and for the next five years, the Cubs ended the season at or near the bottom.

In 1968 Chicago fans saw the Cubs as an up-and-coming team and came to Wrigley Field to watch the team improve. The Cubs finished third again that season, and ratings on TV and radio soared. Attendance at Wrigley climbed to more than a million, the most in sixteen years. Durocher had done his job. The team was ready for the '69 season and all of the players would be back.

As you look at the Cubs roster from that era, you see a team that deserved a great deal of respect. They had three future Hall of Famers: Billy Williams, Fergie Jenkins and Ernie Banks. They also had one player who should be in the Hall — Ron Santo, who was the dominant National League third baseman of his era.[13] They had four more very good, solid

Opposite: The 1968 Chicago Cubs. *Fourth row (left to right):* Ferguson Jenkins, Joe Niekro, Chuck Hartenstein, Bill Hands, Darcy Fast, Ken Holtzman, Dick Nen, Rich Nye, Jim Hickman, Phil Regan, Don Kessinger, Glenn Beckert, Bob Tiefenauer. *Third row (left to right):* Yosh Kawano (equipment manager), Al Scheuneman (trainer), Bill Plummer, Archie Reynolds, Jophrey Brown, Clarence Jones, John Uphamn, Lee Elia, Randy Bobb, Adolfo Phillips, Gary Ross, Willie Smith, Black Cullen (traveling secretary). *Second row (left to right):* Billy Williams, Ron Santo, Randy Hundley, Ernie Banks, Pete Reiser (coach), Leo Durocher (manager), Joe Amalfitano (coach), Rube Walker (coach), Joe Becker (coach), Jack Lamabe, Don Pinkus (batting practice catcher). *Front row (left to right):* Jose Arcia, Bill Stoneman, Jim Flood (batboy), Ken Kamin (batboy), Al Sprangler, Jimmy Lee McMath (National Baseball Hall of Fame Library, Cooperstown, N.Y.).

players in Randy Hundley, Glenn Beckert, Don Kessinger and Phil Regan. In addition, the team had a fair number of able players in Joe Niekro, Kenny Holtzman, Jim Hickman, Bill Hands and Gene Oliver. The only player who didn't carry his weight was Don Young, a .239 hitter who would misplay two fly balls when the Mets beat the Cubs 4–3 on July 8, 1969. He completed the season a forgotten man.[14]

Not least, the Cubs had one of the best managers around in Durocher. With Leo at the helm, the team had every reason to believe that they would make it to the top in 1969.[15]

CHAPTER 6

Miracle Mets

Before the 1969 season opened, it had been predicted that the long-suffering Cub fans would be tantalized all summer, and that then the St. Louis Cardinals, the defending National League champions would break their hearts.[1]

The Cubs were described as a close-knit ballclub, well crafted by Durocher. And Ernie Banks, the 38-year-old first baseman, thought they were ready to win the pennant. On April 8 he began his seventeenth season, saying, "This is my biggest chance to be on a pennant winner. I feel like this year we really do have the talent to do it and I want to do everything I can to make it happen."[2]

On the following day, a newspaper headline boldly announced: "RECORD 40,796 SEE CUBS WIN IN 11th 7 TO 6." Underneath, an article described Chicago fans starting to arrive at Wrigley Field at 8:00 A.M., and about the park being jammed to capacity, including the standing-room areas behind the lower deck. It also talked about Cub fans having "flag fever," as if the first game of the season had a touch of Opening Day and World Series rolled into one.

Cheers went up when team captain Ron Santo introduced Jimmy Durante during the opening ceremonies. But the loudest applause came when Ernie Banks bounced out of the dugout. Ernie did not disappoint his fans in the first when he stepped to the plate against the Phils' Chris Short and hit a two-run homer, the 476th of his career. This put him ahead of Stan Musial and into tenth on the all-time home-run list. In the third, Banks came through again, this time with a two-run homer that gave the Cubs a 5 to 1 cushion until Don Money hit a solo homer in the seventh, shaving the Cub margin to 5 to 2.

Ernie Banks hits his 476th home run, April 8, 1969 (National Baseball Hall of Fame Library, Cooperstown, N.Y.).

Fergie Jenkins cruised through the eighth, seemingly invincible. But in the ninth Callison and Rojas lead off with singles, and then Money tied the game with *his* second homer. Reliever Phil Regan stemmed the tide, though, and the Cubs won in the bottom of the eleventh on a two-run homer by ex-boxer, ex-pitcher, bench warmer Willie Smith.

While the Cubs were beating the Phillies, the Pittsburgh Pirates were taking care of the St. Louis Cardinals, beating them in the fourteenth inning in a night game, 6 to 2.

On the following day Billy Williams pounded four consecutive doubles to tie a major-league record and the Cubs whipped the Phils 11–3.

April 10 was Ron Santo's day to shine. The Cubs' captain powered two home runs against the Wrigley Field jet stream, and Chicago had their third consecutive victory, winning 6–2. The Cubs had not enjoyed such a successful start in many seasons.

On April 11 the Montreal Expos came to town — and were beaten by the Cubs 1–0 in twelve innings. Joe Niekro (nine innings) and Ted Abernathy (three) combined in the shutout. Billy Williams drove in the winning run with a two-out single to give the Cubs their fourth in a row. And so it went for a while. Chicago won eleven of their first twelve games before slowing down and finishing the month 17–7.

May seemed promising when the Cubs beat the Mets 6–4 at Wrigley on May 2, four of the runs coming in the fourth. Ron Santo started the slugfest with two out in the fourth by launching a 435-foot line drive that almost tore a hole in the AstroTurf that covered the old center field bleachers. Ernie Banks followed with a single, Randy Hundley drew a walk, and then Al Spangler spiked an unexpected three-run homer off rookie pitcher Gary Gentry.

On May 13, the Cubs walloped the Padres 19–0 at Wrigley to tie a club record for the most lopsided shutout since 1900. It was also the third consecutive game in which the Cubs shut out the opposition, with Dick Selma spinning a complete game. Ernie Banks was the hitting star with seven runs batted in on two homers and a double.

The shutout derby continued on May 16 when the Cubs exploded for 10 runs in the seventh inning, defeating the Astros 11–0 in Houston. Ken Holtzman pitched the shutout.

Then on May 20 Holtzman pitched his third consecutive shutout, running his scoreless-innings streak to 33, defeating the Dodgers 7–0 in Los Angeles. And there was more to come. On May 22 and 23, Jenkins and Selma pitched their second straight shutouts. On May 25, in the second game of a doubleheader, Bill Hands and Ted Abernathy combined for a shutout. And on May 30, 36,075 fans watched Bill Hands handcuff the Atlanta Braves with his slider to take the game 2–0. The National League Eastern Division standings showed the Cubs in first, 7½ games in front of second-place Pittsburgh, with St. Louis third, 9 games behind.

As the Cubs continued their winning ways on June 15, Ernie had an article in the *Chicago Tribune* titled, "Mr. Cub Tells Inside Story of Team's Success." Banks applauded leadership by Leo Durocher. But he also talked about players like Don Kessinger and Randy Hundley who helped the team by saying the right thing at the right time, thus adding to the morale. Banks pointed out how Kessinger studied the opposition quietly and passed along information to the rest of the team. As for Hundley,

Banks saw him as an all-star catcher who had wonderful control of his emotions.

Below the article by Banks was another headline: CUBS DO IT AGAIN! BEAT REDS IN 10th, 9–8.

On June 29, after the Cubs won a doubleheader, 3–1 and 12–1, opposing manager Red Schoendienst of the Cardinals must have been dismayed when he walked into the clubhouse. The Cubs had just kicked the hell out of his team, and with the way they were playing, the Cubs would be hard to catch.

With those two wins, Chicago was 8 games ahead of the second-place Mets and 14 games in front of the fourth-place Cards.

The Cubs could not be budged out of first. On July 15, Banks had another piece in the *Tribune*, and described the previous day's game when the Cubs had defeated the Mets 1–0. Banks talked about what he called "the big out." The Cubs had been leading 1–0 when an eighth-inning lead-off grounder by Ken Boswell skidded off the third-base bag and into the tall grass near the Cubs bullpen. Ron Santo ran it down, then fired an off-balance throw, without looking, toward second base. Boswell was tagged out and the Cubs' lead was not threatened. If Boswell had beaten the throw for a double, the Mets would have had three power hitters coming up. Santo's desperation throw could have been wild. Boswell would have then reached third and might even have scored. Though Bill Hands was pitching a great game, his opponent, Tom Seaver, would have been given a psychological lift with a tie score.

By July 30, the Cubs had slumped a little. They lost that day for the seventh time in thirteen games, though their lead was still 5½ games. On July 31 the Cubs ripped the Giants, 12–2 at Wrigley, and then the team was off and running again. August 15 found the Cubs 9 games in front of second-place St. Louis and 10 games in front of the Mets.

On August 16 the Cubs stayed even with the Cards (though they lost a ½ game to the doubleheader-winning Mets), as Jenkins won his seventeenth game, a 3-hit shutout. The score was tied 0–0 entering the ninth, but a pinch single by Paul Popovich started a rally that netted Chicago a 3–0 win over the Giants. The Cubs were thus assured that no matter the result of the following day's doubleheader, they would return home from a West Coast trip with a bigger lead in the Eastern Division race than they had when they left.[3]

6. Miracle Mets

On August 26, the Cubs were directed by National League President Warren Giles to begin immediately the printing of tickets for the best-of-five playoffs scheduled to open Saturday, October 4.[4] But their lead had dwindled to 3½ games as the Mets inched their way toward the top.

Struggling to stay in first, manager Leo Durocher went against his hunch at the last minute and started Dick Selma on August 30 in place of right-hander Ken Johnson against the Braves at Atlanta. But Durocher quickly changed his mind when Selma gave up three hits and a walk and two runs in the first. He didn't waste time bringing in Johnson, the veteran right-hander, who quickly took control.

Johnson pitched scoreless ball until yielding a lead-off homer to Hank Aaron in the seventh, but then another veteran pitcher, Phil Regan, came in to rescue the game — and maintain the Cubs' four-game lead. Regan, entrusted with a 5 to 3 lead, yielded two hits and one run in three innings for his fifteenth save of the season.

Another star of the game: Ernie Banks who slammed a first-inning home run off Ron Reed who had beaten the Cubs 6 to 2 ten days earlier. The homer, the Cubs' third consecutive hit in the first inning, followed a double by Billy Williams and a single over short on which Ron Santo drove in his 109th run.

The Mets kept pace, winning on Donn Clendenon's homer in the tenth against the San Francisco Giants.

On September 9, following a sweep of the Cubs by Pittsburgh, the Mets pulled within ½ game of first by sweeping a two-game series with the Cubs, Tom Seaver taking the last game 7 to 1. The dazed and disillusioned Chicago team had lost control of the National League's Eastern Division pennant race. A throng of 58,436 pennant-crazed New York fans in Shea Stadium chanted "Good-bye, Leo, we hate to see you go." Then, the Cubs escaped to Philadelphia, holding onto first place by the slenderest of margins.

For the first time in the season, another team in the East had lost fewer games. The Mets, a half game behind Chicago, had dropped 57, and the Cubs, who had played more games, had lost 58, including their last six in a row.

One must wonder about the rapid turn of events. On August 26, the club was ordered by the National League to print playoff tickets. And two weeks later, the team had virtually lost their lead. Were the players reminded of the curse in a game with the Mets on September 9, as reported by the *Chicago Tribune*, when someone released a black cat in front of the Cubs dugout at Shea Stadium, and the cat then crossed Ron Santo's path as he waited for his turn to bat, then scurried away?

Could this have caused some adverse psychological effect that influenced the way the team played? Did it remind the team of the Curse of the Goat?

The Cubs needed an awakening. Trying to halt the relentless Mets on September 9, Durocher had started Fergie Jenkins with only two days rest, but that move failed. And the next day Rick Wise, a 23-year-old right-hander for Philadelphia, dealt Chicago their seventh consecutive loss, 6–2.

Ken Holtzman, the third Cub starting pitcher whose routine had been altered during this inglorious week, endured a shaky night with his control. Six walks put him in repeated jeopardy while the game was still interesting. And he trailed by only 3 to 2 when it became necessary to pinch hit for him in the eighth. Then the Cubs bullpen let the game get out of hand in a three-run Philadelphia eighth, all runs being charged to Phil Regan.

A black cat crosses between Ron Santo and the Cubs dugout, Shea Stadium, September 9, 1969 (Bettmann/Corbis).

As the Cubs lost, the red-hot New York Mets charged into first place in the National League's Eastern Division by sweeping a doubleheader from Montreal, 3 to 2 in 12 innings and 7 to 1.

Ken Boswell drove in Cleon Jones to decide the opener and Nolan Ryan pitched a 3-hitter in the second contest as the Mets moved to a one-game lead over the Cubs. The double triumph stretched the Mets' winning streak to six games and put the once hapless New Yorkers into first place for the first time in their eight-year history.

Ferguson Jenkins warming up (National Baseball Hall of Fame Library, Cooperstown, N.Y.).

Despite the drop out of first place for the first time all season, the Cubs appeared to have lost none of their confidence and zest for the game. "I'm optimistic, very optimistic," said Ron Santo who drove in the losers' two runs, but blamed himself, along with the rest, for failing to deliver a big hit. "We can have all the confidence we want, but something's got to happen on the field," Santo observed. "We need a big base hit. I drive in one run with an infield out, another with a fly. If either of them had been big hits, we'd [have broken] the game open. But I envision a winning streak, a long winning streak!" he said, with all the confidence he could muster.[5]

It was hard to be confident, though, as evidenced in a September 11 *Chicago Tribune* article by Robert Markus. His "Stops Along the Sports Trail" column said that "everybody in this town is upset. Everybody's got

The 1969 World Champion New York Mets. *First row:* Gus Mauch (trainer), Joe Pignatano (coach), Rube Walker (coach), Yogi Berra (coach), Eddie Yost (coach), Joe Deer (assistant trainer). *Second row:* Tug McGraw, Gary Gentry, Al Weis, Cleon Jones, Manager Gil Hodges, Jerry Grote, Bud Harrelson, Ed Charles, Rod Gaspar, Duffy Dyer. *Third row:* Jim McAndrew, Tommie Agee, Cal Koonce, Ken Boswell, Tom Seaver, Jerry Koosman, Ron Swoboda, Wayne Garrett, Bobby Pfeil, Lou Niss (travelling secretary). *Top row:* Nick Torman (equipment manager), J.C. Martin, Ron Taylor, Ed Kranepool, Don Cardwell, Donn Clendenon, Nolan Ryan, Art Shamsky, Jack DiLauro, Roy Neuer (clubhouse attendant) (National Baseball Hall of Fame Library, Cooperstown, N.Y.).

a long face. The elevator operator in our building is so grouchy, he won't open the door, and I hear Mayor Daley was gonna call off the city council meeting. Everybody is worried."

And why shouldn't they have been? Since the season had started, anyone who'd tried to compare Santo, Kessinger, Beckert and Banks with the Mets' Wayne Garrett, Bud Harrelson, Ken Boswell and Donn Clendenon was convinced the Cubs were superior. Randy Hundley versus Jerry Grote behind the plate? No contest. Yes, the Mets' pitching was better, but not *that* much better.

By mid–August, the Cubs had led by 9½ games, and they led by 5 with only 25 remaining at the beginning of play on September 5. Now, everything turned upside down. As the season began to draw to a close, the Cubs lost 7 straight, 10 of 11, and 14 of 20 before being eliminated on September 24.

During that same 20-day span the Mets kept winning, going 19–5. The Mets took the flag with a record of 100–62, eight games ahead of the Cubs.

Simply put, the Cubs fell apart. Between September 3 and September 15, a 5-game lead became a 4½-game deficit, a swing of 9½ games. And some fans blamed it on the Curse of the Goat.

CHAPTER 7

A Stunning Collapse

After blowing the 1969 pennant, the Cubs must have entered the 1970s in a state of shock. But the same players were still together and ready to give it another shot. Maybe they'd be lucky, be lucky enough to take the flag in 1970.

But good luck was not a commodity the Cubs enjoyed. Two weeks into the season, Randy Hundley tore a ligament in his left knee in a jarring collision at the plate with Carl Taylor of the Cardinals during a 7–4 win at Wrigley Field on April 21. This put Hundley on the disabled list until July 10.

But the Cubs did well at first. On April 27 they won their eleventh game in a row, defeating the Pirates 1–0 in Pittsburgh. This win gave the Cubs a 12–3 record and it seemed to squelch the idea that the team might suffer psychological damage resulting from the collapse of 1969.

Ernie Banks slammed his 500th home run on May 4, but he was now limited to a part-time role because of aching knees, and would play in only 72 games that year.[1] And the Cubs started losing, going 12–14 in May, and 10–18 in June. On June 30 the team lost their twelfth in a row, dropping a 5–4 decision to the Cardinals. This losing streak dropped the Cubs' record to 35–37, and although the team seemed to be in contention at times, something always came along to spoil their chances. The trade of Ted Abernathy to the Cardinals for Phil Gagliano is an example. It was a bad deal. Abernathy had three more good seasons, while Gagliano was a useless addition.[2]

July started out well, though, with the Cubs ending their 12-game losing streak by beating the Cardinals 5–0 in St. Louis, Fergie Jenkins pitching the shutout. And the month ended well when Chicago swept the

Reds in a doubleheader at Riverfront Stadium in Cincinnati 7–1 and 11–7. For the second time in a span of six days, Glenn Beckert collected seven hits in a twin-bill. Going 19–12 in July, the Cubs had high hopes as they entered August. On August 19 they tied a club record by smashing seven homers in defeating the Padres 12–2 at Wrigley Field. Jim Hickman hit two home runs, with Ferguson Jenkins, Billy Williams, Joe Pepitone, Johnny Callison, and Glenn Beckert adding one each. Three days later, Ken Holtzman came with five outs of a no-hitter as the Cubs clobbered the Giants 15–0 at Wrigley. The only San Francisco hit was a single by Hal Lanier with one out in the eighth. On September 2, they scored eight runs in the fourth and defeated the Phillies 17–2 at Wrigley, collecting twenty hits in the contest.

The team was just five games over .500, but still in contention, and the Billy Goat would have been alive with discussions while beer flowed from the taps. On September 23, though, the Cubs suffered a crushing blow to their pennant hopes, losing a doubleheader by identical 2–1 scores against the Cardinals to drop 2½ games behind the Pirates. They would finish the season 84–78, five games out of first.

When season records are examined, the 1970 Cubs may have been bigger underachievers than the 1969 club that blew a 9½-game lead. In 1970, Chicago outscored the opposition 806–679, the largest run differential in the National League that season. The Cubs scored 31 more runs than the Reds and allowed two fewer, yet Cincinnati won 102 games and Chicago won only 84.

For Cub fans, it was another disappointing year. Even William "Billy Goat" Sianis would have been dismayed, because long ago he had decided to end the Curse. He wrote to the Cubs organization, telling them there was no longer a curse on the team. He said he had removed it, and suggested that they all go out and celebrate by breaking bread together.[3]

But fate intervened. "Billy Goat" Sianis died at home on October 22, 1970.[4] He was 76, unmarried, and had no children. He left the Billy Goat Tavern to his nephew, Sam Sianis, who carried on what his uncle had started.

Sam reportedly was born in the same town as his uncle, in Greece. U.S. Public Records, record number 439687501, lists his date of birth as December 1, 1934, while Rick Kogan's book, *A Chicago Tavern*, says it was "on the morning of 12 December 1935." Living off the land without the use of farm implements, Sam worked hard, doing everything needed to run the farm.[5] Since the demands of the farm were so time-consuming, Sam was unable to complete his education. One day, before the age of 20, he decided to go to the United States, and he did, arriving at Ellis Island on May 15, 1955. After visiting relatives, and working for the railroad for a number of years, he decided to join his uncle. Sam arrived in Chicago on July 4, 1960, and began working alongside "Billy Goat" Sianis.[6]

After "Billy Goat" Sianis died, Sam kept the place going, showing everyone that he had the business acumen that his uncle had.[7] On July 4, 1973, Sam and a goat sat in the back seat of a long limo, heading north toward Clark and Addison. Cub fans were gathering and celebrating at Wrigleyville, waiting for the ballpark to open. The chauffeur slowed the limo to a crawl, pulled into a parking space designated for Chicago's Mayor Daley, exited the car, came around to where Sam and his goat sat, and opened the door as if royalty was about to exit the vehicle. Sam stepped out first, holding onto a leash, and then coaxed the goat off the back seat, and onto the walkway that led to the Wrigley Field turnstiles. Once again, in spite of having a ticket, a goat was not allowed into the ballpark.[8]

At the time, the Cubs were in first place. But after a win that day, they lost 30 of their next 37 games in a stunning collapse that brought about the dissolution of most of the last remnants of the 1969 club.

What happened? Could it have been the Curse? Bad luck? Something else? Let's look at the 1973 team and then decide.

CHAPTER 8

Running Out of Gas

When Leo Durocher failed to capture flags in 1970, 1971, and 1972, he was fired and Whitey Lockman took over.

"Morale is a helluva lot better under Whitey," said Ferguson Jenkins, about to face Mike Torres of the Montreal Expos on April 6 before a full house at Wrigley. "If our bullpen can get straightened out, we can do it. People ask why we haven't been able to win the big games in previous years. Well, it was because the same eight players played day after day after day. When big games came along, they were worn out."

"Whitey talked to us individually this spring and told me he planned to play all 25 players. He has the depth to give guys a rest every once in a while and not hurt the team," continued Jenkins, about to try to put together his seventh consecutive 20-victory season despite a case of tendonitis in his shoulder.[1]

Among those in box seats that sunny afternoon, were Mayor Richard Daley and Federal Judge Abraham Marovitz. They watched as the ceremonial first pitch was thrown out by Navy Lt. Commander Robert Naughton, a former prisoner of war.[2] They also watched Jenkins pitch superbly. A standing-room-only crowd of 40,273 at Wrigley saw the Cubs, down 2–1, rally in the last of the ninth, winning on bases-loaded walks by Mike Marshall to Randy Hundley and Rick Monday.

Opening day over the years had always been an exhilarating spring event for Chicago fans. The Cubs always seemed to look their best in the first game of the season. It was the other 161 games that caused trouble.

The next day, April 7, the Cubs again demonstrated that they could come from behind and win the close ones. Mike Marshall, perhaps baseball's best relief pitcher, was again unable to stop them.

Whitey Lockman, manager of the 1973 Cubs (photograph by George Brace).

Manager Whitey Lockman called four "hit-and-run" plays that day. Two led directly to runs as Chicago won 3–2 over Montreal in 10 innings. Ron Santo, though, swinging the bat better and with more savvy than at any time in his career, did the obvious damage by nailing a Marshall screwball into left center field with two out in the tenth for the game-winning hit.[3] A few weeks earlier, his mother and stepfather had been killed in an auto accident on their way to visit him during spring training.[4]

Although Santo had to take some time off, Lockman, true to his word, shuffled all 25 of his athletes as regularly as possible, and maneuvered them into games when needed. On April 29, he summoned Gene Hiser and Paul Popovich as rather surprising pinch-hitters in the sixth inning of a 3–3 contest with San Diego. The result was a tie-breaking single by Hiser and a two-run single by Popovich, leading to a 10–4 romp for the North Siders. The triumph completed a three-game sweep against the Padres.

"I think everybody is going to have a better mental attitude because of the way Whitey uses all the players," said Popovich. "It's better for the guys on the bench and also for the regulars, who know they're going to get a rest now and then."[5]

With Pittsburgh dropping a doubleheader to the Dodgers, the Cubs climbed to within a half-game of the Eastern Division-leading Mets.

By May 29, one month later, the Cubs had passed and were pulling away from New York, leading the second-place Mets by 5 games. They continued playing splendid baseball, as two days later they scored ten runs in the first inning, defeating the Astros 16–8 at Wrigley. All ten runs were scored after the first two hitters were retired.

By June 25, though, most of the Cubs looked and felt as if they had been on a four-month Yukon expedition. They felt as if they were carrying 40-pound backpacks, swinging 20-pound hammers at bat and wearing snowshoes when they ran. In fact, they had been on the longest road trip ever, sixteen games eventually. Nevertheless, on June 25, with an almost nonexistent offense, Santo and Kessinger kicked the team into high gear at the last possible moment, with a three-run ninth-inning rally that brought the Cubs a 3–2 triumph over the New York Mets.

Seldom, if ever, had the Cubs rallied so dramatically at Shea Stadium, site of their 1969 collapse, and they appreciated its significance, even if they were too tired to generate an overt celebration. Actually, they were very quiet about the whole thing, much like their bats had been thru eight innings against Jon Matlack.

"It was a real morale booster, for me and the team," Santo said of the victory, and of his bases-loaded, game-tying double off Tug McGraw with none out in the ninth. "I was looking for a screwball and saw a fastball. I couldn't get all the way around on it, but I got the good part of the bat on it."[6]

Santo's double drove in Glenn Beckert and Billy Williams and three batters later, Kessinger singled to center, chasing home the winning run.

After another win in New York on June 26, the Cubs went home at last for a series with the Expos. The second game of a June 27 doubleheader went so long that it had to be called because of darkness, to be continued on June 28. That contest, featuring game-tying homers in the ninth and thirteenth by Ron Santo, was eventually won by the Expos in 18 innings.

In the regularly scheduled game played on June 28, Rick Monday tied the score with a home run in the third, then snapped a 2–2 draw in the seventh with a two-run homer, his 18th of the season, matching his best home-run output ever. Additionally, Monday participated in the game's pivotal play, insisting afterward that he'd made a legitimate catch of a sinking line drive hit by Ken Singleton with the bases filled and one out in the third. It led to a rare appeal play, forcing Ron Hunt out at third after he failed to tag up after the catch. A television replay left the impression that Monday trapped the line drive, on which second-base umpire Tom Gorman started to give the "safe" sign, then signaled out. Hunt took one step back toward third but never tagged the bag before trotting home with what he thought was the Expos' second run.

The Cubs were now leading the Eastern Division, 7½ games in front of Montreal. The New York Mets had slipped to last, 10½ games out.

On July 1, playing before 42,497 at Wrigley, the Cubs salvaged a doubleheader, scoring three runs in the ninth on a homer by Randy Hundley to beat the Mets 6–5 in the second game. After a loss on July 3, the Cubs came from behind again on July 4 when Ron Santo ended the game with a two-run homer in the tenth, beating the Phillies 3–2 at Wrigley.

Two days later the *Chicago Tribune* published an article headlined "If Cubs Blow It, Look for the Goat." Dave Condon reviewed the historical background of the Curse, and talked about William "Billy Goat" Sianis leaving the curse in his will and passing it on to his heirs. He also talked about Sam Sianis, one of the heirs who tried to break the curse, but was not successful.[7]

On that same day in the *Tribune*, July 6, George Langford talked about the Cubs closing out a 10-game home stand, one which had been a disappointment, by surrendering seven early runs and falling to the Philadelphia Phillies, 7–4. Langford quoted Don Kessinger who had admitted to the team being a little flat. Whitey Lockman talked about Rick Reuschel, the Cubs' most consistent hurler, suffering his first bad outing of the season in 18 starts. But he was hopeful as the team departed on an 8-game, 10-day tour of the West Coast.[8]

By July 17, though, the Cubs were losing games and a grip on first as San Diego's Steve Arlin blanked the team 1–0, extending the North Siders' losing streak to five in a row and giving them 11 losses in their last 15 games. That game, plus the Cardinals' victory of the day, shaved the Cubs' division lead to a half game — their smallest margin since assuming first place on May 9.

Then people began wisecracking, poking fun at the Cubs in the July 18 edition of the *Tribune*. Wilmar: "The Cubs are merely victims of the times — they've run out of gas." Crigley: "Lets not panic. The Cubs are still the best team on the north side." Stachowski: "Some people go on their honeymoon to Niagara Falls. The Chicago National League baseball club goes to Cub Falls."

Nevertheless, George Langford did his job in a professional manner when he wrote a July 19 article for the *Tribune*, headlined "Santo Hurt as Cubs Lose Again 8–5." Langford wrote, "Friends, the Cubs are in serious trouble and it is only mid–July. Yesterday, they not only lost their sixth consecutive game and twelfth in the last 16 thus falling out of first place for the first time in 70 days, but they were confronted with the following burdens in the wake of San Diego's 8–5 victory:

> Ron Santo suffered a strained muscle in the left side of his lower back attempting to avoid a tag at first base, was carried from the field on a stretcher and likely will be lost to the team until after the All-Star game next week.
>
> Fergie Jenkins, once their best pitcher, continued in his pitching slump which has been punctuated by home runs at the alarming rate of one every six innings. Three were stroked off him yesterday, for a total of 28 in 23 games, and the Padres beat him for the first time in their five-year existence.
>
> Thus, in just six days, the Cubs have lost the five-game lead they held over the St. Louis Cardinals and inevitably Chicagoans are recalling the specter of 1969, that nightmare that was a reality when a nine-game lead was wasted in late August.
>
> Just 19 days ago they enjoyed an eight-game lead. The latest loss dropped the Cubs out of first place for the first time since May 9 by eight ten-thousandths of a percent — the Cards had a winning percentage of .5384 to the Cubs' .5376 — but the Cubs regained the lead by a margin of .005 last night after St. Louis lost to San Francisco 8–3.

The Cubs fought on. On August 4 in Montreal, under the headline "Reuschel Fans 11 in 4-hitter," Bob Logan opened his column by saying, "It was about time to hold a séance, call Hertz Rent-a-Poltergeist, hire a friendly neighborhood warlock, or do something to break the spell that has been haunting the Cubs." Logan continued:

> Nothing all that drastic was required for Rick Reuschel to quell the Expos 3–0 tonight in a truly brilliant four-hit, 11-strikeout effort. A couple of lucky charms sufficed to snap a three-game losing streak and

bring the Chicagoans within 2½ games of the lead in the National League East.

A bat and a hat did the trick, not to mention Reuschel's own keen powers of observation. The hat was Ron Santo's, a Navy Pier fisherman's cap he sported in the hotel lobby this afternoon.

"I don't fish," Santo replied to a query about the snappy headgear. "When things are going bad, I try to change our luck with a new hat."

The bat belonged to Bill Robinson of the Phillies who had just clubbed the Cubs into submission three straight times. He gave it to Andre Thornton, a fellow fugitive from the Philadelphia minor-league chain gang. Thornton used it tonight to chalk up his first major league hit and set the Cubbies on the road to recovery.

The article went on to quote Reuschel, who had been toying with his delivery in the bullpen, trying to recapture his form from earlier in the season: "Everything just fell into place when I found I was coming off the mound too much toward first base. I started throwing like I had been earlier in the season and tonight was the best game I've pitched since then."[9]

As the Cubs struggled to stay in contention for the flag, the New York Mets continued to flounder along in last place. By August 28, they were still in last while the Cubs had slipped to third, still 2½ games behind the Cards and a half game behind the second-place Pirates.

Added to the downward trend was a medical report on Ferguson Jenkins who had injured his pitching hand on August 27 in Atlanta. Although there were no fractures, and despite the almost constant application of ice to his two middle fingers, it was said to be likely that he would miss his next starting turn in Pittsburgh.

As to the injury, not even Jenkins could explain exactly what happened when he was at bat and suddenly found Jose Cardenal coming home from third in a surprise maneuver, colliding with Jenkins as catcher Skip Jutze moved out of the way in pursuit of the ball. The Cubs ace lost his balance and tumbled to the ground.[10]

Nor could Fergie explain why his pitching for the year had slumped — to a 12–12 record. Because of his poor showing, many Cub fans had come down hard on Jenkins. But Robbin Chark of Chicago came to his defense in the *Tribune* when she said, "I am a great Cubs fan who is upset and angry to see so many people picking on Fergie. How in the world do you expect him to do good if you boo him? He needs encouragement, and lots of it."[11]

In the same article, G. L. of Kenosha, Wisconsin, had something to say about the entire Chicago team. "The Cubs right now are strictly on their own. They are only a few games out of the division lead — and they either have it or they don't. There are no more Leo Durochers to blame. I always remember what Connie Mack once said: 'I've seen boys on my baseball team go into slumps and never come out of them, and I've seen others snap right out and come back better than ever. I guess more players lick themselves than are licked by an opposing team. The first thing any man has to know is how to handle himself.'"[12]

Apparently, the Cubs did not know how to handle themselves, as reported by Richard Dozer in the *Chicago Tribune* on September 7. Under the headline "Cubs Limp Home 6 Games out of First after 5–3 Defeat," Dozer reported on the Cubs as being beaten and bedraggled, now within three games of the bottom. This was the same team that had been at the top of their division for nearly three months. Now that they were home, they were going to try to break a three-game losing streak when they opened a weekend series against the first-place Cardinals at Wrigley Field.

The Cubs not only won the opener, they swept the series, and were again only three games back. Now, the Pirates were coming to town. And there must have been hope that they could still win the pennant. That was not asking too much from a team that boasted the National League batting champion, the best-fielding shortstop in the game, and a pitcher who had won 20 games six years in a row.

In their first game with the Pirates, the Cubs knew it was an absolute necessity that they win. It was a moment of truth. It was a matter of being two games out or four out.

The result? The Cubs fumbled afield, stumbled at the bat, bumbled on the bases, and the Pirates easily defeated them 11–3. Burt Hooton pitched a 4-hit shutout the next day but the Pirates took the next two games and were in first, one game over .500. Richard Dozer wrote that the Cubs needed to win 12 of their last 17 to finish at .500, a figure that could still win the championship.[13]

On September 25, the Cubs rallied in a game against the Cardinals for a 4–3 win. Jose Cardenal drilled a two-run double into left center field with the bases loaded and two outs in the ninth inning. The Cubs were technically still alive, four games below .500.

Besides the Cardinals and Pirates, the Mets had been battling for the lead. They had risen from the cellar to contend for the title. On September 28, they came to Wrigley Field with a one-game lead over the Pirates and a 4-game lead over the Cubs with four games remaining. It had been raining and Wrigley Field was muddy, so the Mets-Cubs skirmish was rescheduled as part of a doubleheader on September 30.

The Cubs still had a chance of tying the Mets for the title, but it was not to be. George Langford wrote in the *Tribune* on October 1, under the headline "That's All, Folks! Mets R.I.P. Cubs":

> Because the Cubs have let so many sure things slip away in recent years, it didn't figure that their official elimination yesterday — when a miracle was required — would cut too deeply.
>
> But it did.
>
> They defeated the Mets 1–0. Then they saw the scoreboard tell them at 3:45 P.M. that St. Louis had won, thereby ending all hope on the North Side.
>
> Twenty-seven minutes later, the Mets tossed the first shovel of dirt on them with a 9–2 triumph in the second half of a doubleheader that assured the New Yorkers no worse than a tie for the National League East title.
>
> The Cubs' chances had been ridiculously small in the first place, needing to sweep this doubleheader and another one today. Still it hurt.

Langford went on to describe the reaction of Ron Santo, who had gotten the game-winning single in the first half of the doubleheader but had made two crucial fielding gaffs in the second game. "All I know is that three months ago we were in first place by eight games and the Mets were last and all the writers were trying to fire Yogi Berra.... Now here I sit and there they sit over there. The first three months don't mean anything. It's those last three," said Santo.[14]

On October 1, in misty, foggy Wrigley Field, before only 1,913 fans, the New York Mets won the National League's Eastern Division title. The Chicago Cubs came in fifth, five games out.

The Mets thus established a record for mediocrity. Their 82 victories and 79 losses represented the worst mark to win anything — division title or pennant — in the history of the major leagues.

What can be said about the Cubs with their 77–84 record? How does one explain the fall of a team that had been on top for months? Is anyone or anything to blame? Pitching staff? Batter slumps? Morale? Bad luck? Psychological hang-ups? Manager? The Curse of the Goat?

8. Running Out of Gas

No one can tell for certain. But on July 6, 1973, in mid-season, the *Chicago Tribune* carried a comment on page 1 that referred to an article in the sports section. "Cubs reject Billy's Goat," the paper said.

"Billy Goat Sianis's hex lives on. Cubs refuse to admit Socrates the goat to Wrigley Field, so David Condon fears their pennant bid is doomed." Condon's remark was interestingly timed. It was around mid-season that the Cubs began their decline.

CHAPTER 9

Managers Coming
and Going

When the Cubs failed in 1973, they must have also lost heart, because the team was then seen as not just losers, but perpetual losers. Nevertheless, Whitey Lockman stayed on as manager for the '74 season, and Chicago finished in sixth place, 22 games behind Pittsburgh. Naturally, it was his fault. Right? So Lockman had to go.

Jim Marshall took over the helm in 1975. But his club didn't do much better, coming in fifth, still 22 games out. Marshall stayed on as manager in '76, and the Cubs came in fourth, 26 games behind Pittsburgh. Goodbye, Marshall.

In 1977, Herman Franks took a shot at the head-honcho job. Again the Cubs finished fourth, 20 games back.

The struggling Cubs, with managers coming and going, would certainly have continued to be a topic of discussion at the Billy Goat Tavern. After all, much had been written about the Curse of the Goat, and many of these writings had been posted on the walls of the tavern, particularly those by Mike Royko, who used the place as an oasis.[1]

Beginning many years before, Bill Sianis would entertain customers by shouting "Cheeseborger! Try the double cheese! No fries, cheeps!" The routine caught on and became a staple at the Tavern. Besides Mike Royko and other journalists, the Billy Goat Tavern counted a number of young Second City comedians among its customers, including Don Novello (better known as Father Guido Sarducci) and Bill Murray. In January of 1978, there would have been serious discussions about whether Herman Franks would stay for the season, but on January 28 all eyes in the Billy Goat

Tavern were glued to the television, the regulars bursting with laughter as John Belushi and the cast of *Saturday Night Live* mimicked the goings-on at the Billy Goat in a Novello-penned skit:

> Standing behind the diner's counter was Nico (Bill Murray), a waiter. A patron enters, seats self. "I'll have eggs," he says. Waiter nods.
> WAITER: "Cheeseburger?"
> PATRON: "No, eggs. Don't you speak English?"
> JOHN BELUSHI, as Pete Dionasopolis, the owner, interrupts: "No eggs! Cheeseburger?"
> PATRON: "Just a couple of eggs."
> BELUSHI: "No eggs! Cheeseburger! Everybody got a cheeseburger. Cheeseburger?"
> PATRON: "It's too early in the morning for a cheeseburger!"
> BELUSHI: "Too early? Look! [He points around] Everybody has cheeseburger!"

The skit continues, with Belushi endlessly entreating customers to have a cheeseburger. If they asked for a Coke, they were met with shouts of "no Coke! Pepsi!"

Sam Sianis didn't see the TV program. He heard about it at a party where people, instead of saying cheeseburger, screamed "cheesborger." And after the *Saturday Night Live* episode had been explained to Sam, he found everyone telling him to say cheezeborger instead of cheeseburger, and it didn't take long for Sam and his crew to greet his customers with "Cheezeborger, Cheezeborger! No fries, cheeps! No Coke! Pepsi!"

What the skit did not portray were the frequent practical jokes William Sianis sprang on his customers, as told by his nephew Sam in an interview November 9, 1983. The elder Sianis would ask someone to drop a package in the mail for him; when handed the package, the customer would receive an electric jolt. He would pass someone the telephone, saying there was a call for them; only when they picked up the receiver would they realize that it was piping hot. Another phone might squirt water into the user's mouth. If you played a tune on the oddly handy flute, you'd find yourself with a black circle around your mouth and a sooty mustache to match. Air from a fan strategically placed beneath a grate would blow lady's dresses up as they walked over it on their way into the bar.

Belushi's "Cheezborger! cheezeborger!" routine made the tavern famous, more people came to the Billy Goat, and this would have resulted in even more heated debates about baseball, the Cubs, and the pros and cons of Herman Franks, the manager who had agreed to stay on for the 1978 season.

That year, Franks did much better, the team moving up to third, 11 games back, so he stayed on again. But near the end of the 1979 season, with the team doing poorly, Franks had to go, and Joey Amalfitano managed the club for the last seven games as Chicago finished fifth, 18 games behind Pittsburgh.

Preston Gomez took the job in 1980, and when the club could not improve, Amalfitano again became skipper. The Cubs dropped to sixth with a miserable record of 64–98.

In 1981, the team went nowhere again. Led by Amalfitano, the Cubs finished sixth, 17½ games down.

It was Lee Elia in 1982. The Cubs came in fifth, 19 games behind St. Louis. Charlie Fox in 1983 did no better. Again, the team came in fifth, 19 games back.

For ten years, with managers coming and going, the Chicago Cubs didn't do much of anything. It had been 38 years since the team won a pennant, and 85 years since they won a World Series championship. About the only thing Cubs fans could do was voice their mantra, "Wait till next year."

CHAPTER 10

Hello, Mr. Frey

James Gottfried Frey developed a reputation for striking pay dirt when he led the Kansas City Royals to their first American League championship in 1980, his first year with the team. He was available, so the Chicago Cubs hired him for the 1984 season.[1] Hiring him was part of a grand plan, started on October 15, 1981, when new owners, the Tribune Company, made Dallas Green the executive vice president and general manager of the Cubs.

Acquiring Green wasn't easy. As manager of the Phillies, he had led the team to their first World Championship in the franchise's 97-year history in 1980s. Nevertheless, when the Tribune Company told him he could build the Chicago club in whatever way he thought best, he signed with the Cubs.

Phils fans were at a loss for words when they read the *Philadelphia Bulletin* headline: "Dallas Green to Take Over Cubs." Chicago fans too were thunderstruck. It was the first Cubs personnel move by the Tribune Company, and one week later Green hired Lee Elia as the Cubs' new manager, replacing Joe Amalfitano. Green told the media that a losing team like the Cubs had an attitude problem. It was something that had to be changed.

He knew that the players had to be changed and that the entire system needed a major overhaul. No one predicted that Green would come up with a pennant contender quickly. As he dealt with much uproar, he knew that the job of rebuilding the organization would be done as long as he was in charge.[2]

In fact, the team should have known within a month of his hiring that change was coming. He had written each player a letter, telling them that physical conditioning started immediately, not at spring training. He also told the players that they would soon be hearing from Tony Garofalo (the Cubs trainer) and Lee Elia about the new conditioning program. Every player knew that come spring training, they had to be ready to work on fundamentals instead of spending time getting in shape.[3]

When Jim Frey came aboard in 1984, Dallas Green knew the team was ready, and the April 3 season opener in San Francisco must have been a delight for both Green and Frey as they watched the Cubs defeat the Giants 5–3.

But their joy was short-lived. The Cubs didn't do too well in the seven games played in California, finishing the short West Coast tour with a 2–1 loss to Rick Honeycutt and the Dodgers, and a 3–4 record. This loss put the Cubs into a three-way tie for fourth, 3 games behind the league-leading New York Mets. And come Friday afternoon, weather permitting, the Cubs and the Mets would square off in the Friendly Confines, Wrigley Field, in front of a standing-room-only crowd.

Since 1976, the Cubs had opened at home against the Mets six times. Chicago fans could now view the 3-game weekend as a tradition. If the rain eased, it was going to be Steve Trout, the only Cubs' left-handed pitcher against the Mets' rookie, Dwight Gooden. Both were fastball pitchers, but Gooden was viewed as one of the best young pitchers around.

The grounds crew did their part. They worked hard and long. In fact, they worked around the clock, just so the players wouldn't have to play the game in deep mud.[4]

Cubs management did their part too by allowing Sam Sianis and his goat into the ballpark and onto the field for the opening game at Wrigley. Sam marched around the field, close to the stands, greeting fans with a broad smile, holding his cap high in the air with one hand and the leash for his goat with the other. The goat was elegantly attired, and wearing a Cubs cap. And it was readily apparent that Sam Sianis was there with his goat in an attempt to break the Curse.

Besides Trout, the Cubs' starters at the beginning of the season were Scott Sanderson, Dick Ruthven, and Chuck Rainey. But the key was their skipper, Jim Frey. His abilities as a judge of talent and as a leader were never questioned.[5]

On Friday the 13th, in the home opener at Wrigley, the Cubs bashed the Mets 11–2 before 33,436 fans. The team showed their power when Ron Cey, Jody Davis and Gary Matthews hit home runs, abetted by a blustery

Sam Sianis and his goat at Wrigley Field, April 13, 1984 (as published in the *Chicago Sun-Times*. Copyright 1984 by *Chicago Sun-Times*. Reprinted with permission).

wind. The Cubs pounded out 14 hits and evened their record at 4–4. The Mets slipped to 6–2.

Trout, the lanky left-hander, tossed a complete game, allowing just seven hits, struck out four and walked none. Trout even contributed a pair of hits, including a bunt single in the Cubs' five-run fourth inning.

On the following day the Cubs did it again, beating the Mets 5–2 in front of 15,789 chilly fans. Leon "Bull" Durham, who had been booed the previous day, answered on Saturday with an eighth-inning home run into the teeth of a 10-mile-an-hour wind. It gave him two runs batted in for the day. Dick Ruthven earned his second victory of the season by pitching six strong innings, allowing only six hits while striking out five.

The North Siders continued to play good baseball. One of their fans, Indiana Congressman Elwood Hillis, crowed to his colleagues on Capitol Hill when the Cubs defeated the St. Louis Cardinals 3–2 on April 24 and moved into sole possession of first place in the National League's Eastern Division.[6]

The next day the Cubs lost to St. Louis and fell out of first.

Not losing heart, they continued to show their power. Leon Durham hit a home run in each of three games against the Padres at Wrigley on May 4, 5 and 6. And on May 7 the Cubs scoring seven runs in the second inning to take a 9–0 lead, and then held on to beat the Giants 10–7. And Durham hit a homer for the fourth game in a row.

One week later, on May 14, Ryne Sandberg was named NL Player of the Week. During a 16-game hitting streak, he'd gone 13-for-29 [.448] with 3 doubles, 3 RBIs and 2 stolen bases.[7]

Two days later, the Cubs beat the Reds 10–4 at Riverfront Stadium, pummeling five Reds pitchers for 13 hits, and moving past the Mets into first place in the NL East. Sandberg extended his hitting streak to 18 games, but it was the three homers by Ron Cey, Leon Durham and Jody Davis that ruined the Reds.

The Cubs hit the ball hard on May 24 with Bob Dernier collecting five hits in five at-bats during a 10–7 win over the Braves in the first game of a double-header at Wrigley. Leon Durham contributed six runs batted in with a pair of three-run homers. And the Cubs won the second game 7–5.

And so it went. By June 13, with a Cubs' record of 34–25, Dallas Green found himself wanting another pitcher to help his team win the pennant. In May he'd traded Bill Buckner to the Red Sox for pitcher Dennis Eckersley. This time he sacrificed four promising players under the age of 25 for three Cleveland veterans, including Rick Sutcliffe who had a herky-jerky delivery that kept batters off stride.

On June 23, in one of the most dramatic and unforgettable victories in the history of the franchise, Ryne Sandberg slammed two home runs and three singles, driving in seven runs to spark the Cubs to a thrilling eleven-inning 12–11 decision over the Cardinals at Wrigley.

But the Mets too were playing great ball, holding on to a slight lead. Many Chicago batters were firmly convinced that they could overtake and pass the Mets if the team administration would only change its landscaping policy. The Cubs bosses had ordered the infield grass cut high to help slow ground balls to compensate for the lack of range by 38-year-old shortstop Larry Bowa and 36-year-old Ron Cey.[8]

In spite of this, on July 29, the Cubs swept the Mets 3–0 and 5–1 in a doubleheader at Shea Stadium to cut New York's lead in the pennant race to 1½ games, and on August 1, Chicago took over first with a 5–4 win over the Phillies at Wrigley. A sacrifice fly by Jody Davis in the ninth plated the winning run.

On the following day, the Curse of the Goat was forgotten when the Cubs turned a bizarre double play in the ninth to stave off the Expos 3–2 at Wrigley.

With runners on first and third and one out, Pete Rose hit a liner that bounced off reliever Lee Smith's shoulder to shortstop Dave Owen, who caught the rebound. Owen threw to first to double up Don Stanhouse to end the game. The play has gone down in Cubs lore as the "immaculate deflection."[9]

By August 8, luck was still with the Cubs as they completed a four-game sweep of the Mets at Wrigley with a 7–6 win. The Cubs downed the Mets 9–3 on August 6, and 8–6 and 8–4 in a doubleheader on August 7, increasing their lead from a half game to 4½ games with the four wins.

By August 24, the Cubs were still going strong, and still on top, leading the second-place Mets by four games. Rick Sutcliffe had been superb, with nine straight wins. The team kept winning.

The Mets searched high and low for a crack in the Cubs' armor and could hardly find a dent. They tried to poke base hits past bulletproof second baseman, Ryne Sandberg. He stuck them to his Gold Glove. They tested the tender back of pitcher Scott Sanderson. He showed them more backbone than a dinosaur. They pushed relief pitcher Lee Smith to the last out in the ninth. He gave them only false hope. After 2 hours and 52 minutes of hardball on September 15, the Mets lost 5–4 to the Cubs, heirs apparent to the National League East title.

"They don't look too vulnerable to me," Mets' manager, Davey Johnson said. "Their pitchers pitched remarkably well against us. We've still got spirit. We battled back. If we had caught a few breaks, it might have been different."

Such is the lament of losers. The Mets fell 9½ games behind in the NL East standings, while the Cubs' magic number shriveled to five in front of 38,653 fans.[10]

Who would've thought that the 5 foot 9 inch Cub manager could have made it happen. Who would have thought that a guy who had plugged away for most of his life as a CPA, and who sold insurance on the side, would one day bring the Chicago Cubs to the brink of a National League East Division championship title?

Frey's German-born father would never have believed it. All he wanted was for his son to be an accountant. His aunt and great-aunt would not have believed it. They kept asking Rose Frey if her son was ever going to get a job. Even if these elderly ladies from the old country understood baseball, they couldn't imagine how little Jimmy could work into it. Frey himself would never have believed it. "No one ever accused me of having an athletic body," Frey said, referring to the days before that body, in an atavistic change, turned into a potato dumpling. "How many little, half-bald fat guys are there walking around? There's millions," Frey said. "I think you would say I am the type of person that would go unrecognized under normal circumstances."[11]

Under normal circumstances, the city would not be denying 53-year-old Jim Frey his wish to manage, go home and be inconspicuous. The Clark Street parking lot attendant would not have waived the fee for him. Half the bar patrons at a North Side restaurant wouldn't be trying to buy him vodka tonics. A salesman wouldn't drop off a bottle of liqueur on his table.

Nothing could be more unusual than the Cubs' success in a town starving for it. On September 23, with a Sunday sweep of a doubleheader against the St. Louis Cardinals, 8–1 and 4–2, Frey's Cubs reduced their magic number to one, increasing the possibility of a celebration in Pittsburgh where they were going to open a three-game series the next day.

On Monday, with one out to go, Cubs general manager Dallas Green leaned over and kissed his wife. Ryne Sandberg looked across the infield at Larry Bowa and smiled. Then Rick Sutcliffe won the game with a called third strike on the Pirates' Joe Orsulak.

By clinching the National League East Division championship title with a 4–1 triumph over the Pirates at Three Rivers Stadium, the Cubs set off a celebration. It was Sutcliffe's 14th win in a row, running his record as a Cub to 16–1. Overall, Sutcliffe was 20–6 in 1984, counting a 4–5 mark with the Indians.

"This ball club has suffered for 39 years. They've not been first in anything, and that's long enough," said Frey in his postgame interview, popping the cork on a bottle of champagne. "Everybody said this club had a monkey on its back. Now the monkey's off."

Hadn't Frey heard about the Curse of the Goat? In order to really get the monkey off the team's back, the Cubs would have to beat the West Division champs, the San Diego Padres, in a best-of-five National League Championship Series beginning October 2.

Nevertheless, winning half a title was a Cinderella story. The Cubs had finished fifth in 1983. They had lost 11 straight preseason games in the spring, and the team finished with the worst exhibition record in all of baseball. Now, the Cubs had topped their division. That was something to applaud.

The Cubs won the Eastern Division title in 1984 mainly with players obtained from other clubs. Among the starting eight position players, Ryne Sandberg, Larry Bowa, Bob Dernier, Gary Matthews, and Keith Moreland all came from the Phillies; Leon Durham and Jody Davis had been Cardinals; and Ron Cey came from the Dodgers. The starting five in the pitching rotation included Rick Sutcliffe (Indians), Dennis Eckersley (Red Sox), Steve Trout (White Sox), Scott Sanderson (Expos), and Dick Ruthven (Phillies). The only two players on the 25-man post-season roster who had spent their entire career in the Cubs' organization were Lee Smith and reserve outfielder Henry Cotto. The roster had been almost completely remade since Dallas Green's takeover in October 1981. The only three 1984 Cubs who were on the team during the 1981 season were Smith, Durham and Davis. Only 14 of the 25 had been with the Cubs in 1983.[12]

The Cubs' rise to the top of the standings created a dilemma because of the absence of lights at Wrigley Field. With the World Series due to open in the National League city, it would have meant playing the first, second, sixth and seventh games on weekday afternoons if the Cubs reached the Series. Under its contract with NBC-TV, midweek games would have cost baseball millions of dollars in revenue because of reduced advertising income that would have been realized by the network. Each major league team stood to lose between $400,000 and $700,000 as its share of the television proceeds. The Cubs were asked to move the home post-season games to either Comiskey Park or County Stadium in Milwaukee, but the club adamantly refused. The Cubs also vetoed the suggestion to use a portable lighting system at Wrigley for the post-season. To solve the situation, commissioner Bowie Kuhn arranged for alternative schedules. They provided for the Fall Classic to start in the American League city if the

Cubs won the NL pennant. This would have placed the three games in Chicago on Friday, Saturday, and Sunday afternoon. One Cubs season ticket holder filed a lawsuit in Cook County Circuit Court seeking $1 million in damages against Kuhn and NBC because he might miss a fourth home game if the Series went the limit.[13]

The court waited as Game 1 of the Championship Series opened at Wrigley on October 2. The Cubs continued their Cinderella story. They overwhelmed the Padres 13–0, hitting five homers, including one by Rick Sutcliffe that cleared the right-field bleachers and landed on Sheffield Avenue. Gary Matthews hit two homers and Bob Dernier and Ron Cey added one each. Sutcliffe pitched seven innings and allowed only two hits.[14]

With the Cubs leading 5–0, the Padres had loaded the bases with two outs in the fifth when former Cub Carmelo Martinez smacked a 2–0 pitch on a line to right field.

"I started forward thinking it was a line drive hit," said Moreland, who often had been maligned for his supposed immobility as an outfielder. "As I was running in, I saw that with the wind blowing out, the ball had stayed in the air, so I just took a shot at catching it." Moreland made a tumbling grab, taking the ball just inches off the turf. "That catch really ended the ballgame," Rick Sutcliffe said. First baseman Leon Durham called it "the catch of the game.[15]

On October 3 the Cubs moved to within one game of ending their 39-year absence from the World Series with a 4–2 win over the Padres before 36,282 fans at Wrigley. Trout scattered five hits over 8⅓ innings, and Lee Smith picked up the save by retiring the final two batters.

Cub fans could not control their frenzy. Sitting on a curb behind the left-field bleachers Wednesday afternoon, Antoinette Nilsen, 74, and Jo Petricca, 72, couldn't have been happier. The sisters grew up a couple of blocks from Wrigley Field and they said that their affection for the Cubs had been lifelong. Even if they couldn't get a ticket to the playoffs, they were not about to be far from the ballpark.

Relying on the scoreboard, they savored every pitch as the Cubs defeated the Padres to take a 2–0 lead in the National League playoffs.

"We were watching the balls, the strikes, and the hits on the scoreboard," Nilsen said. "Not only did we know what was going on at the game, but we took part in the excitement. When they hollered, we hollered."

"We were enjoying it as much on the outside as they did on the inside.

Sitting on the curb is the next best thing," Patricca agreed. "We wouldn't have missed this for the world."

Some fans seemed unable to believe it was all true. "I'm dreaming. I must be dreaming and I'm going to wake up soon," Nancy Mikus, 32, of Bartlett, said after the game.[16]

But it was true. The Cubs demonstrated a versatility of offensive styles that changed with the wind. They used an aggressive, derring-do style of base-running that helped them to an early 3–0 lead.

It marked the first time the Cubs had won two postseason games in the same year since 1935, when the Detroit Tigers beat them in the World Series in six games. For the Cubs to play in their first World Series in 39 years, all they needed was one more victory over the Padres in their next three games.[17]

On Thursday, October 4, at Jack Murphy Stadium, the Padres stayed alive with a 7–1 victory, scoring 3 runs in the fifth and four more in the sixth. The Padres ripped Eckersley, but to take the brass ring they would have to make playoff history by coming back from a 2–0 deficit.

"I think the pressure is on them now," said San Diego second baseman Alan Wiggins. "There's just too much history of Cubs failure."[18]

Every other misery was temporary. It might rain for weeks, but the sun would always come back out. No matter how long the winter, spring would follow. Mothers-in-law would go back home, but the Cubs' failure seemed eternal.

It has been argued that the Cubs brought despair to millions by their long-standing failure. Maybe so, but they brought happiness to many more. Nothing cheers a loser faster than having somebody less fortunate to feel sorry for, and the Cubs collected sympathy like a navel collects lint. That was a significant contribution to the mental hygiene of a nation, better than therapy, more reliable than drugs, and cheaper than either.

It had been such a nice, orderly world. When was it? Just the week before? The only reasonable, honorable thing for the Cubs to do was to lose three straight to the Padres in the National League playoffs. Believers would have been happy enough. Instead, in the first two games at Wrigley Field, the Cubs crushed the Padres with the wind blowing out and ran past them with the wind blowing in. Just like bullies.

Then they came to San Diego, needing one more win, an advantage no National League team had ever wasted. And they lost Game Three.[19]

On October 6, 6 foot 5 Scott Sanderson was ready to face his old teammates despite the pain in his lower back. He had spent 21 days on the disabled list after suffering recurring back spasms earlier in the season. But he was selected against Padres left-hander Tim Lollar in Game 4 which was to start at 7:25 P.M. Chicago time.

Cubs' manager Jim Frey resisted the temptation to panic and bring back ace Rick Sutcliffe on three days' rest. He reasoned that if it went to a fifth game, he'd want to put his best guy into the biggest and most important game, and he would want Sutcliffe to be 100 percent.[20]

As fate ordained, Sanderson had to leave the game after 4 and ⅔ innings, having allowed three runs. Lee Smith took over, and became the losing pitcher when Steve Garvey, the veteran San Diego first baseman, drilled a line-drive, two-run homer to right field, with one out in the bottom of the ninth to give the Padres a 7–5 victory. Jim Frey would now have to call upon Sutcliffe.

It was down to the wire. For Chicago, it had been almost four decades of frustration, bad jokes and good-natured indulgence waiting for the lovable but bumbling Cubs to turn into champions.

After all that waiting, Game 5 on October 7 took on historic proportions. A bookie could lay odds that no one anywhere in Chicago was going to miss that game if they could help it. The partying and the nail biting must have started early in Wrigleyville where the bars began filling up wall to wall.

Once the game began, all eyes were on the televisions, tensions rising when the Padres took the lead. But when the Cubs pulled even and then ahead with back-to-back home runs in the fourth, the cheers must have rocked Wrigleyville and the mood must have been exhilarating. But fate intervened.

On October 8, the headline of the *Chicago Tribune*'s sports page summed it up: "Paradise Lost — Sutcliffe Fails to Stop Padres."

"Today, the Cubs pennant hangs at half staff," sportswriter Fred Mitchell wrote. "The franchise's fervent hopes of capturing its first National League flag in 39 years died Sunday when the San Diego Padres rallied for four runs in the seventh inning to defeat the Cubs 6–3 in Game 5 of the National League Championship Series. A raucous crowd of 58,359 sun-baked creatures at Jack Murphy Stadium became an extension of the world-famous San Diego Zoo. The Padres' dramatic victory fed the animals. For many Chicagoans and a nation of Cubs followers, this one really hurt."

"It's an empty feeling," said manager Jim Frey in an isolated office adjacent to the morgue-like clubhouse. It's like we got half a taste of what it was supposed to be like. We didn't get the whole thing. We had it, and it just slipped away from us."[21]

There was little consolation for Cubs players. If Leon Durham had sunk further in his chair, he would have become a seat cushion.

Durham's seventh-inning error opened the door for the Padres to gain a three-run lead. Rick Sutcliffe, with red beard and eyes, couldn't mask his feelings. He'd lost his first game since June 29, ending a streak of 15 consecutive victories.

The Cubs had been rolling along with a 3–0 lead and their Sutcliffe pitching a two-hitter through five innings. "I must admit, I felt pretty confident at that point," Frey said.

But the Padres scored two runs in the sixth, after loading the bases with none out and then getting a pair of sacrifice flies.

In the ugly seventh inning, San Diego scored four runs after Durham's error at first base opened the flood gates. Carmelo Martinez led off with a walk. Garry Templeton sacrificed him to second. Then pinch-hitter Tim Flannery hit a grounder to first, and Durham dropped to one knee. But the ball went between his legs into right field, allowing Martinez to score the tying run.

"It was a routine ground ball and it stayed real low," Durham said. "It was about a nine-hopper. I just knew it was going to come up but it didn't. I could see it big as day. It wasn't nothing like a hot shot. I'm sorry it happened. I'm sorry it started something for them."[22]

Durham, a good first baseman, forgot the fundamental in fielding a ground ball: keep the glove down. There is always the chance the ball won't come up. It's easier and quicker to bring the glove up for a bad hop. Coming up is instinctive. More time and thought is required to lower the glove. Durham played it safe — or so it seemed. He dropped to one knee, the ideal position to block the ball. But the tip of his glove, which should have been scraping the dirt, was at ankle height. The ball scooted under Durham's glove and through his legs for only his fifth error of the year and the first on a ground ball. What a way to lose a pennant.[23]

If nothing else, the Cubs collapse after being up 2–0 did much to revive popular interest in the Curse of the Goat.[24] And in their hearts, Cub fans were already voicing a familiar phrase, "Wait till next year."

As for the Cubs ticket holder who had filed the $1 million lawsuit seeking damages because he might miss a fourth home game if the World Series went the limit, the situation was moot.

CHAPTER 11

Goodbye Mr. Frey

The next year, 1985, with Jim Frey again as manager, the Cubs dropped to fourth, 23½ games behind St. Louis. In 1986, they did even worse, finishing fifth, 37 games behind.

Goodbye, Jim Frey, hello, Gene Mitchell in 1987. Mitchell managed the Cubs to sixth place, 18½ games behind. In 1988, Don Zimmer became manager and moved the team up to fourth, but 24 games out of first.

In 1989, with Don Zimmer still guiding the ship, the Cubs were given little chance at the beginning of the season of even posting a .500 record.[1] They began play in frigid weather. On April 8, with a lot of fans huddled under blankets, Domingo Ramos came to bat with one man on in the fourth, and launched a towering drive through a bitter 15-mile-an-hour wind that just reached the basket in left field.

The homer erased a 2–1 Pittsburgh lead and propelled the Cubs toward a 5–3 win, making Mike Bielecki a winner in his first start of the year. It gave the team a record of 3–2, and put them in third place in the East Division, one game behind Montreal. Not only was it Ramos's first Cubs homer, it was only his sixth lifetime in 689 at-bats and his first big-league homer anywhere since 1987 when he was with Seattle.

The next day at Wrigley found 11,387 die-hard Cub fans shivering in 33-degree conditions with a wind chill of eight above. But they were rewarded as they watched Rick Sutcliffe strike out 11 batters and beat the Pirates 8–3.

Four days later, April 13, the Cubs were tied with Philadelphia for first place, both with a record of 6–2. A month later, though, the Cubs were 17–18 and it looked like another long year for their fans. Then they won eight of nine games and moved back into first.

The Billy Goat Curse

On May 25, Alan Solomon of the *Chicago Tribune* wrote a column headlined "Fun Is New Cub Motto." The Cubs' clubhouse was rocking, he said.

The team had just beaten Mike Scott and the Houston Astros to move into first place, and the chatter/giggle level was at a season high. Shawn Dunston, who had homered for the first time all season, was sitting in front of his cubicle, his post game meal on a plate balanced on his lap, when he looked up and smiled to acknowledge the presence of an even larger smile.

"That's my boy!" said Andre Dawson, and the two joyfully clasped hands.

It was almost a shout.

Now Dawson is supposed to be the "quiet" leader — that's what he has been since joining the Cubs in 1987 — but this wasn't that Dawson. This was a man thoroughly enjoying what was happening around him.

And this, remember, is a man on the disabled list.

"I'm very encouraged by the spirit of the ball club," said Dawson, who may be able to play a little by late next week. "This is a real loose group, about as loose as you can get, considering all the youngsters that we have."

It wasn't always a loose group. There hadn't been much looseness since late last season, when "fun" became a clubhouse issue. Hotfoots were barred under penalty of fine. The August 8 wet-tarp slide cost four players $500.

Manager Don Zimmer let it be known that pranks and silliness, while they had their place, weren't always appropriate. Some of the players took that directive personally. Most of them are gone.

"Everything they said was negative," Zimmer said. "Not bad people, but just enough to aggravate you: I wanted to get rid of them."

Along came spring training. With so many jobs open, with so many insecure players, with so many veterans clearly on the bubble and with so many players of all ages wary of offending the skipper, the clubhouse in Arizona was, well, less than rollicking.

It's rollicking now. And no one is happier about it than Zimmer.

"Sliding on a tarp sure isn't my idea of having fun," Zimmer said. "And my idea of having fun isn't giving somebody a hotfoot, where somebody could get seriously hurt. To me, that's just ignorant. Now, practically anything else they want to do is fun. I hear guys kidding each other on the bus. And as long as they go about it the right way, they can still have fun and laugh on the bus, even if we lose three in a row.

"But when you're going good and winning some games, I don't care what team you watch, there is that little edge you have, of having even more fun."

It's tough to imagine any team having more fun than this team is having right now.[2]

One month later, on June 25, it was certainly no fun when the Montreal Expos completed a 3-game sweep of the Cubs, extending their scoreless-inning streak to 22 and dropping Chicago to second place, a percentage point behind the first-place Mets.

And it was no fun one day later when the second-place Cubs became the third-place Cubs after Doug Drabek extended their hitting slump, pitching the Pittsburgh Pirates to a 2–1 victory before 35,407 at Wrigley Field. It was the fourth straight loss for the Cubs, and in those four games, they had been outscored 17–2 and outhit 34–19. Ryne Sandberg had gone 0 for 11, Andre Dawson 0 for 11, and Dwight Smith 1 for 11.

The Cubs were having trouble, but it was not as if the club was sinking deep into the standings. They were in third place, but only half a game off the lead. Don Zimmer may

Jim Frey, Cubs manager, 1984–1986 (photograph by George Brace).

have felt like cutting his throat after the fourth straight loss, but he must have known that sooner or later his team would start hitting.

After another thirty days, Chicago was in sole possession of second place, 3½ games behind Montreal. They occupied that position only because Shawon Dunston came to bat on July 25 and powered a solo homer against St. Louis, giving the erratic lefty Mitch Williams the breathing room he needed for the Cubs to beat the Cardinals 4–2 in muggy Busch Stadium. It was the Cubs' fourth straight win, and second win in two nights against the Cards as the Cubs faced a big 6-game stretch against St. Louis and New York. After sweeping the Mets, Chicago began inching its way toward the top. Even at times when it appeared a game was lost, the Cubs came back.

On July 30 a two-out, two-run, homer by Mark Grace in the bottom of the ninth beat the Mets 6–4 at Wrigley Field. The next night Dwight Smith powered a grand slam off Greg Harris in a 10–2 win over the Phillies at Veterans Stadium in Philadelphia. And on August 5 a three-run, ninth-inning charge beat the Pirates 4–2 in Pittsburgh. The win put the Cubs into a tie for first with the Expos, both teams having a record of 63–47. Two days later the Cubs took possession of first with a 5–3 win over the Expos at Wrigley.

The North Siders continued to battle for the top spot. On August 11, Ryne Sandberg homered in his fifth straight game, tying a club record set by Hack Wilson in 1928. August 12 saw Shawon Dunston driving in six runs with a homer, a double and a single. On August 15, Andre Dawson powered a three-run game-winning homer in the twelfth. And so it went.

On August 29, Houston's Mark Portugal had a 5-hit shutout going with Chicago trailing 9–0. With two outs in the sixth inning, Shawon Dunston bounced a high chopper to the mound. One might have thought that the inning was over, but Portugal threw the ball away and Mark Grace scored the Cubs first run. Another run made it 9–2 after six innings. Then it was 9–5 after seven, and the Cubs tied the game with four more runs in the eighth. After Dwight Smith won it for the Cubs with a single in the tenth, shame on anyone among the 25,829 fans in Wrigley Field who left early.[3] Those who left missed seeing the biggest deficit the Cubs had overcome since September 28, 1930, when Hack Wilson's 189th and 190th runs batted in helped the Cubs overcome a nine-run deficit, beating Cincinnati 13–11 at Wrigley.

Chicago was now at the top, 2½ games ahead of St. Louis, 3½ in front of New York, and 4 in front of Montreal. Their three pursuers in the National League East would have to play well to stay within striking distance. And so they did, while the Cubs slipped a little. September 9 saw the team a half game ahead of second-place St. Louis. But when Luis Salazar drove in the winning run with a single, beating the Cardinals 3–2, that lead was extended. It became even larger when the Cubs beat St. Louis 4–1 at Wrigley the next day. And it continued to expand with a 4–3 win over the Expos on September 11 and a win the next day as Mike Bielecki pitched a two-hitter to defeat the Expos 2–0. After completing a sweep of the Expos on September 13, the Cubs traveled to Pittsburgh where on September 15, Shawon Dunston powered a grand slam in the sixth to lead a 7–2 win over the Pirates. The victory gave the Cubs a 5½-game lead with 15 games left on the schedule.

Dunston now had 9 homers and 57 runs batted in, raising his average to .277. On May 20, he had been hitting .158. The usually ebullient Dunston tried to downplay the significance of his slam, but he admitted he had become more patient at the plate. Chicago now had six wins in a row, and they were 5½ games ahead of New York, and 6 games in front of St. Louis and Montreal.[4]

On September 26, the red-hot Cubs whooped it up, clinching their division title as they beat the Expos 3–2, while the second-place Cardinals lost to the Pirates 4–1.

For the second time in six years, a street party had begun on Chicago's North Side. Chicagoans clogged the streets outside the ballpark, climbing light poles and shouting into the night.

The City of Chicago also planned an official celebration. A big bash was set to begin at noon the next day at Daley Plaza with members of the 1969 Cubs as guests of honor. The City rounded up as many members of that ill-fated team as it could and planned several activities for the rally, including singers and dancers and a giant television screen to show videotaped highlights of the Cubs' 1989 season. Banners on lightposts were going to proclaim, "The People of Chicago Salute the 1989 Chicago Cubs." But city officials remained mum on what plans they had should the Cubs win the National League pennant or the World Series.[5] They had been down this road before, full of anticipation in the early stages of the playoffs. Then a few unexpected mishaps had taken their dreams away. Then they remembered the Curse of the Goat.

On Wednesday, October 4, an eager 39,195 fans braved the cool temperatures to behold Wrigley Field's first night playoff game. The gates did not open until 5:30, but by then many had been at the park for hours. Some sat on sidewalks outside the bleachers, even though there was no need to line up for an all-reserved-seat event.

Traffic streamed into the neighborhood. National League president Bill White and Commissioner Fay Vincent were among the early arriving luminaries. Governor James Thompson and Mayor Richard Daley showed up later, in time to see the flag presented by the Ft. Sheridan color guard. It was a nice enough night for everyone except for pitchers and maybe the hordes on the Sheffield Avenue apartment roofs, who undoubtedly felt the chilly wind.

Boos began early when Clark doubled off Greg Maddux to drive in the Giants' first run in the first inning. Clark kept hitting, including a solo homer in the third and a grand slam in the fourth, both off Maddux. The Cubs got mainly the silent treatment from their fans after that, unless one counts the sound of feet shuffling out of the stadium by the start of the eighth inning. The way the Cubs played, you would have thought they had turned back the clock to spring training. In the 11–3 Giants win, Will Clark had knocked in six runs and scored four, with four hits in as many at-bats.

"It won't haunt me," Maddux said, "I've been hit before. It's a bad time to get hit like this, but I'll think about it tomorrow morning, go over what I did wrong and go from there. I felt good in the bullpen, good stuff, strong. I felt fine. I just didn't have good command of some pitches."

"Will this demoralize us?" Maddux asked. "I don't think so. We've been bouncing back all season. I don't see any reason why we can't again."[6]

Don Zimmer swore that the series was a long way from over.[7] Since the Cubs had played in the 1984 Championship Series, the format had changed to seven games.

In Game 2, on Thursday October 5, the Cubs didn't merely make amends, they made history: a six-run first-inning burst, the largest first inning in a League Championship Series, more than enough to carry them to a 9–5 victory over the Giants and square the playoffs at one victory each.

It was superb theater for the overflow crowd of 39,195. The sweet-swinging Mark Grace led the assault, with three hits and four runs batted in. The difference between Games 1 and 2 might have come down to two pitches. On Wednesday night, Don Zimmer had let Greg Maddux stay in with the bases loaded in the fourth, and Will Clark deposited a pitch onto Sheffield Avenue. On Thursday night, Zimmer went to reliever Paul Assenmacher in the fifth and Clark bounced it to first. That fifth-inning groundout, which stranded two runners with the Cubs leading by four, was the biggest putout in the Cubs 9–5 series-tying victory. It proved the Cubs could retire Clark, who had reached base his first seven trips of the series, and it prevented Kevin Mitchell from coming up as the tying run.

Assenmacher had been warming up on Wednesday night when Zimmer went to the mound and decided to leave Maddux in before Clark unloaded. What made Zimmer decide to keep Maddux in the game?

One must also wonder about Cub fan Florence Zangora, who brought a bit of voodoo to Wrigley Field on Thursday night in the form of a Will Clark doll. She put a hex on the doll and Clark went 1 for 4 as the Cubs won.[8]

As Chicago gathered a bit of momentum, Giants home-run king Kevin Mitchell roared to the press, "You're going to see what kind of team we've really got. We're very confident. That's what you've got to be. You can't go in there fakin' and shakin.' It's all about the money makin.'"

It was uncertain who was shakin' and fakin' — the Giants or the Cubs. What was known was that Game 3 was to be played on Saturday night in San Francisco, with Rick Sutcliffe pitching against Mike LaCross. Both were tall right-handers in their twelfth major-league seasons. LaCross had a so-so 10–10 record that year. Lifetime, he was three games under .500. Sutcliffe had a much more distinguished career. He had won the 1984 National League Cy Young Award and, despite arm and shoulder problems, was 16–11 for the season.

Appearing at a Friday press conference in Candlestick Park, Sutcliffe said that his arm was well-rested and felt as strong as ever. He was starting with six days' rest and had pitched only 13 innings in the last 16 days, an indication that he would have his best fastball. When he did, he almost always won.

Sutcliffe also revealed that he had developed his sinker, a fastball with a sudden drop. If it worked it would be invaluable because it could prevent the Giants' sluggers from hitting the ball in the air, then being aided by a sympathetic wind in San Francisco, the kind of breeze known to carry the ball into the outfield seats.[9]

On October 7 in Game 3, Rick Sutcliffe felt something give in his right leg as he turned to throw out Matt Williams on a chopper to the mound in the first inning. He then handed the Giants three first-inning runs to wipe out a 2–0 Cub lead. But he hung tough, pitched five strong innings, then doubled to set up the Cubs' lead run in the seventh, again pulling a muscle in his right leg.

Team doctor Michael Schafer proclaimed Sutcliffe fit, but manager Don Zimmer was more cautious and took him out of the game. Assenmacher came in to pitch the seventh, and gave up a single to Butler. Three times the Cubs pitcher would throw to first before delivering a pitch to Robby Thompson, and when that was a ball, Les Lancaster was summoned to relieve Assenmacher and protect his team's 4–3 lead. But Thompson homered over the left field fence, and then the Giants hung on to win 5–4.

The next day the Giants moved to a 3–1 series lead, after Steve Wilson surrendered a game-winning homer to Matt Williams, giving the Giants a 6–4 victory.

Batting in the fifth with one on and the score tied, the red-hot Williams, a right-handed swinger, fouled off pitch after pitch and ran the count to 3–2. Don Zimmer visited the mound after 11 pitches. First base was open and the next two batters were lefties.

"We don't care if you walk him. Just don't give him anything out over the plate,"

Zimmer told Wilson. Twice Williams fouled off what might have been ball four. Then Wilson came across with a fast ball, over the middle and a little above the knees. Williams hit the ball over the left-field fence, and then the Giants held on to win.

Steve Wilson's tears couldn't bring Williams's drive back into the ballpark. But the Cubs still had a chance. With two down in the ninth, the Cubs were poised to pull off another of their patented comebacks. Ryne Sandberg and Lloyd McClendon singled and Mark Grace walked to load the bases for Dawson.

Steve Bedrosian was on in relief for the Giants. "There was no doubt in my mind that I was going to hit the ball on the nose somewhere," Dawson said.

Bedrosian broke off a slider that Dawson could only wave at. "My thinking changed after I swung and missed at the first pitch," Dawson later said. "I should have just been trying to make contact."

After a fastball inside for a ball evened the count, two more perfect sliders finished the kill. Dawson went down swinging. "It's a good pitch," Bedrosian said. "The fastball is what I'm known for. The slider just gave him something else to think about."

Dawson later confessed he was thinking the wrong thing. He couldn't time the slider right to stroke it to right field or up the middle. He whiffed at his biggest at-bat, and the game went to the Giants.[10] Now it was do or die for the Cubs.

The next day, October 9, a glorious summer ended as the Cubs lost Game 5 — and the pennant — to the Giants, 3–2. Will Clark knocked in the game-winning run with a single in the eighth. For the series, the Cubs had left 43 men on base, 17 by Andre Dawson alone. Cubs pitchers had a collective ERA of 5.57. Ace Greg Maddux set a NL playoff record with 12 runs allowed in 7 and ⅓ innings.

The Cubs were beaten by 40-year-old Rick Reuschel who had been dropped unceremoniously from the Cubs roster after the 1984 season, and come back to pitch well for the Pirates and then the Giants. On Monday, he stymied the Cubs, especially Andre Dawson, with a tantalizing sinker that looked hittable but wasn't — at least when the Cubs seemed only one hit away from bringing the series back to Chicago.[11]

First they groaned, then they cheered, then they sighed, and finally loyal Cub fans resigned themselves to the fact that no pennant would fly at Wrigley Field for the 44th straight year. An uncredited piece in the *Tribune* summed up the situation, and the fans' feelings:

> Yes, Cubs fans, the fat lady does sing. She came waddling into my office, a heavy-jowled woman who had to weigh at least 250 pounds. To my amazement, she stood in front of my desk, opened her mouth wide and began singing in an ear-shattering soprano voice.
>
> "You looooose," she sang, "You lose, it's over, it's all over, the end has come, doom, doom, doom, gloom, gloom, gloom...."
>
> I jumped up and demanded to know who she was and why she was in my office.
>
> "That should be obvious," she said. "You have heard the expression: 'It is never over until the fat lady sings.' Well, I am that fat lady, and I am here to sing because it is over for the Cubs."
>
> "What you say is true. But the hard fact remains: you have been singing your sad song for Cub fans longer and more frequently than for anyone else. It is obviously discriminatory, and I would appreciate an explanation."
>
> "Well, there is your image as lovable losers. I'm sure you have read

that description in many a sports column written by sports experts, some of whom have IQs greater than that of a chipmunk. Don't you wish to maintain that image?"

"First of all, we are not lovable. We are a mean, tough, hard-nosed city. This is the city that gave the world Butkus, Ditka, and Capone. It is Frisco that is cuddly and lovable.

We are like New York and Detroit. We punch first and talk later. In Frisco, they dance first and kiss later, a terrible sight to behold. So forget that lovable, cuddly stuff. We do not enjoy losing."[12]

The dialogue with the fat lady went on and on, and at no time did she mention the Curse of the Goat.

CHAPTER 12

Just Plain Bad

Before the '94 season started, the Cubs' management traded Jose Vizcaino to the Mets for Anthony Young and Otis Smith. When Young was acquired, he had a lifetime record of 5–35, including a major-league record 27 losses in a row. Why trade for a loser?

Opening day, April 4, 1994, saw First Lady Hillary Rodham Clinton toss out the ceremonial first pitch. Wearing a blue Cubs blazer and cap, she threw from the front row of seats on the third-base side. She also sang "Take Me Out to the Ballgame" with Harry Caray during the seventh-inning stretch.[1] A Cubs fan, Clinton was hopeful for a victorious year, yet she knew about the believers in the Curse and how they had watched the Cubs fail to gain prominence so far in the nineties. On opening day, a 22-mile-per-hour gale was blowing out at Wrigley, Karl Rhodes hit three home runs in his first three at-bats for the Cubs. In spite of this, the Cubs lost to the Mets 12–8 before a crowd of 38,413.

And the Cubs continued losing. When Anthony Young, a new acquisition, came to the mound on April 15, he gave up consecutive home runs to Fred McGriff, Terry Pendleton and Tony Tarasco in the first inning. Naturally, with that kind of pitching, they chalked up a 19–5 loss to the Braves at Wrigley.

On May 3, the Cubs lost their twelfth consecutive home game, falling to the Reds 5–2. The 12 losses in the first 12 home games of the 1994 season broke the club record of 11, set in 1902 when the Cubs played at the West Side Grounds.

Tom Trebelhorn, one of a string of ten successive managers to last no more than a year in the job, had suffered through this horrible start. It was the Curse, it had to be, and he wanted to get rid of it.

One story claims that Trebelhorn arranged for Sam Sianis and Cubs great Ernie Banks to join a group of robed, chanting monks in what was intended to be a curse-cleansing procession around the vine-covered interior walls of Wrigley Field.[2] But when Sam and the goat, named "Billy," arrived at the ballpark, there was some reluctance to let them in. Reportedly, though, the fans chanted, "Let the goat in! Let the goat in!" and management intervened. So Banks, Sianis, the monks and the goat did their thing, and the Cubs won that game 5–2, ending their worst home start ever.[3]

Another source says that the goat came from a group of ministers in Waterton, Wisconsin, and that this goat had no connection to Sam Sianis and his Billy Goat Tavern.

Tom Trebelhorn, 1994 Cubs manager (photograph by George Brace).

When the ministers had the idea of breaking the curse, they called radio station WMAQ, and talk-show hosts Steve Oiken and Tom Greene made all the arrangements for the curse-breaking event. When the ministers arrived at the ballpark, they ran the goat around outside of Wrigley Field. But when the Cubs' execs were notified, they brought the goat inside the ballpark, and Sam Sianis and Ernie Banks were part of the festivities.[4]

Steve Trachsel told how upset he was when dozens of people and the goat came walking through the bullpen in front of him as he was warming up for the game. He talked of the event as if it was garbage and went on to say that he did not appreciate the idea that the goat was responsible for the win against the Reds that day. Trachsel pointed to excellent pitching as having more to do with the win than a goat.

In spite of Steve Trachsel's comments, Tom Trebelhorn felt good about the goat parading around Wrigley Field. But it's fair to say that he mostly felt good about the 5–2 win over the Reds and the end of the 12-game losing streak.[5]

It has been suggested that Trebelhorn made a mistake. He should have involved an exorcist to get rid of the curse.[6]

How do former Cubs players view the Curse of the Goat? Sammy Sosa believes in God and himself, not in curses. Ernie Banks and Glenn Beckert, although not rendering an opinion on the validity of the curse, were among the ex-Cubs at Wrigley Field, offering advice on how to break it. Therefore it seems fair to say that they may believe in the curse. Otherwise, why give advice on how to break it?[7]

The Cubs won their first 1994 home game on May 4, after the curse-breaking event, but further good fortune did not follow. On June 13, Ryne Sandberg announced his immediate retirement from baseball. This came without warning and stunned Cubs management, teammates, friends and everyone in baseball. Sandberg said that he had lost the drive that made him a success and that the game was no longer fun.[8]

On August 12, with about 70 percent of the season completed, major-league players went on strike. The Cubs finished fifth in the shortened season, with a 49–64 record, 16½ games behind. Was the Curse still at work?

I talked with Andy Pafko, outfielder for the Cubs in the 1945 World Series, who scoffed, "What's a billy goat got to do with winning and losing? The goat doesn't have anything to do with hitting and running, and nothing to do with winning a World Series." He said that he did not see a goat in the box-seat section of Wrigley Field when the Cubs played Detroit in the fourth game of the 1945 World Series. He became aware of the Curse afterwards, and none of the players believed in it.

When I pointed out that the Cubs went from first in 1945 to third in 1946, sixth in 1947, and eighth (and last) in 1948 and '49, Andy replied, "We didn't have the personnel. You gotta have pitchers. You gotta have a catcher who knows every man on every other team. The catcher has the most important job in baseball."

Leonard (Lennie) Merullo, Cubs' shortstop in 1945, did not agree

Andy Pafko, outfielder for Chicago Cubs in 1945 (courtesy of Andy Pafko).

with Pafko about the Curse. He has come to believe in it. He talked about the Cubs losing, and losing, and losing, and said, "You get to believe. There must be something to it." In talking with Sam Sianis at the Billy Goat Tavern on Chicago's Michigan Avenue, he said, he has come to be absolutely certain the Curse is real.

Karen Kasparaitis, a Cubs fan I talked with outside of Wrigley Field, does not believe in curses. But she would consider the possibility of a psychological influence on the players merely by their awareness of an alleged curse.

However one views the Curse, Cubs' players and fans alike would have to agree that 1994 was another year of misfortune. Besides the twelve

Lennie Merullo, Cubs shortstop in 1945 (National Baseball Hall of Fame Library, Cooperstown, N.Y.).

straight home-game losses early on, the Cubs also lost ten straight starting on May 31.

In 1994, individual Cubs with great potential didn't develop. One example was outfielder Karl Rhodes. On opening day at Wrigley, he had homered in the first, third and fifth innings. George Bell of the Blue Jays is the only other player to hit three homers on opening day, but Rhodes did it in his first three at-bats. But subsequently Rhodes faded into obscurity. With another 306 at-bats, he had only five more homers and batted just .206.

Later Rhodes went to Japan and became a recognized home-run hitter. In 2001, with the Kintetsu Buffaloes, he hit 55 homers to tie a single-season Japanese League record set by Sadaharu Oh in 1964.[9] Why the difference in performance?

This same question must be asked of the Chicago Cubs. For their first 80 years, prior to and including 1945, the Cubs were generally assumed to be contenders, playing well and winning the occasional pennant. For the next 38 years, the Cubs were the least successful team in baseball, never making the playoffs, not even once. Since 1984, the baseball gods have granted the Cubs only a glimmer of hope.[10]

CHAPTER 13

Those Wild Crazy Cubs

That faint glimmer of hope flared up in 1995 when a new manager, Jim Riggleman, came aboard. He took the Cubs through the National League's first wild-card race, and the team was in it until the final weekend of the season, but they finished third in the Central Division with a record of 73–71.

In 1996 the Cubs were unable to develop any consistency all season, dropped 14 of their last 16 games, and finished with a 76–86 record.

In 1997, Chicago experienced one of the worst seasons in franchise history. The Cubs lost their first 14 games, and finished with a record of 68–94. In the wild-card race, the Cubs were tied for last place, 24 games behind.

While the Cubs were experiencing these misfortunes, Sam Sianis and his Billy Goat Tavern were doing well, in no small part because of a legend that had been ongoing for fifty years, namely the Curse of the Goat.

Sianis received a letter from United Airlines in 1995, inviting him to send his "Cheezeborger" into the sky for one month, starting on June 5. The airline told him that his famous cheeseburger would be served aloft during June to hundreds of thousands of passengers going to and from O'Hare Field. Other Chicago food sellers were invited to take part in the campaign to promote the Taste of Chicago, conceived as a small-scale spectacle during Mayor Jane Byrne's administration. Sam planned to send 100,000 cheeseburgers to the airport where United would cook them and put them in Styrofoam boxes that would show the Billy Goat logo.[1]

The contrast between the Sianis family's successes and the Cubs' failures was striking in '97 when the Cubs broke the all-time National League record for the worst start in a season. But better days were on the horizon. With Riggleman still at the helm, a good season might have been anticipated when on April 2, 1998, after the Marlins had scored six runs in the first inning, the Cubs rallied in the ninth to an 8–7 victory. Jeff Blauser broke a 7–7 tie with an RBI single.

The next day, back in Chicago, the Cubs won their home opener against the Expos before 39,102. Steve Trachsel, the winning pitcher, drove in three runs with a pair of singles.

During the game, the Cubs wore a patch with Harry Caray's caricature on the sleeves of their jerseys to pay tribute to the late broadcaster who died on February 18. A large image of Caray was placed over the broadcast booth at Wrigley Field facing the playing field. Additional homage to Caray took place during the seventh-inning stretch when the club brought in guests of widely varied musical abilities to carry on his tradition of leading the fans in singing "Take Me Out to the Ballgame." The first was Caray's wife, Dutchie. Standing beside her was her grandson, Chip, who joined Steve Stone on the telecasts of Cubs games in 1998.[2]

Did Harry Caray have anything to do with the Curse? A photo exists of Caray at Wrigley Field, mike in hand, talking with Sam Sianis who is standing next to a goat. The goat's blanket indicates that it was the Chicago-Cook Area mascot. This status could not be confirmed with Cook County officials, however, and a letter of inquiry to Sam Sianis received no answer.

Maybe Caray *did* have something to do with the Curse. He died in early 1998 and then the Cubs won eight of their first ten games, a year after beginning the '97 campaign 0–14. And the team continued playing great ball.

On April 18, Kerry Wood won his first major league game. His teammates gave him eight runs in the first inning. It was more than enough as he pitched five shutout innings, beating the Dodgers 8–1.

Wood continued to dazzle. On May 6, in the most dominating performance in Cubs history, he pitched a one-hitter and tied a major-league record with 20 strikeouts to defeat the Astros 2–0. Wood surpassed the National League record of 19 K's previously held by four pitchers, and the major-league rookie record of 18.

And the Cubs continued to win more than they lost, sometimes dramatically.

On May 8, after the Giants scored in the top of the fourteenth, the Cubs came back with two in their half to win 5–4 at Wrigley. Mark Grace drove in the tying and winning runs with a bases-loaded single.

Three days later, Chicago played Arizona at Bank One Ballpark in Phoenix, and won the game 4–2. Kerry Wood struck out 13 batters in seven innings. Combined with his 20 strikeouts on May 6, Wood set a major-league record for most strikeouts in consecutive games with 33.

Interleague play had been introduced in 1997 so now the Cubs and White Sox met in regular-season play. On

Harry Caray interviewing Sam Sianis at Wrigley Field, with the billy goat standing by (undated photograph by George Brace).

June 6, pinch-hitter Derrick White hit his first major-league homer in five years (his first hit in three years), which put the Cubs ahead 6–5 in the sixth inning against the Sox at Wrigley. The Cubs went on to win 7–6, their eighth win in a row.

On June 8, the Cubs won their tenth in a row, taking an 8–1 decision over the Twins in Minneapolis. Sammy Sosa tied a Cubs record by hitting a home run in his fifth consecutive game. With the victory, Chicago had a record of 38–24 and were tied for first place in their division with the Astros.

Sosa continued to clobber the ball. On June 15, he powered three homers, giving the Cubs a victory over the Brewers 6–5 at Wrigley. On June 20, he hit two homers, one a 500-foot blast off Toby Borland in a 9–4 win over the Phillies. The Cubs remained within striking distance of first until early August when Houston pulled away, but they hung tough in the race for the wild-card.

Besides following the race for the playoffs, excited Cub fans cheered day after day as Sammy Sosa battled it out with Mark McGwire in the home-run race to break the Roger Maris seasonal record of 61.

On August 31, Sosa tied McGwire for the second day in a row, hitting his 55th home run in the third inning of the Cubs 5–4 victory over Cincinnati, putting Chicago eleven games behind first place Houston in the National League Central Division.

On September 2, Paul Sullivan, a *Chicago Tribune* staff writer, noted, "The Cubs have won six of their last seven games, going 15 games over .500 to their high-water mark for the year. They lead the Mets by a game in the NL wild-card race and are two games ahead of the San Francisco Giants."[3]

Three days later, the Cubs were still a game ahead of the Mets in the wild-card race, and three games ahead of the Giants, when Sosa's 57th homer, an opposite-field blow off Pittsburgh right-hander Jason Schmidt on a 2–0 pitch in the first, sent him past Hack Wilson all-time Cubs' seasonal home-run list. It would have broken the National League record, except that McGwire had already done that.

On September 7, Mark McGwire hit his 61st home run to tie Maris's 1961 record. Sosa then had 58.

On September 11 Sosa hit his 59th homer, and on September 12, his 60th in a thrilling win over the Brewers 15–12 at Wrigley. That blow ended up on the steps of a house across Waveland Avenue.[4]

Sosa kept the Cubs near the top of the wild-card race when he hit his 61st and 62nd homers on September 13, as the Cubs beat the Brewers again. This tied Mark McGwire for the homer lead, but two days later McGwire powered his 63rd in an 8–6 Cardinals loss to the Pirates.

On September 16, Sosa tied McGwire again as he launched a two-out, 434-foot, upper-deck grand slam for his 63rd of the year, snapping a 2–2 tie with San Diego and leading the Cubs to a 6–3 win over the Padres. The Cubs were now a half game in front of the Mets, and 4½ games in front of the Giants in the wild-card race.

13. Those Wild, Crazy Cubs

Kerry Wood, Cubs pitcher (AP/Worldwide Photos/Nam Y. Huh).

September 20 saw McGwire pull ahead in the home-run derby, reaching 65 in an 11–6 win for the Cardinals over the Brewers in Milwaukee.

Three days later it was Sosa's turn, as he broke out of a 0–21 slump by hitting his 64th and 65th homers, again tying Mark McGwire for the league lead, but the Cubs suffered a devastating 8–7 loss to the Brewers in Milwaukee.

The Cubs had led 7–0, but the Brewers fought back. With the Cubs ahead 7–5 going into the bottom of the ninth, reliever Rod Beck loaded the bases. With two out, Geoff Jenkins lifted a fly ball to Brant Brown, who was put into the game in the eighth for his defense. It should have been a routine out, but Brown apparently lost the ball in the sun, it dropped out of his glove, and all three runners scored to give Milwaukee the win.[5]

Was it the sun? Or could there have been a goat, sitting high in the bleachers, sipping a beer and laughing. The Cubs were now tied for first place in the wild-card race with the Mets. The Giants were 1½ games back. The Cubs and Mets had three games left to play while the Giants had four.

As the Cubs battled to win the race with the Mets and the Giants, Sosa battled McGwire for the homer title. The races were on parallel tracks.

On September 25, Sosa smacked his 66th home run of the season. Forty-five minutes later, McGwire answered with *his* 66th, but the Cubs did not keep pace with Sosa. They lost 6–2 to the Astros in Houston. At the end of the day, the Cubs, Mets and Giants were tied for first place in the wild-card race, each with a record of 88–72.

Besides being tied for the wild-card race, the Cubs experienced an unusual incident. Brown, who had dropped the fly ball on September 23, was attacked in left field at the Astrodome by a pigeon, which he swatted with his cap before it disappeared.[6] Was there a connection between the pigeon and the Curse of the Goat?

On September 26, one day later, the Cubs continued to maintain a tie with the Giants in the wild-card race by beating the Astros 3–2. The Mets fell one game behind after losing 4–0 to the Braves in Atlanta.

Sosa meanwhile, fell behind McGwire when the latter homered twice to lift his season total to 68 during a 7–6 Cardinal loss to the Expos.

The Cubs too, temporarily lost their tie with the Giants when they blew a 3–1 lead, losing 4–3 in eleven innings to the Astros. All the Giants had to do now was win one last game from the Colorado Rockies, but fate intervened and the Giants blew a 7–0 lead. Colorado bounced back at Coors Field to beat the Giants 9–8 on Neifi Perez's ninth-inning homer. That left the Cubs and Giants tied for the National League wild-card play-off berth at 89–73.

A one-game, winner-goes-to-Atlanta game was scheduled for the following night at Wrigley, and the Cubs brought in a goat to ward off the Curse.

Gary Gaetti put the Cubs in the lead 2–0 when he walloped a two-run homer in the fifth. Pinch-hitter Matt Mieske drove in two runs with a bases-loaded single in the sixth. The Cubs added another run in the eighth and headed into the ninth with a 5–0 lead before the Giants threatened with a three-run rally. The game ended with a pop-up by Joe Carter, leaving Jeff Kent on first base. The Cubs won 5–3, and walked away with the National League wild-card berth. Starter Steve Trachsel got the win, allowing just one hit and no runs (but six walks) in 6⅓ innings.

The Cubs might have known that they were destined to win the wild-card race in their winner-goes-to-Atlanta game after Trachsel loaded the bases in the fourth on a hit batter and two walks, but then made Brian Johnson look positively catatonic on a called third strike to end the inning.[7]

Off they went to Atlanta, with Sammy Sosa and his 66 homers, four behind Mark McGwire's record-setting 70. Besides Sosa, the Cubs had another secret weapon.

His name was Kerry Wood. Out since August 31 with a strained elbow, it was anticipated that Wood would pitch Game 3 at Wrigley. The Braves must have remembered his three starts against them in his rookie season. In the last of those, he proved that smoke can beat mirrors, outclassing four-time Cy Young Award winner Greg Maddux. After that game, Chipper Jones, one of the classiest hitters in baseball, admitted that Wood had made him and his teammates look silly. Because of Sosa and Wood, the Braves had reason to fear the playoffs with the Chicago Cubs.[8]

In Game 1, on September 30, with John Smoltz pitching for Atlanta, the Cubs had to keep it close until Smoltz tired, as he did in the sixth and seventh innings. They could not afford to make one significant mistake against a team that had won 106 games. But they made one in the second inning.

With two outs, outfielder Andruw Jones topped a chopper to shallow short. Even if a charging Jose Hernandez had snagged it, only a perfect off-balance bullet might have nipped Jones. Hernandez was given an error he probably didn't deserve. Then Mark Clark made the dumbest pitch he has ever thrown, aided by a manager who let him throw it. He tried to bounce a 3–2 pitch in the dirt with Braves starter John Smoltz on deck. Clark wound up grooving a forkball to Michael Tucker, who poked a two-run homer to spark the Braves on their way to a 7–1 victory.

"I wanted to throw it in the dirt and get him to swing at a bad pitch or else walk him," Clark said. "I didn't give him any pitches to hit until then. Then I just made a mistake by leaving that pitch over the plate with the pitcher on deck."[9]

Later the Braves scored four in the seventh on three walks and Ryan Kiesko's grand slam off Matt Karchner. The Cubs were now down 1–0 in the best-of-five series.

The next day, in Game 2, the Cubs were two outs from tying the series, with Kevin Tapani pitching the game of his life for the Cubs, and then, with one stunning swing, Javy Lopez hit a one-out home run to tie the game in the ninth, and the Braves won it 2–1 in the tenth on Terry Mulholland's botched play at first and Chipper Jones's run-scoring single.

This loss must have been tough for the Cubs to stomach. Instead of going home with a 1–1 tie in the series, they headed back to Wrigley two down, needing three straight wins.

The Braves knew they would be facing Kerry Wood on October 3. And the Cubs knew they would be facing not only Braves' pitcher Greg Maddux, but also Steve Garvey, Lee Smith, Leon Durham, Don Young, Lou Brock, Ernie Broglio, Les Lancaster, Mitch Williams, the Billy Goat curse and everything else associated with their 53-year streak of avoiding the World Series.

The Cubs also knew that they hadn't done anything the easy way all year long. Sammy Sosa's confidence level was so high that he predicted the Cubs would take the next three from the Braves and go on to the National League Championship Series.[10]

The Cubs and their fans knew that their last chance was in the hands of Kerry Wood. And they knew that the last time he threw off the mound at Wrigley, he struck out 7 of the last 11 batters he faced. They knew that the last time Kerry stood in the batter's box at Wrigley, he hit a home run to left field. And no one could have guessed after Kerry's 13th victory on August 31 against Cincinnati that the next time he would pitch would be in the National League playoffs against the Atlanta Braves, facing Greg Maddux at Wrigley Field, with the Cubs' season on the line.

After a 32-day rest, and repeatedly insisting that his elbow felt fine, after endless speculation about whether he would, could or should pitch again this year, and after the Cubs lost a Game 2 heartbreaker in a "must win" game, here was Wood, ready to save the day. That's what everyone must have thought.

After all, he had tied the record for strikeouts in a game (20) in his fifth start, and led the National League with the lowest opponents' batting average (.196) and most strikeouts per nine innings (12.6). He was almost unbeatable at Wrigley (9–1, with a 2.97 earned-run average in 13 starts).[11]

On October 3, in Game 3, the hopes of the Cubs came to an end, as Greg Maddux, former Cub, walked onto the mound for the Braves on a cool, gusty evening at Wrigley, and retired hitters with typical control capturing the National League division series with a 6–2 win before a crowd of 39,597.

Sammy Sosa in his race with Mark McGwire for the single-season home run record (National Baseball Hall of Fame Library, Cooperstown, N.Y.).

Kerry wasn't what he had been. Considering that it had been more than four weeks and about a 40-degree temperature swing since he had last pitched, he guided the team through five innings doing fairly well, allowing just one run (scored by Maddux who had doubled in the third). He faced the minimum three batters in just one inning, though, and had thrown 97 pitches by the time he was pulled, and he'd had to refrain from throwing breaking balls to avoid putting too much torque on his tender elbow.[12]

Sammy Sosa, too, wasn't what he had been. In the last of the eighth, the Cubs began rallying as Hernandez singled up the middle. It was the first of four eighth-inning hits that gave Chicago two runs and offered a last hope. Season-long hero Sosa struck out with two men on and a run in.

Would it have made a difference if Sam Sianis and his goat had gone to Atlanta with the team?

CHAPTER 14

The Curse Lives On

In 1999, with Jim Riggleman at the helm, the Cubs were 32–23 when they suffered a monumental collapse, losing 63 of their next 87 games and finishing twelfth out of thirteen in the wild-card race.

In 2000, when Don Baylor took over as manager, another new building project began. The Cubs suffered 97 losses and again finished twelfth in the wild-card race.

The next year the Cubs showed more promise. Kerry Wood returned to the dominating form that made him Rookie of the Year in 1998, striking out 217 batters in 174½ innings, fourth best in the National League. Sammy Sosa had the best season of his career, hitting 64 homers, driving in 160 runs, scoring 146 times, and hitting .328 with an on-base percentage of .437. Sosa became the first player in baseball history to hit 60 or more home runs in a season three times in a career. But the Cubs gave up a six-game lead on June 21, and failed to reach post-season play. They were fourth in the wild-card race, four games behind.

In 2002 there were high expectations, but the team went 8–16 in April and Don Baylor was fired on July 5. Bruce Kimm became the interim manager and did no better. The Cubs didn't have a .500 month all season and finished eleventh in the wild-card race, 28 games behind. Rumors surfaced that the Cubs wanted Dusty Baker to replace Kimm.

On November 19, General Manager Jim Hendry introduced Baker as the Cubs' 55th manager. Baker said that he found Chicago to be a great sports town, with passion, where people ate, drank and slept Cubs.[1] When he met the media at Wrigley Field, he was firm in saying that he was not a miracle worker, but he said that things were about to change. When the interview was over, the press knew that he was in Chicago to do away with the idea that the Cubs were "lovable losers." They knew that he was in Chicago to win. He didn't want to hear about billy goats, curses or any other kinds of excuses that had been voiced in the past for the team's failures.[2]

Jim Hendry did his best to give Baker a formidable team. He convinced the Dodgers to take Todd Hundley for Eric Karros and Mark Grudzielanek. Karros was a great hitter, but concerns had been raised about back problems that threatened to diminish his ability to continue hitting the ball hard. Grudzielanek also had physical problems but Hendry liked him and wanted him in case Bobby Hill, the regular second baseman, could not be called upon to play every game.

With Hundley gone, a good-hitting catcher was needed. So, Hendry traded two potentially good players to Arizona for Damian Miller and dealt with Milwaukee for Paul Bako, for a player to be named later.

But the Cubs' bullpen was an absolute disgrace in 2002. They threw away 25 saves while saving only 23. Before the 2003 season, Mike Remlinger then signed on as a free agent, and the hard-throwing lefty was expected to carry a fair share of the load. As for right-handed throwers, Baker had Kyle Farnsworth and veteran Dave Veres.

When the Cubs pulled up spring-training stakes in Mesa, Arizona, and headed toward the opening day of the season in 2003, the team had Bako and Miller behind the plate, either Hee Seop Choi or Karros at first, Grudzielanek at second and Alex Gonzalez at short. Third base, a continual problem for the Cubs since the departure of Ron Santo, was handed over to Mark Bellhorn, a switch-hitter who had smacked a surprising 27 home runs in 2002. The outfield was set, with Corey Patterson, a speedster with remarkable power, in center, Moises Alou in left and Sammy Sosa in right. The extra men, in a time of need, were Tom Goodwin, Troy O'Leary and Ramon Martinez. Jim Hendry and Dusty Baker knew that the roster was bound to change during the season. But Baker liked the team as it was and voiced his opinion that the club was going to surprise some people.[3]

With everything in place, the Cubs began a wild ride toward the 2003 pennant, and just when the team was within reach of the flag, the Curse of the Goat reared its head and dashed all hope.

On March 31, the Cubs thrashed the Mets 15–2 in New York on Opening Day. Corey Patterson set a Cubs opening-day record for most runs batted in, with seven on two homers and two singles. Mark Grudzielanek was 3-for-3 in his first game with the Cubs, and Mark Bellhorn drove in four runs. The team tied a club record for the most runs scored in the first game of the season, matching the 15–1 win at Louisville in 1899. That was quite a start and hopes were high.

April 6 saw Paul Bako prove his worth to the Cubs when he drove in six runs on a triple and two singles in a 9–7 win over the Reds in Cincinnati.

On April 8, the Cubs beat the Expos 6–1 before 29,138 fans in their home opener at Wrigley. On the following day, the team continued their winning ways with a 3–0 defeat of the Expos, Mark Prior fanning 12 and walking none in a complete game.

But the Cubs were losing, too. Two weeks into the season, Dusty Baker defended his team, insisting that the Cubs were working to turn around poor early-season hitting, and saying that he didn't understand the perspective of some critics. Baker said he was not about to allow negative mindsets into his clubhouse, nor was he going to dial up his own rhetoric just to satisfy those who believed he had to be harder on his players. At the time he made these remarks, the Cubs were in third place with a 6–5 record, 1½ games out of first.[4]

The Cubs hitting did improve, with an 11–1 victory over the Reds on April 15. The next day Sosa's three-run homer off Paul Wilson in the first, put the Cubs in charge, and they never looked back. Damian Miller and Hee Seop Choi added solo homers and Alou blasted a three-run shot in the seventh, his first of the year. They beat Cincinnati 10–4, putting them atop the National League Central division.

The Cubs swept the series on April 17, reaching double figures for the third game in a row against the Reds at Wrigley, winning 16–3.

On April 19, the Cubs scored five runs in the tenth to beat the Pirates at Pittsburgh 6–1, but the next day gave a sign of bad things to come.

After a two-run Sammy Sosa homer in the first off Pirates pitcher Salomon Torres, Sosa came up again in the fourth. Torres threw a high, tight fastball that hit Sosa, destroyed his helmet, and caused splinters of plastic to go into his face, inflicting small cuts. Sosa left the game. He was swinging the bat two days later, but he didn't do well for the rest of April. He then had toenail surgery, putting him on the disabled list. Then it was a beaning and his stats went down.

In June, bad things continued to happen. With one solid swing, Sosa's bat broke in half, and the umpire discovered that the Cubs superstar had used an illegal corked bat. Although Sosa swore it was an honest mistake, it resulted in a seven-game suspension. Worst of all, it destroyed Sosa's reputation. He would never be the same. All told, he missed 20 games because of toe surgery and his suspension.

While all of these things were happening to Sosa, from April 20 on, the Cubs continued winning. Mark Prior heated up when on April 25 he drove in four runs on a homer and a double in an 11–7 win over the Rockies in Denver. On May 1, Alex Gonzalez slammed a three-run homer and Sosa added a solo shot, both in the tenth inning, to sink the Giants 5–1 in San Francisco.

On May 28, the Cubs still occupied the number one slot, 1½ games ahead of St. Louis, but they began slipping some and by June 26 had dropped back to share first with Houston. The losing continued — eight out of eleven games at the end of June, and the Cubs soon found themselves in third place, with Houston first and St. Louis second.

On July 11 at Wrigley, Mark Prior ran into Atlanta second baseman Marcus Giles on the base paths and somersaulted over Giles, landing on his pitching shoulder. The collision was so severe that both men had to be helped from the field. Although Prior claimed he was only bruised, the pain lingered, and on July 21 he was put on the 15-day disabled list.[5]

Yet, once again, the Cubs turned on power, beating the Florida Marlins 16–2 on July 20 and the Braves in Atlanta the next day, 15–6. In Houston on July 25, the Cubs stunned a sellout crowd of 43,013 when Carlos Zambrano tied the game in the seventh with a two-out, two-run homer off Wade Miller, followed by Moises Alou's game winner an inning later.

The 5–3 win put Chicago 4½ games behind Houston. This could have been one of the most important wins of the year for the Cubs because the Astros, playing .600 ball since May 1, had started to pull away, and Chicago faced a tough week ahead with two additional games with the Astros and a series with the Giants.

The Cubs also faced a tough time because their rotation was in a state of flux due to Mark Prior's sore right shoulder. His recovery was taking longer than expected. In addition, there was inconsistent pitching by

Shawn Estes which forced the Cubs were to bring up Juan Cruz from Triple-A.[6]

Prior came back. After missing three starts, he stunned other teams by winning seven in a row. The big right-hander's sharp-breaking curve and bullet-like fastball were two good reasons why Chicago was creeping back up in the standings.

On August 22, Carlos Zambrano took a no-hitter into the eighth, and Sammy Sosa hit his 499th and 500th career home runs in Phoenix, and the Cubs beat the Diamondbacks 4–1. The no-hitter was spoiled with two out in the eighth when Shea Hillenbrand put a ball down the third-base line. Ramirez charged it and fired it to first, but umpire Kelley called Hillenbrand safe. TV replays later showed Hillenbrand was out. Nevertheless, the Cubs had won one more.

Yet Shawn Estes continued to have problems. By August 24, he had allowed more base runners per nine innings (15.9) than any other National League pitcher. Opposing hitters had a .307 average against him, the league's third worst mark.

There were other problems, too. After Tony Womack joined the team in August, he sustained a freak injury on August 23 when as a base runner his knee struck Arizona's first baseman Shea Hillenbrand in the back of his head in the sixth inning, putting Womack on the disabled list. (The Cubs lost that game 13–2.)

The Cubs were a half game behind Houston.[7] For a couple of weeks they lingered near the top. In his first full year as general manager, Jim Hendry's makeover of the 2002, 95-loss club was no nip-and-tuck job. Only three position players remained from the previous year's team — Sammy Sosa, Moises Alou and Alex Gonzales, along with three starting pitchers and three relievers. Injuries and unfulfilled expectations by some young players in 2003 forced Hendry to acquire four new regulars: Kenny Lofton, Aramis Ramirez, Randall Simon and Tony Womack. Since they had been added, the Cubs had shown remarkable staying power and were in contention.[8]

Hitting and fighting also helped keep the Cubs near the top. On September 3, down 6–0, the Cubs came back to beat the Cardinals 8–7 at Wrigley. The Cubs scored three runs in the sixth, three in the seventh, and two in the eighth. Moises Alou broke a 7–7 tie with a run-scoring single. It was his fifth hit of the game in five at-bats. Alou had four singles and a homer. The tension-filled game featured a shouting match between managers Dusty Baker and Tony LaRussa. Starting pitchers Matt Clement and Danny Haren went at it by hitting each other with pitches.[9]

With a doubleheader split with the Pirates on September 19 the Cubs were a game and a half out of first. Sosa's misfortunes continued, including an ejection for cursing himself, a cork-throwing spectator confronting him at Camden Yards, and a tidal wave of scrutiny. Despite the first barrage of criticism in his career, Sosa seemed to be having the time of his life.

"It's unbelievable," he said. "A great team. Everybody steps to the plate. It's awesome. That's how you win divisions and championships. Don't focus on one guy. Everybody has to do it together."

That's what the Cubs were doing. On September 21, in a game the Cubs could not afford to lose, Mark Prior dominated Pittsburgh, striking out 14 Pirates in a 4–1 victory, putting Chicago ½ game out of first. Reliever Mike Remlinger got the Cubs out of an eighth-inning jam.[10]

On September 23, Kerry Wood put the Cubs in first, beating the Reds 6–0, combining with two relievers for a two-hitter. And the next day Shawn Estes took the mound and pitched an 8–0 shutout against the Reds, keeping the Cubs one game ahead of Houston.

The following day, though, the Astros beat the Brewers 6–1 and the Cubs lost to the Reds 9–7, stunned by Cincinnati's six runs in the sixth. This put Chicago and Houston in a tie for first.

The Cubs had three games left in the regular season, against the Pirates at Wrigley Field, three games to wrap it up — or lose it.

On September 26, the Cubs' game against the Pirates was postponed by rain, but Chicago took sole possession of first place because the Astros lost 12–5 to the Brewers in Houston. The postponement meant for a doubleheader the next day.

And the Cubs came through, sweeping the Pirates 4–2 and 7–2 to clinch the NL Central title. At the end of the game, Sammy Sosa sprayed fans in the right-field bleachers with celebratory champagne. Many of his teammates jogged around the perimeter of the outfield, followed by Dusty Baker, saluting the fans. Thousands stayed in the park for more than an hour after the game as the players celebrated on the field.[11] The Cubs had clinched their first division title in 14 years.

A couple of hours after a meaningless loss to the Pirates the next day, a rainbow appeared behind the center-field scoreboard, which could have been interpreted as a good omen. The Cubs wound up with an 88–74 record, and headed to Atlanta for a workout in preparation for Game 1 of the National League Division Series against the Braves.[12]

September 30 was a day to remember as thousands of Cubs fans made Turner Field seem like Wrigley, providing an electric atmosphere during Game 1. The Braves took a 1–0 lead in the third inning on a homer by Marcus Giles off Kerry Wood, which held up until the Cubs scored four runs in the sixth. Wood himself drove in the tying and go-ahead runs with a double off Russ Ortiz. The 4–2 victory ended an eight-game, post-season losing streak by the Cubs on the road, dating back to the 1945 World Series.[13]

Atlanta came back on October 1, to even the series in Game 2, when Mark DeRosa broke a 3–3 tie in the eighth with a two-run double to the gap in left-center off Dave Veres, to gave Atlanta a 5–3 victory. But back in Chicago on October 3, the Cubs regained the advantage when they took Game 3, beating the Braves 3–1 before 39,982 at Wrigley Field. Mark Prior was brilliant, pitching a complete game, a two-hitter. The only Atlanta hits off Prior were a single by Giles in the third and a double by DeRosa in the eighth. The Cubs had all the runs they needed with two in the first off Greg Maddux.

On October 4, 39,983 fans came to Wrigley Field poised to celebrate, but Chipper Jones slammed two-run homers from both sides of the plate, giving Atlanta a 6–4 win. The series was tied 2–2 with one game to go.

The series moved back to Atlanta for the deciding game the next day. Cubs starter Kerry Wood was given a 2–0 lead in the second inning with a solo homer by Alex Gonzalez, and he protected it with ferocity. Gonzalez made it 4–0 with a two-run shot in the sixth. The game ended when Wood induced Chipper Jones to hit into a rally-killing double play, giving the Cubs a 5–1 win and their first post-season series victory since 1908.[14]

This post-season win ended a streak of ten consecutive post-season series losses, and it allowed the Cubs to move on to the National League Championship Series against the Marlins who had upset the Giants in the other division series.

For those who saw the game, it was one to remember. They will recall where they were, and who they were with, and how they were feeling.

They'll remember Kerry Wood's fastball and the way he befuddled the Braves with his off-speed pitches. They'll remember how Aramis Ramirez's two-run homer in the sixth gave the Cubs a 4–0 lead and made breathing easier. And they'll remember thinking, "Ballgame."

They'll remember Vinny Castilla's hot shot to short in the seventh, how the ball bounced off Alex Gonzalez and caromed perfectly to second baseman Mark Grudzielanek who threw to first to get Castilla. They'll remember mumbling through a weak smile something about divine intervention and feeling sick to their stomach.

They rooted for a team that hadn't won a postseason series in 95 years, and some couldn't help but remember — the Curse of the Goat.

On a warm night in Atlanta, in a town where the local team had won 12 straight division titles, the Cubs came in and did what Cubs had unfailingly failed to do. They won. They beat the Braves 5–1 in Game 5 of their best-of-five National League Division Series, and Cubs fans will remember the wild scene between second base and the pitchers mound, the Cubs celebrating in a big blue pile.[15]

Chicago itself was in a state of euphoria, and superstitious fans were not taking any chances. A restaurateur broke a plate outside his restaurant as part of a ritual to lift the Curse. A realtor went to a closet and took out an old, beat-up Cubs' cap that he wore only when his team made it to the playoffs. Another fan refused to get a haircut until the playoffs were over. Other fans had other rituals.[16]

On October 7, in the first game of the National League Championship Series, the Cubs took a 4–0 lead in the first inning, but the Marlins scored five times in the third off Carlos Zambrano. After Florida scored in the sixth, the Cubs tied it with two in their half on a homer by Alex Gonzalez. The Marlins went ahead again 8–6 in the ninth, but again the Cubs evened the score with two tallies on a two-out homer by Sammy Sosa that landed on Waveland Avenue. The Marlins got a pinch-hit home run by Mike Lowell off Mark Guthrie in the eleventh, and this time the Cubs had no answer. The Marlins won 9–8.

But the next day the Cubs bounced back by crushing the Marlins 12–3 before 39,562 at Wrigley to even the series at one game apiece. The Cubs led 11–0 at the end of the fifth inning. Alex Gonzalez hit two homers, and Sosa and Ramirez added one each. Sosa's homer in the second off Brad Penny traveled 495 feet and banged off a television-camera booth about

100 feet beyond the center-field wall. Kenny Lofton collected four hits, and Randall Simon had three, including a bases-loaded single in the first that put the Cubs ahead 2–0. Mark Prior was the winning pitcher.

On October 10, the Cubs took Game 3 with a 5–4 win in eleven innings in Miami. In the eleventh, Kenny Lofton hit a one-out single and scored on a pinch-hit triple by Doug Glanville. Randall Simon had hit a two-run homer in the eighth to give the Cubs a 4–3 lead before the Marlins tied the contest in their half.

On October 11, Chicago beat the Marlins 8–3 to take Game 4. This put them within one game of the World Series. Aramis Ramirez paced the attack with two homers, a single, and six runs batted in.

On October 12, Game 5 was scoreless until Carlos Zambrano allowed a two-run homer in the bottom of the fifth. With the Marlins facing elimination, Josh Beckett, who threw as hard as Wood and Prior, cooled off the Cubs with a two-hit 4–0 shutout in Miami. He struck out 11 and held the Cubs hitless until Alex Gonzalez singled in the fifth inning.

The Cubs now headed back to Chicago with a 3–2 lead in the series, knowing that they needed only one more win to take the National League pennant, and then go on to the World Series.

Wanting the Cubs to win Game 6 on October 14, Sam Sianis decided to take his goat to Wrigley Field, hoping to break the curse. He talked to the press about his intentions and arrived at the ballpark before the game.[17]

The goat was not allowed into the ballpark. So Sam and the goat mingled with fans outside who seemingly enjoyed seeing them. The Sianis family had become part of a Chicago legend that had been handed down to Cubs fans for decades. One

Sam Sianis and his goat mingling with fans outside of Wrigley Field, October 14, 2003 (John Zich/New-Sport/Corbis).

fan wearing a Cubs jersey apparently didn't believe in the legend. He carried a sign that read, "WHAT CURSE?"

Chicago took a 3–0 lead with runs in the first, sixth, and seventh innings.

After Mark Mordecai flied out for the Marlins to start the eighth inning, the Cubs were only five outs away from their first World Series since 1945. With a three-run lead and no one on base, Mark Prior stood tall on the mound, working on a three-hit shutout, and since August 4 Prior had been 12–1 with an ERA of 1.44, including post-season play. There was every reason to believe that the Cubs would be successful in winning the pennant.

Vendors in Wrigleyville were waiting outside of the ballpark with T-shirts proclaiming the Chicago Cubs as National League Champions, but the game wasn't over.

In the top of the eighth, with one on and one out, Luis Castillo of the Marlins hit a high foul ball to left field where it was heading into the stands. The Cubs' Moises Alou, thinking he could nab the ball for the second out, headed toward the stands with his glove held high. He was just about to fit his glove around the ball when a Cubs fan, Steve Bartman, interrupted Alou's poise and the ball deflected off Bartman's hand and into the stands. The Cubs tried to get a fan-interference call, but the field umpire labeled it foul, declaring it "up for grabs."

Then the Cubs unraveled. Prior ended up walking Castillo. Then, Marlins catcher Ivan Rodriguez singled to score Juan Pierre. Miguel Cabrera then hit a ground ball to Cubs shortstop Alex Gonzalez, who had a .984 fielding percentage (with just 10 errors) for the season, the best among

Steve Bartman (in hat, wearing headphones) deflecting a ball about to be caught by Moises Alou (John Zich/ NewSport/Corbis).

all National League shortstops. Instead of fielding the ball cleanly, Gonzalez closed his glove a split second early and the ball dropped into the dirt, loading the bases. The Marlins went on to score eight runs in the inning to take an 8–3 lead, then held on to win. The series, instead of ending with the Cubs being National League champs, was now tied at three games each.

In Game 7, the Marlins faced Cubs pitcher Kerry Wood, who was arguably the best pitcher in the National League. This should have made Cubs fans feel a little better. But the Marlins scored three runs in the first on a homer by Miguel Cabrera. The Cubs countered with three runs in their half, the last two on a Wood home run. Alou then put the Cubs ahead 5–3 with a two-run homer in the third.

However, the Marlins zeroed in on Wood, scoring three in the fifth and one in the sixth, and then added two in the seventh off Kyle Farnsworth. The last Cubs run came in the seventh on a Troy O'Leary pinch-hit home run. It was Chicago's only hit during the last six innings.

The 9–6 win gave the Marlins the National League Championship and Wrigleyville soon became a ghost town. Players and coaches cleaned out their lockers. A worker removed the red, white and blue bunting from the top of Wrigley Field. TV crews did their postmortems in front of the famous Wrigley marquee.[18]

The eighth inning of Game 6 gave evidence that the Curse of the Goat lived on, and the Cubs and their fans, trying to put the heartbreak behind them, waited for the destruction of the "Bartman ball" in an attempt to end the continuing misfortunes that had befallen their team.[19]

Frustrated fans had to do something to end the accursed Curse. Grant DePorter, a Chicago restaurateur, bought the ball for $113,824.16, and arranged to have it destroyed. Prior to its destruction, outside Harry Caray's restaurant on February 26, 2004, the ball was put into a sealed, transparent case, and treated as if a prisoner being sent to the electric chair. Guarded by a team

The Bartman ball awaiting its destruction (Tannen Maury/epa/Corbis).

of 13 security men, it was given a last meal of lobster, steak and a cold beer.[20]

As the final hour drew to a close and the governor refused to grant a reprieve, the switch was pulled, setting off an explosive charge, ending the existence of what had been an official Major League baseball. The execution was covered live on CNN, ESPN and MSNBC. And the story was reported in newspapers around the world.

Death of the Bartman ball (Tannen Maury/epa/Corbis).

Yet, the story did not end. One year later, DePorter, in a further attempt to end the Curse, took the ingredients of the doomed ball, soaked it in vodka and beer, and added it to a pasta dish at his restaurant. The menu called it "Foul Ball Spaghetti." Naturally, the supply was limited, but thousands of diners must have relished this unique recipe.[21] Many of them were probably Cubs fans who once again voiced the mantra, "Wait till next year."

CHAPTER 15

As Bad as Usual

Spring training in 2004 at HoHoKam Park in Mesa, Arizona, saw Cubs fans giving Greg Maddux a standing ovation prior to his first Cactus League start with the Cubs that year. He was back with the team after signing a three-year, $24 million deal, after eleven years with the Braves.

Maddux's return was a feel-good story because after his departure in the winter of 1992 he went on to establish a 194–88 record with Atlanta, with a 2.63 earned-run average, winning three Cy Young Awards along the way. Now he was back, and he would pitch at least through 2006.[1]

Dusty Baker's Cubs were about to open the season as favorites to win the National League pennant, and there was every reason to believe they would take it. After Prior's shoulder injury, he had come back stronger than ever in 2003, going 10–1 with a 1.52 in his final 11 regular-season starts. The rest of the rotation was strong enough to keep the ship on course, and Joe Borowski had a year as closer under his belt. He came through in his final 14 save opportunities and posted a 0.77 earned-run average in September, proving himself down the stretch.

The Cubs' bench was better than any in recent memory. The two Todds, Hollandsworth and Walker — free agents coming from the Marlins and the Red Sox — had been key contributors to their respective playoff teams in 2003. Now, they were content to be role players behind Moises Alou and Mark Grudzielanek. Tom Goodwin was and continued to be the glue in the clubhouse and a top-notch pinch hitter, while Ramon Martinez was steady and unselfish. The Cubs therefore had subs to call upon in the late innings, and the addition of Derrek Lee was expected to help immensely.

But Sammy Sosa had a chip on his shoulder. After the corked-bat incident, toe injury and other problems of '03, Sosa wanted to prove he was one of the game's pre-eminent sluggers. He was ready.

The Cubs were due. The talent was in place. The manager was a proven winner. The ball that came to symbolize the Cubs cursed history had been reduced to a pile of thread by a Hollywood special-effects expert. The Cubs' storybook year was about to begin.[2]

Or was it? Before the season even started, Prior was out with an inflamed Achilles tendon, and the Cubs had to be prepared to win without him.

It was time for Kerry Wood to be the pitcher he could be, with the commensurate number of victories to prove it. It was time for Cubs hitters to support Wood every time he pitched and not to assume that Woody was going to take care of everything. In other words, it was time for Cubs hitters to give him more than two runs per game.

It was time for Corey Patterson to pick up where he had left off before his knee betrayed him in 2003. It was time for Carlos Zambrano to harness his emotions and the energy in his fastball, and be a consistent winner. It was time for Matt Clement to be the pitcher he was when he shut down Pittsburgh to help the Cubs clinch the National League Central title the year before and not the pitcher who too often ambled along at .500.

It was time for Greg Maddux to not change a thing. It was time for Moises Alou to stay healthy. It was time for Joe Borowski to give Dusty Baker no reason to contemplate a change in closers. It was time for the rest of the bullpen, led by LaTroy Hawkins, to make everybody forget the way Baker had to rely on his starters in 2003. Now was the time. April was the most important month of the year for this team. Even though the pennant wouldn't be won in April, it could be lost in April. This was the month.[3]

On their way to their season opener, the Cubs had a scare coming into Cincinnati when the plane bounced on one wheel in a stiff wind before landing safely.[4] On April 5, Vice President Dick Cheney threw out the first pitch, and Corey Patterson celebrated his return to the lineup with a home run in his first at-bat, kick-starting the Cubs to a 7–4 victory before 42,122 fans at Great American Ball Park. Kerry Wood got the victory, the bullpen was perfect, and Alou delivered the big hit with a three-run double off starter Cory Lidle in the third inning.

In their second game, two days later, Greg Maddux took the mound. His very first pitch hit Reds leadoff hitter D'Angelo Jimenez on the left leg. Then he plunked Ken Griffey Jr., the No. 3 hitter, in the right calf, making it the first time he had ever hit two batters in the same inning during 3,968 major league innings.

In the second inning the Reds' Adam Dunn sent a Maddux fast ball 415 feet into the right-field stands, and Griffey hit a two-run homer to dead center in the third, that one traveling 426 feet. The Reds then hung on for a 3–1 win.[5]

Sammy Sosa, too, was not his usual self. During spring training he led the Cubs with a .407 average, but now he was hitless in his first eight at-bats, though he wasn't concerned with his slow start. The most important at-bat came in the eighth inning when Sosa came to the plate as the tying run with two outs and runners on the corners. Reliever Ryan Wagner fell behind 2–0 and Sosa took a called strike before flailing away at two outside pitches, ending the threat.[6]

The Cubs continued to have good days and bad days. On April 11, Kerry Wood tied a Cubs record by striking out seven batters in a row during a 10–2 win over the Braves in Atlanta, but on April 12 the Cubs lost 13–2 in their first game of the season at Wrigley before 40,483 fans.

On April 16, Sosa and Alou hit back-to-back homers in the ninth to beat the Reds 11–10 at Wrigley. But on April 18, the Cubs *lost* to the Reds 11–10 in ten innings, though Sammy Sosa became the all-time career home-run leader in Cubs history, passing Ernie Banks, with numbers 513 and 514 as a Cub, and 542 and 543 in his career.

The team hung in there, though, and they stayed within striking distance in the National League Central Division.

On April 19, Derrek Lee hit a grand slam in the seventh for an 8–1 Cubs win. And the next two days they thrashed the Pirates 9–1 and 12–1. On April 25, Mark Clement and Joe Borowski combine on a two-hitter to defeat the Mets 4–1, and complete a three-game sweep.

On April 28, the Cubs survived three home runs by Steve Finley to defeat the Diamondbacks 4–3, and avoid being swept by Arizona who'd clobbered them 9–0 and 10–1 the previous days. On May 6, Derrek Lee slammed five hits, including a homer, as the Cubs won over the Diamondbacks 11–3, and the next day Carlos Zambrano pitched a two-hitter to defeat the Rockies 11–0. On May 16 a win over the Padres capped a three-game series sweep and garnered the Cubs a tie for first. The same day, though, Sammy Sosa sneeze brought on severe back spasms, in turn causing a sprained ligament, putting him on the disabled list for at least a month.[7] Was this just bad luck, or could it have happened because of the Curse?

Even without Sosa, the Cubs battled on. On May 28, Michael Barrett powered a pinch-hit grand slam home run off Mike Johnston of the Pirates in the seventh to give the Cubs a 5–4 lead in the second game of a doubleheader, but Pittsburgh rallied with five runs in the ninth to take the second game 9–5 on a walk-off grand slam by Rob Mackowiak. Two days later, the Cubs broke a five-game losing streak by walloping the Pirates 12–1.

In June the Cubs had a stretch in which they won nine of ten and got to within one game of the top. But then they lost four of five and dropped to five back. Sosa hit a walk-off homer on July 1 to begin a four-game winning streak, but the Cubs then proceeded to lose five in a row.

They were frustrated, as evidenced by the suspension of Carlos Zambrano for five games because he threw at Jim Edmonds twice on July 20. LaTroy Hawkins was also suspended for three games after an argument with umpire Tim Tschida on July 21.[8] On that day Luis Pujols collected five hits, including three homers and a double, to lead the Cardinals to an 11–8 win at Wrigley. It was a devastating loss for the Cubs, who led 8–2 at the end of the fifth.

The Cardinals swept the two-game series, and the Cubs fell ten games behind the division-leading Cardinals with a record of 49–44. Nevertheless, Chicago was in the wild-card chase, three games behind the Giants.

By July 29, Chicago was in second place, 10½ games behind St. Louis even though they had just lost 6 of their last 11 games. In the wild-card race, the Cubs were third, two games behind San Diego.

Jim Hendry, Cubs general manager, wanted to do something to bolster the team. He wanted a good hitting shortstop, like Nomar Garciaparra of the Boston Red Sox who was hitting .388 for the month of July with a season average of .321 and a career average of .323. By the end of July, he had his trade.

On August 1, there was a highly charged atmosphere at Wrigley when Garciaparra made his first appearance in a Cubs uniform and Greg Maddux took the mound in a bid for his 300th career win. Garciaparra managed an RBI single and Maddux failed to earn the decision, as the Cubs beat the Phillies 6–3.

Maddux finally had his 300th win with an August 7 decision over the Giants 8–4. Then the Cubs lost six out of eight.

They were hitting home runs: Lee, Sosa, Alou, Garciaparra, Patterson and Grudzielanek all joined in. And by late August the team was alive, winning eight of nine games beginning August 18, and extending their National League home run total to 188. The team was also close to becoming the sixth franchise in history to have four players with 30 home runs. In spite of this, they were still number two in the division race, 12 games behind St. Louis, though they did inch up to the number one spot in the wild-card race, 1 game in front of San Francisco.[9]

The one game lead didn't last long. On August 27, after giving up six ninth-inning runs in a 15–7 loss to the Astros at Wrigley, Kyle Farnsworth was injured after kicking an electric fan in the runway on the way to the clubhouse. He sprained and bruised his right knee and ended up on the disabled list.[10]

On September 2, the games between the Cubs and the Marlins on September 3, 4 and 5 were postponed because of the approach of Hurricane Frances toward Florida's East Coast.

The wild-card race became a nip and tuck battle between the Giants and the Cubs, and it took some heroics for Chicago to stay near the top. On September 16, Cubs third baseman Aramis Ramirez put on a one-man show when he went 4 for 5 with three home runs and five RBIs, accounting for all the Cubs runs and all but two of their six hits in their 5–4 victory over the Reds.

"If it's not me, it's going to be somebody else," Ramirez said. "This is the time to make our move and get on a roll. We only have 18 games left. San Francisco is playing pretty good right now, so we have to play every game like it's the last one."[11]

The Cubs now trailed the Giants narrowly in the wild-card race and they needed every player for the final push to the top. Ready or not, they needed Kyle Farnsworth who was slated to return to the Cubs' bullpen in a day or two. He had been sidelined for three weeks, and this hurt the depth of the Cubs' bullpen at a most inopportune time.

The Cubs had also been hurt by injuries to their two ace pitchers — Prior and Wood, and when Kerry Wood made the cover of *Sports Illus-*

trated, an inside feature article talked about him being off two months with a triceps injury, and noted that he was only 8–7 in his 19 starts. The idea that the misfortunes were due to a curse led ESPN to run a special comparing the curses surrounding the Cubs and the Red Sox, and came to the conclusion that the Red Sox had it worse.

Baker's comment: "I don't believe in curses."[12]

Curses or not, Garciaparra had been out because of an Achilles tendon injury, then a wrist injury and by September 22, he had missed ten games because of a groin injury. He was acquired because he was seen as the man to lead the team down the home stretch. When questioned, Garciaparra said his wrist injury had healed but that he needed an off season to take care of his Achilles tendon and groin injuries even though they were coming along well.

Dusty Baker wasn't about to wait until the injuries were completely healed. He was putting his shortstop back into the game *now.* The wild-card race was tight. The Cubs were a half game behind the Giants.[13]

With Garciaparra back and hitting, and with Greg Maddux winning his 15th game of the season on September 23, the Cubs took over the wild-card lead, now a half game in front of the Giants. Maddux beat the Pirates 6–3, reaching an unprecedented streak of 17 consecutive seasons with 15 or more victories, while giving his team a three-game sweep over Pittsburgh.

Heading into New York, the Cubs had won 12 of their last 15 games. They were definitely on a roll. In spite of injuries, they were clearly strong in all three phases of the game, fine pitching, defense and clutch hitting.

On September 24, the Cubs won again. When Derek Lee's one-out RBI single off Braden Looper in the tenth inning brought home the go-ahead run in a 2–1 victory over the New York Mets, Cubs fans cheered wildly. They were now 1½ games ahead of the Giants in the wild-card race. The win left the Cubs with a 16–11 record for September and a 35–19 record over the last two Septembers.

September had changed dramatically for the Cubs since Dusty Baker's arrival on the scene in 2003. He brought along the experience needed to create a winner, as demonstrated by his last five seasons managing San Francisco and the Cubs. Baker's teams had an 85–45 record in September and October, an enviable .654 winning percentage.

Then, with two swings of a bat, the Cubs' lead in the wild-card race was cut, and Rick Morrissey, a *Chicago Tribune* sports writer had something to say about it in his September 26 column:

> It's bad enough that the kid who killed the Cubs on Saturday was playing in the seventh major-league game of his career. But when it turns out the kid played ball at Clemente High School on Chicago's West Side, idolized the Cubs growing up and used to hang out with Sammy Sosa, well, you figure that if this thing falls apart, Victor Diaz will go down in Chicago lore as further proof a curse exists.
>
> "Is this going to be in the *Tribune* tomorrow?" Diaz said cheerfully in the Mets' clubhouse.
>
> You wouldn't hear Mike Piazza or Tom Glavine say that. But this is September, when wide-eyed young players get the chance to shine and the Cubs get a chance to be the Cubs. Diaz hammered a game-tying, three-run homer in the ninth inning off befuddled closer LaTroy Hawkins. And then Kent Mercker served up the game-winning homer in the 11th inning to Craig Brazell, another September call-up.
>
> "Diaz and Brazell, whew," said Cubs manager Dusty Baker, the reality of it almost overwhelming him. That "whew" said: Not exactly Ruth and Gehrig.
>
> But for a day at least, the 22-year-old Diaz felt like a future Hall of Famer, even if it did threaten to damage the Cubs' playoff hopes. San Francisco beat the Dodgers and cut the Cubs' lead in the National League wild-card race.[14]

If you do not believe in the Curse of the Goat, think about Sammy Sosa during that game. He was 0 for 5, striking out four times and hitting into a double play. And his batting average on the current road trip was .132. How bad can a superstar suddenly get?

If you are still a non-believer, think about the Cubs being on the verge of a 3–0 victory with two outs in the bottom of the ninth and then Diaz's two-strike, three-run homer tying the game, sending shock waves through the Cubs' dugout. Think about two innings later, and Brazell's first major-league home run snapping the Cubs' four-game winning streak.

Two days later, on September 28, the Giants beat the Padres and the Cubs lost to the Reds, tying the two in the wild-card race. On the following day, the Cubs lost the wild-card advantage to the Giants when LeTroy Hawkins surrendered a 2–1 lead with two outs in the ninth and then Cincinnati toppled Chicago 4–3 in twelve innings.

The Cubs were red-faced again on the next day with Prior on the mound. He pitched the best game of his career in his biggest game of the season, allowing one home run — which struck the foul pole — and striking out 16 light-hitting Cincinnati Reds in nine tidy innings.

In spite of superb pitching, his teammates deserted him, scoring only once, and the Cubs eventually lost 2–1 in 12 innings.

What happened to the Cubs' hitting? "I can't speak to that," Prior said. "That's really not my department."

The Cincinnati pitching staff started the four-game series with the league's second-worst ERA of 5.03. The Cubs averaged 4.75 runs in four games, and that's factoring in the 12 runs in their only victory. For a team leading the National League in home runs and total bases and second in slugging percentage, it was amazing that the bats had crumbled into sawdust. The Cubs had just lost five of six games to the Mets and Reds.

In these six games the Cubs scored in only nine of 53 innings. They hit only three home runs, one of them by pitcher Glendon Rusch. They stranded 44 runners and twice grounded into three double plays in one game. On September 30, they failed to score in the last two innings off pitcher Juan Padilla, who came into the game with a 12.71 ERA and had been scored on in eight of his last nine appearances.

Could anyone explain what happened?

"No, I can't," manager Dusty Baker said.

"I wish I knew," catcher Michael Barrett said. "It's hard to say."[15]

Jack Rakove wrote an op-ed titled "The Curse That Won't Quit." Published in the October 1 issue of the *Chicago Tribune*, its comments seem to be as valid as any others:

> This was a team of high expectations from the start and even higher expectations when it led the wild-card race a week ago. All in all, the Cubs were ready to be branded for life as underachievers if they didn't win their final three games against the Braves.
>
> True to their reputation, the Cubs blew it when they lost to the Braves 8–6 on Saturday, October 2. The previous Saturday saw Chicago two games ahead in the wild-card race. A week later they were two games behind after losing five games to the also-ran Mets and Reds and one to the National League East champion Braves who officially eliminated them from the playoffs.

Although there could be many explanations for the collapse, the one that Moises Alou refused to accept was, the Curse. "I'm sick and tired of fans bringing that up," Alou said. "You're lucky or unlucky."[16]

Not everyone agreed.

CHAPTER 16

It Never Ends

Most players and fans were probably not surprised when Sammy Sosa was traded to the Orioles in early February 2005. On October 3, 2004, the last day of the season, the Cubs had defeated the Braves 10–8 at Wrigley. Sosa had arrived only seventy minutes before the start of the game and he left fifteen minutes after the first pitch without putting on his uniform. He had then been fined $87,400 by the Cubs for the unexcused absence.[1]

The Cubs were inconsistent throughout the 2005 season. Injuries to Mark Prior, Kerry Wood and Nomar Garciaparra once again robbed the team of key players, but they managed to finish in fourth place with a 79–83 record. The two bright spots were the performances of first baseman Derek Lee (.335 batting average, 46 home runs, 107 RBIs) and the rise of closer Ryan Dempster (33 saves in 35 save opportunities).

So the Cubs retooled for the 2006 campaign. During the off-season, they revamped their outfield, acquiring speedy centerfielder Juan Pierre from the Florida Marlins in a trade. The Cubs also signed free-agent outfielder Jacque Jones to a three-year deal to fill a hole in right field. Veterans Bob Howry and Scott Eyre were brought in to bolster the bullpen — each received a 3-year contract. Former blue-chip prospect Corey Patterson, who despite short flashes of brilliance never played consistently well at the big league level, was traded to the Orioles for two minor leaguers. Nomar Garciaparra left via free agency to the Los Angeles Dodgers. And starting pitcher Wade Miller, formerly of the Red Sox and Astros, was signed, getting a one-year, $1 million contract.

The Cubs roared out of the gate in 2006, but an injury to All-Star first baseman Derrek Lee sent the team into a tailspin of historic proportions. In early May, the team set a franchise record for offensive futility by scoring only 13 runs in 11 games. On two separate occasions within a month, the Cubs tied a team record by allowing eight home runs in a single game.

On July 16, the Cubs had a 5–2 lead over the Mets in the sixth, and then the Mets had an 11-run rally that included two grand slams, the first time the Cubs had ever given up two grand slams in a single inning. It was also the first time the Mets had scored as many as 11 runs in a single inning.

By August, Wade Miller had yet to throw a single pitch all season. On September 22, Miller had a record of 0–2 with an ERA of 4.97.

The Cubs' misfortunes prompted me to stroll through Wrigleyville on July 16, several hours before game time, and talk with fans waiting to see Chicago and New York square off. I asked one woman, "Do you have anything to say about the Curse of the Goat?"

"They need to stop blaming the goat," she said. "I think they have a lousy team."

"What about 2003, when they had a good team, and were only five outs away from winning the pennant?"

"Fire Dusty Baker!" she replied without hesitation. "My father and I were talking about each of the Cubs players, today's players. They need to be taken into the alley and have the shit kicked out of them. They have no heart this year. I'd rather watch a T-ball game. But over the years, I admire the fans. I love the fans. They root for the team with every pitch, and until the last out, even when the team is losing 9–0."

A young man said, "I believe in curses. They can't do nothin' to get rid of the curse."

A fan at a bar said, "It's bad karma. I don't believe in curses." Another chimed in, "I don't believe in a Curse of the Goat. It's bad luck. Someone doesn't want them to win. Maybe it's God."

A fan outside the stadium said, "I believe in curses."

"What makes you believe in curses?"

"The Cubs," he said.

Another fan, standing nearby agreed. "Definitely," she said.

Another had doubts, and he offered a way of getting rid of the curse should there really be one. "To get rid of the curse," he said, "get pitchers that don't get hurt." He went on to say, "The curse will go on for not more than ten more years."

"Why should fans remain loyal to a losing team?"

"History keeps fans loyal," he replied.

Nearby, two other Cubs fans who were listening and waiting to get into the ballpark had this to say: "I don't believe in the goat. Dusty lost the games. It's the manager's fault." The other said, "They gotta rebuild. They need a new manager."

The Cubs needed something. They ended the 2006 season at the very bottom of the National League's Central Division with a 66–96 record.

CHAPTER 17

Curses and Beyond

The Curse of the Goat and its impact on the Chicago Cubs, has been woven into baseball lore as have other curses, both in baseball and other sports.

In 1918, George Herman Ruth pitched the Boston Red Sox to their fifth World Series championship. In spite of Ruth's phenomenal ability, Red Sox owner Harry Frazee sold the Babe's contract to the Yankees for $100,000 so he could help his girlfriend on one of her theatrical productions.

The Yankees had never won a World Championship before acquiring Ruth, but since then they have won twenty-six. The Yankees franchise is one of the greatest success stories in the history of baseball. The Boston Red Sox, on the other hand, have appeared in only four World Series since 1918, losing all of them in seven games. The performance of the Red Sox after selling Ruth has been nothing short of a disaster for 83 years and some consider this to be the Curse of the Bambino.[1]

For 83 years, Boston could not win it all. Then came 2003, and the Red Sox came within five outs of reaching the World Series. And the following season they broke free of the curse by sweeping the Yankees in the Championship Series after being down by three games, and then sweeping the Cardinals four straight in the World Series.

The Chicago White Sox are another team that some say played ball under a curse since 1919. It was that year that a gambling scandal was uncovered that entailed the intentional throwing of the World Series by eight members of the White Sox. A curse that allegedly befell that team afterward has been referred to as the Curse of the Black Sox.[2] For the next 85 years the White Sox failed to win a world championship. At last, on

October 27, 2005, the White Sox broke the curse by taking the flag from the Houston Astros.

Then there was the Curse of William Penn whose statue stands in Philadelphia atop City Hall. As a tradition, no building in the city rose above it, but in March 1987, One Liberty Place was completed, a 945-foot skyscraper that dwarfed the 548-foot height of the Penn statue. Soon, Two Liberty Place followed to a height of 848 feet.

Prior to the erection of the two structures, Philadelphia sports teams had been successful: the Philadelphia Phillies won the 1980 World Series, the Philadelphia Flyers won back-to-back Stanley Cups in 1974 and 1975, and the NBA's Philadelphia 76ers won the championship in 1983.

Unlike the baseball-only curses, the Curse of William Penn can be seen as having smitten four professional teams in Philadelphia. The Flyers lost the Stanley Cup finals in 1987 (in 7 games), only two months after One Liberty Place opened, and again in 1997 in a sweep by the Detroit Red Wings. The Phillies lost the 1993 World Series in 6 games. The 76ers lost the 2001 NBA Finals in 5 games. The Eagles lost Super Bowl XXXIX by three points in 2005. In addition, losses in conference finals have occurred seven times since the opening of One Liberty Place, including four by the Flyers, in 1989, 1995, 2000 and 2004. The 2000 team was one win away from a Stanley Cup Finals appearance. But after leading the New Jersey Devils 3–1 they lost three straight. In the following year, the 2004 team lost Game 7 of the Eastern Conference Finals to the Tampa Bay Lightning. The Eagles accounted for the other three conference-final losses.[3]

In considering the Curse of the Goat, it is interesting to note the number of players who have won World Series titles after leaving the Cubs. These include Andy Pafko (who played in the 1945 World Series as a Cub, the year that the Curse of the Goat was hurled at the team), Smoky Burgess, Don Hoak, Dale Long, Lou Brock, Lou Johnson, Jim Brewer, Moe Drabowsky, Don Cardwell, Ken Holtzman, Bill North, Bill Madlock, Manny Trillo, Rick Monday, Burt Hooton, Bruce Sutter, Willie Hernandez, Joe Niekro, Dennis Eckersley, Joe Carter, Greg Maddux, Joe Girardi, Glenallen Hill, Luis Gonzalez, Mike Morgan, Mark Grace, Mark Bellhorn and Bill Mueller.

It is also interesting to note that Hall of Famer Ernie Banks, with 512 lifetime home runs, never played in a World Series — he was never traded by the Cubs.

Also, consider the "Ex-Cubs Factor," when former Cubs players played a key role in the loss of a World Series. Boston Red Sox first baseman Bill Buckner was blamed for the Red Sox 1986 World Series loss after a routine ground ball rolled through his legs. Former Cubs reliever Mitch "Wild Thing" Williams gave up the 1993 World Series winning home run to Joe Carter in Game 6.

Curses go hand in glove with superstitions. Superstitions are sometimes applied to unusual patterns that have no logical explanation, and help people assert some feeling of regulation over phenomena that cannot be controlled. It is therefore not surprising to find an abundance of superstitions in sports.

Curses and superstitions are used to explain why a few teams come up short of winning championships for decades on end, and why some players suddenly experience precipitous drop-offs in performance, and why a particularly good player makes a bad play that ends his team's championship hopes.

With the application of superstition, the inexplicable is explained.

CHAPTER 18

The Kiss of Death

Deuteronomy 28:45–46 says that curses are applicable today: "All these curses shall come upon you, pursuing and overtaking you until you are destroyed, because you did not obey the Lord your God by observing the commandments and the decrees that he commanded you. They shall be among you and your descendants as a sign and portent forever."

A curse can be defined as a prayer or invocation expressing a wish that harm, misfortune, or any other injurious event be brought upon another person, place, etc. The curse has been a regular part of ancient cultures, and effigy has been a universal method of laying on a curse. Waxed effigies were common in ancient India, Persia, Egypt, Africa and Europe, and currently are still used. As the effigy is harmed, so the victim is said to be harmed. When the effigy is destroyed, the victim supposedly dies.

Curses as well as blessings have been bought and sold throughout the centuries as a service to others, calling upon supernatural powers to effect a change, and there is evidence that changes have occurred.[1]

Bukala Buki, a motel employee in Skokie, Illinois, says:

> I believe in a curse because of where I'm from. I'm from Nigeria, and in my country it's more of a voodoo kind of thing. For example, if someone offends someone, they put a curse on you — [to] go crazy or die, and it does happen. Like someone I know, she is ill mentally and we think someone put a curse on her. She came to the U.S., did well and someone is jealous because she made it, or is upset at her for not sending money home as much as that person would like. Her dad had many wives and many kids and one of them did it.
>
> In Nigeria, breaking a curse depends on whether you are a Muslim, a Christian or a traditional medicine person. Muslims pray, using the

Koran. The Koran is very powerful. Christians use the Bible. Those who rely on traditional medicine go to an herbalist. Some herbalists can actually see who did the curse and try to use herbs of various kinds. I've seen it work. For example, back home, a lady was crazy, and she saw an herbalist and got well.

In support of this claim regarding the validity of curses, consider the countless number of superstitious athletes who believe that an appearance on the cover of *Sports Illustrated* (*SI*) is the **kiss of death.**

Alexander Wolff, senior writer for *SI*, attempted to validate that belief by gathering information on *SI* covers from Eddie Mathews, on the cover of the inaugural issue in 1954, to Michael Jordan, who took his 51st turn on the *SI* cover in September 2006. All total, Wolff investigated 2,456 *SI* covers and found 913 "jinxes" wherein there was a misfortune or a decline in performance following an appearance on a *SI* cover. Here are a few examples:

- Tiger slugger Kirk Gibson appeared on SI's 3/24/1980 cover. He then started the season and went 4 for 35 as Detroit opened 2–9.
- George Brett appeared on 4/13/1981. He started the season hitting .208 and his Royals started 3–10. The SI cover ran again in August after a strike was settled. Brett then went 1 for 20.
- Dale Murphy made the 8/9/1982 cover. He had a stretch of 6 for 31 and the Braves dropped 14 of 15 games.
- Commissioner Bart Giamatti's photo did not make the SI cover, but his words about Pete Rose did on 9/4/1989. He died of a heart attack that week.
- Jack Nicklaus appeared on 4/21/1986, winning the Masters. In his next outing, he tied for 42nd in the Houston Open.
- Steffi Graf appeared on 3/27/1989 and suffered her first loss of the season two weeks later.
- Mark Gastineau of the Jets posed with the Giants' Lawrence Taylor on 9/29/1986. After the SI cover came out, Gastineau missed his first game in seven years.
- Wayne Gretzky appeared on 12/18/1989. Days after his photo made the cover, he failed to get a single assist, thereby settling for a tie for the NHL record of consecutive games with at least one.[2]

- Ramon Martinez appeared on 9/30/1991. On this date the Dodgers had a two-game lead in the NL West. Martinez lost his next two starts, and the Dodgers finished the season a game behind the Braves.
- Barry Bonds made the cover on 5/24/1993. In two weeks his batting average dropped 40 points.[3]

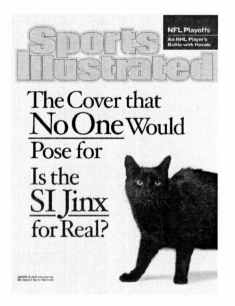

The Cover that
No One Would
Pose for
Is the
SI Jinx
for Real?

January 21, 2002, *Sports Illustrated* cover (Walter Iooss, Jr./*Sports Illustrated*).

To illustrate Wolff's story, St. Louis Rams quarterback, Kurt Warner was asked to pose for the *SI* cover along with a black cat. But Warner refused, so the cat did a solo.

In trying to explain his findings, Alexander Wolff turned to sports psychologist Jim Loehr who was of the opinion that there was an *SI* cover jinx of a sort. Loehr called it "a failure to efficiently metabolize heightened expectations," and Loehr works with athletes on this matter.[4] He emphasizes physical condition, sound nutritional practices, points to the mental and emotional side of competition, and teaches athletes the skills to reach their optimal performance.[5]

Alexander Wolff's favorite instance of the *SI* is that of University of Washington's quarterback Bob Schloredt, an All-American who was on a 1960 cover taking a long snap. "A week later, the heavily favored Huskies lost to Navy when the Middies scored in the final minutes following Schloredt's fumble of—you guessed it—a snap."[6]

Jinxes, curses, and superstitions continue to have a profound influence. Just think how many superstitions exist and are commonly known:

Finding a four-leaf clover brings good luck.
Friday the thirteenth is an unlucky day.
Breaking a mirror will bring you seven years of bad luck.
If a black cat crosses your path, you will have bad luck.

The Billy Goat Curse

A rabbit's foot brings good luck.
Finding a horseshoe brings good luck.
Step on a crack, break your mother's back.
An itchy palm means money will come your way.
To open an umbrella in the house brings bad luck.
A cat has nine lives.
A beginner will always have good luck: beginner's luck.
Garlic protects from evil spirits and vampires.
Clothes worn inside out will bring good luck.
Eating fish makes you smart.
A cricket in the house brings good luck.
It is bad luck to sing at the table.
Crossing your fingers helps a wish come true.
An acorn at the window can keep lightning out of the house.
If the bottoms of your feet itch, you will take a trip.
When a dog howls, death is near.
It is bad luck to chase someone with a broom.
To find a penny heads up brings good luck.
To cure a sty, rub it with a gold wedding band.
A person cannot drown before going under three times.
A drowned woman floats face up, a drowned man floats face down.
Evil spirits cannot harm you when you are standing in a circle.
Smell dandelions, wet the bed.

Enough said.

CHAPTER 19

Wackiest Guys on Earth

Kevin Rhomberg played in only 41 games for the Cleveland Indians, batting .383 with just 47 at-bats from 1982 to 1984. It's not Rhomberg's baseball prowess for which he is known but for his obsessive-compulsive need to carry out a superstitious act, over and over again. Rhomberg was indeed the Sultan of Superstition in baseball. Just ask Dan Rohn, the manager of the Mariners' Class AAA team in Tacoma.

Rohn and Rhomberg were teammates in Venezuela for winter ball. Rohn touched him one night after his last at-bat and ran away to hide. Rhomberg looked for hours, but could not find him. Rohn eventually returned to his hotel, believing he had outfoxed his teammate. But early in the morning there was a knock on the door awakening Rohn. He opened the door.

"It was Rhomberg," Rohn said. "He touched me and ran away."[1]

Rohn will tell you about Rhomberg's need to touch back anyone who had just touched him. If a person touched him and ran away without being tagged back, Rhomberg would send that someone a letter, saying, "This constitutes a touch."[2]

His teammates called him "Touch Me, Touch Me." They would playfully taunt him and drive him into a near panic by touching him and running away. Rick Sutcliffe reportedly reached under a bathroom stall and touched Rhomberg on the toe. Not knowing who it had been, Rhomberg stormed around the clubhouse and touched everyone.[3]

Few players carry such behavior to an extreme as did Rhomberg, but superstitions and rituals are rife in sports in general and baseball in particular. It has been this way dating back to the 1800s when St. Louis third baseman Arlie Latham would spit on a horseshoe for good luck.[4]

"In the case of baseball, it's something you acquire when you join the club," says Stuart Vyse, author of *Believing in Magic: The Psychology of Superstition* and professor of psychology at Connecticut College.

In baseball, it is very impressive to watch the lengths to which a ballplayer will go in an attempt to manipulate fate.

Outfielder Larry Walker was obsessed with the number 3. He set his alarm for 33 minutes past the hour, took practice swings in multiples of three, wore No. 33, was married on November 3 at 3:33 P.M., and bought tickets for 33 disadvantaged kids when he played in Montreal, to be seated in Section 333 at Olympic Stadium.

Relief pitcher Turk Wendell chewed four pieces of black licorice when he pitched, spit them out after each inning and brushed his teeth in the dugout, and leaped (not stepped) over the baseline (described as a "kangaroo hop").

Mark Fidrych would not reuse a ball that had been hit safely "because it had a hit in it," he said in a phone interview. "I didn't want to see that ball again." Fidrych once told an interviewer he wanted it to go back in the ball bag "so it would goof around with the other balls in there. Maybe it will learn some sense and come out as a pop-up next time."

John Smoltz did jumping jacks in the clubhouse during an Atlanta Braves rally, and was afraid to stop lest he be held responsible for the end of the Braves' scoring. He once ended up doing jumping jacks for nearly half an hour.

What can one say about pitcher Greg Swindell, who would bite the tip off one of his fingernails before each start and hold it in his mouth for good luck the entire game. Or Dave Concepcion, who once tried to cleanse a slump by taking a couple of spins in a large commercial dryer. Or Joe Niekro, who lined up nine cigarettes in the dugout and smoked one after every inning.

And what about Hall of Famer Wade Boggs who always ended his pregame infield practice by stepping, in order, on the third, second, and first-base bags, then on the baseline, then taking two steps in the coach's box and trotting to the dugout in exactly four steps.

Then there is the legendary Cincinnati manager Bill McKechnie who was said to imbue his ratty old necktie with magical power, to the point of wearing it to bed.

There is also **John McGraw**, the manager of the New York Giants. This hard-as-nails manager once gave a job to a farmer who couldn't play because he believed the man, Charlie Faust, was a magnet for good luck. Faust received a tryout when he approached McGraw and told him a fortune teller predicted success for him as a Giants pitcher. Faust was horrible, but his arrival coincided with a Giants winning streak and he was fitted for a uniform. McGraw also once employed a brewery to send a horse-drawn beer wagon across the Polo Grounds for 10 straight days because the first day it happened, one of his players had a great day at the plate.[5]

These are only a few of the hundreds of superstitions and rituals in baseball. When it comes to habits, rituals and superstitions, baseball players and managers are some of the wackiest guys on earth.

According to Dr. Richard Lustberg, superstitions help create self-confidence. "Athletes begin to believe," he said, "and want to believe that their particular routine is enhancing their performance."[6] Some may laugh, but psychological factors help teams win.

Need one wonder why so many fans and players believe in the Curse of the Goat when time and again the Cubs have seemed to be at arm's length of taking the National League flag, only to let it slip away?

Chapter 20

Losing Stinks

Will the Cubs' losing go on forever? It seems as if it will. In 2005, Chicago fans witnessed a horrible year for the Cubs. They finished last in the National League Central with a record of 66–96, 17½ games behind St. Louis.

Worst of all, the Cubs ended up in this quagmire with a talented team, and they did it after General Manager Jim Hendry had devoted his time early in the season to the acquisition of players such as Derrek Lee, Aramis Ramirez and Nomar Garciaparra.

Jim Hendry had a reputation for making such excellent acquisitions, but with the Cubs, fresh acquisitions always seemed to go sour.

Consider what happened to Garciaparra. He was part of the "Holy Trinity" of shortstops, which included Alex Rodriguez and Derek Jeter. They were considered to be the best shortstops in baseball.

Garciaparra emerged as one of the better hitters of the Holy Trinity, with the highest on-base plus slugging percentage (OPS), finishing with 35 home runs and 122 RBIs in 1998, runner-up for the American League MVP. He then led the AL in batting for the next two years, hitting .357 in 1999 and .372 in 2000, finishing in the top ten in MVP voting in both years.

In mid-season 2004, Garciaparra was traded from the Boston Red Sox to the Cubs. In 2005, a torn left groin muscle forced him onto the disabled list for more than three months, and his inability to perform for the Cubs resulted in his being let go. He then signed on with the Los Angeles Dodgers in 2006.

In Los Angeles, Garciaparra was moved to first base so as to minimize the risk of injury. He regained his offensive stroke, batting .303 for the year remaining constantly productive. At the 2006 Major League Baseball (MLB) All-Star Break, Garciaparra was tied with Pittsburgh's Freddy Sanchez for the lead amongst all MLB infielders and all NL batters with a .358 average, to go along with 11 home runs and 53 RBIs, carrying a 21-game hitting streak into the break. On October 7, Garciaparra was named the National League's Comeback Player of the Year.

With the Cubs, Garciaparra performed sub-par. With another team, he was once again a star. And there were others.[1]

Kerry Wood and Mark Prior, two young pitchers, had great potential. Fans looked to them to put the Cubs at the top. But injuries plagued both of them. Wood had been a starter his entire career until 2005 when he pitched in relief while dealing with shoulder problems. At the end of 2006, he decided not to have surgery for a partially torn rotator cuff in his right shoulder, and accepted the idea that he might have to pitch in relief rather than start when he returned to the lineup.

As for Mark Prior, nobody could say whether or not he would be able to return following his injury-plagued 2006 season. His absence certainly affected the off-season plans for the rotation.[2]

How could the Cubs possibly win when something always came along to strike them down? Case in point: sudden hospitalization of pitcher Glendon Rusch after a blood clot was discovered in his right lung. So many injuries and calamities. It's enough to make a person believe in the Curse.

In 2006, Derrek Lee, the defending National League batting champion, broke his right wrist in a collision with Rafael Furcal, forcing him to miss two months, and then go back on the disabled list again to give his wrist more time to heal. After his return, he was batting .345 in 15 games, but could not finish the season. A tearful Lee said he could no longer play because he had to be with his 3-year old daughter who had lost vision in one eye. "We just ask for everyone's prayers," Lee said. "We need a miracle. We need your prayers. We need everyone to believe she's going to be OK."[3]

After Lee addressed his teammates before leaving, Dusty Baker had something to say: "It's tough, especially when you have kids involved. You wonder sometimes. There are no answers. We just have to pray for him. It's been a tough year. Some strange things have happened this year to say the least. Every time there's one thing that you think is the most serious, there comes a more serious one."[4]

With all of the injuries and all of the tragedies the previous year, Jim Hendry had been busy all winter, using his genius trying to shore up a losing team, all the while listening to complaints from unhappy fans who pointed to the stunning success of the Chicago White Sox in winning the World Series. The pressure was now on Hendry to produce a better team for 2006 and he knew it.

Hendry also knew that money was not a problem. He reported that the Tribune Corporation's payroll was more than adequate to field a competitive team.[5]

But when the Cubs started losing in 2006, it didn't take long for Cub fans to go berserk. Some began writing letters to manager Dusty Baker that began with a racial epithet. Some letters had death threats. Cubs' right fielder Jacques Jones, who had a baseball thrown at him during a game, received a threatening early-morning phone call.

"We ran your nigger friend out of town, and we're going to do the same thing to you," the caller said. The caller referred to former Cubs reliever Latroy Hawkins, who in 2005 received the same abuse as Dusty Baker and who was moved to have Major League Baseball security open his mail. He was stunned by the hatred and found relief only after he was traded to the Baltimore Orioles.

Apparently, Dusty Baker was able to tough it out, even though the letters arrived as regularly as the loud boos at Wrigley. "I'm not going to let them beat me up," said Baker, "and they aren't going to run me out of town."[6]

It was readily apparent that the Cubs were no longer affectionately known as "loveable losers." They were treated with the same disdain as any other underachieving major-league team. Let's face it. Losing stinks.

At the end of 2006, the Cubs were still a losing team. They finished last with a record of 66–96, 17½ games out of first. The fans had had it. They began venting on the Internet. "Can't we option Dusty to Iowa," one comment said, "so he could work on his managing skills? He could build some confidence! Of course, he couldn't field a team with his allergy to rookies."[7]

One Web page showed Cub fans holding up a sign that read, "Fire Dusty." A note below the sign said, "They shud [sic] shove the sign in Hendry's face."[8]

Some fans bashed Jim Hendry. One said, "Hendry should be fired, but don't blame him completely for the way Dusty chooses to mismanage his roster."[9]

Another group of die-hards created a spoof of a book cover. Instead of *The DaVinci Code*, it said *The DaVinci Cub*. The fans went on to say that this new novel had information on Dusty Baker's hold on the Cubs managerial position. They claimed that painstaking research of documents going back to 1908 revealed that Dusty Baker was secretly married to Jim Hendry.[10]

From comments of Cubs fans on the Web site and it was obvious that by poking fun at the team and management, people were laughing instead of crying. A drawing of Charlie Brown in his baseball uniform, appeared, standing on the mound with Lucy and Snoopy beside him. A ball had just come down and hit Charlie on the top of his head. A caption read, "What else can happen?" And it went on: "I am starting a petition to move ALL Cubs related news from the sports section of the *Trib* to the Funnies page. All those in favor chime in." Beneath the drawing, a fan said, "I second the motion."[11]

But maybe all the joking was avoiding what some think is the Cubs' problem — the Curse. Is it real? And, if so, can it be removed?

CHAPTER 21

Looking Back

What is the truth about the Curse? The Billy Goat Tavern Web site talks about the circumstances surrounding it and of how P. K. Wrigley refused to allow the goat into the ballpark because it smelled bad.[1]

Another Web site claims that William Sianis and his goat were allowed into Wrigley, and occupied their box seats until ejected from Wrigley before the game was over due to the animal's objectionable odor.[2]

A third Web site claims that William Sianis had been bringing his goat to Wrigley Field throughout the late 1930s and early '40s, and that Sianis brought the goat to Wrigley Field to see the first game of the 1945 World Series, the same day Harry Truman was there to see Game 1. Trying to paint a nice picture of the city and the team, it was then that Phil Wrigley would not allow Sianis to bring his goat into Wrigley Field. As he was escorted away from the stadium, Sianis turned, raised his hand, and put a hex on the Cubs.[3]

Did any of this really happen? If so, which version is correct?

Shortstop Lenny Murello who played with the Cubs in the '45 Series, does not remember seeing a goat in Wrigley Field at the Series opener. Neither does Andy Pafko who also played that day.[4]

Nevertheless, many years have gone by and memories may have faded. Two things are for certain. The Cubs have not won a pennant since 1945, and the Sianis family, now headed by Sam and his son Bill, have expanded their Billy Goat Tavern "empire" from a single location to six additional taverns in Chicago and one in Washington, D.C. One can even order souvenirs from the Web site: Billy Goat T-shirts, sweatshirts and hats.

One can hardly argue that William "Billy Goat" Sianis was not an entrepreneur extraordinaire. Seeing him in a photo in his later years, behind the bar with a white apron wrapped round his waist, seeing his smiling face, gray hair, and nicely trimmed goatee, is to smile back and say to this Greek immigrant, "Well done."

Sianis came to this country with nothing and made it big thanks to his own ingenuity. Then, after he died, his nephew Sam Sianis took hold of the entrepreneurial spirit, ran with it and continues to enjoy the benefits fostered by a legendary curse.

CHAPTER 22

Righting the Cubs' Ship

In 1994, Tom Treblehorn, one of a string of ten successive Cubs managers to last no more than a year on the job, wanted to cleanse Wrigley Field of the dastardly Curse, and he really went all-out to get rid of it. He arranged for Sam Sianis and Ernie Banks to come to Wrigley to join a group of monks who proceeded to walk around the field close to the vine-covered walls, chanting in an attempt to drive the Billy Goat Curse out of the ballpark.

Instead of the curse leaving, it was Treblehorn who found himself departing at the end of the season.

It has been suggested that Treblehorn should have invited Father Guido Zamponi, a Xaverian who had volunteered to come to Wrigley to see if he could exorcise the Curse. It was a noble gesture for this 77-year-old priest, and in view of his fifty years of experience, what did the Cubs organization have to lose if they allowed the priest to try?[1]

Father Guido was ordained as a priest in 1956, at the Church of Our Lady of Pity in Cambridge, Massachusetts. After a number of assignments in other countries, he went to Italy in 1974, where he was asked to serve in various Xaverian communities. For the past eleven or twelve years he has lived in the beautiful Liguria region, at the Xaverian house in Genoa, helping in the correspondence office, writing personal letters and hosting visits from benefactors who call on him in special moments of their lives, especially when they want to receive sacraments, or during times of illness.

Although Father Guido's health is now failing, as is his vision and hearing, he prays daily for everyone and gives all he can give. He would have been the perfect individual to visit Wrigley and perform an act of exorcism.[2]

Exorcism is the act of driving out or warding off demons or evil spirits from places or things believed to be possessed or infested by them. This is done by earnest and solemn commands in the name of God.

The word "exorcism" is not biblical. It is derived from *exorkizo*, which is used in the Septuagint (Genesis 24:3 = cause to swear; 1 Kings 22:16 = adjure), and in Mathew 26:63, by the high priest to Christ, "I adjure thee by the living God...."

Expulsion by adjuration is therefore the primary meaning of exorcism, and when, as in Christian usage, this adjuration is in the name of God or of Christ, exorcism is a strictly religious act or rite.

If Father Guido is still willing and able to visit Wrigley, it seems reasonable to allow him to do so. If he is not able, he or another may be willing to recommend someone. Whoever that person might be, consideration should be given to the formation of a believing prayer group. They might be able to help in breaking the spell by applying the cross or other religious symbolism to the problem. As one example, if everyone agreed, the prayer could be, "Our Chicago Cubs seem to be under a spell, Lord. Therefore, in the name of Jesus we renounce the curse and break it, and free the team, its manager and all its players from all occult bondages. Free the team from the injustice and the dominion of Satan and make them strong and full of the light of the Lord. In the name of Jesus, Amen."[3]

Exorcism and/or the formation of a believing prayer group, it should be said, will be ineffective without a winning attitude in the team.

CHAPTER 23

A Winning Attitude

The Chicago Cubs at one time had a winning attitude, and it started with its manager.

When tuberculosis took hold of Frank Selee in 1905, he knew he would have to turn over the stewardship of the Cubs to Frank Chance, his husky first baseman, and it wasn't long before the new manager laid down a dictum for his players:

Every opposing team was the enemy, and you don't fraternize with the enemy. Every baseball game was a war, not a pink tea. There was a $10 fine if anyone shook hands with a member of the opposing team (a lot of money in those days). And there were other fines for other rules.

The team learned from the outset that their manager was not averse to doing anything necessary to bring a message home to an unruly player.

He was the model to inspire the best from his men.[1]

With this attitude and these rules in place, the Chicago Cubs had record in 1906 of 116–36 (.763 percentage), a record that has never been equaled. The Cubs also hold the best combined records for two seasons in a row, three seasons in a row, 4, 5, 6, 7 and 8 seasons in a row. They won four pennants and two World Series in five years. They dominated baseball, and a lesson to be learned from this is the need for a tough manager, and a management to support him.

Perhaps the present-day Cubs have this in mind. On October 1, 2006, Cubs President Andy MacPhail issued a press release, announcing his resignation. "I was brought to Chicago to accomplish one goal," he said, "and that was to win the World Series. Despite plenty of time and resources, I was unable to get the job done."[2]

John McDonough, Cubs senior vice president of marketing and

broadcasting, was to serve as interim president. Jim Hendry was to continue as general manager in charge of all baseball operations, and an announcement on Dusty Baker was expected.

The next day many Cub fans rejoiced when they learned the news: "The Cubs confirmed that Dusty Baker would not be offered a contract to return as the team's manager."[3] Four years after coming to Chicago as the team's most high-profile manager since Leo Durocher, Dusty Baker was out of a job.

Some viewed Baker's tenure as a failure and his legacy in Cubs history as one of great expectation followed by great disappointment. In reality, Baker had a winning attitude. He would jump right in and argue with an umpire when he saw a call that he disagreed with as he did when Aramis

Dusty Baker arguing with first-base umpire Tom Hallion (AP/Worldwide Photos/Brian Kersey).

Ramirez was called out at first during a game against Pittsburgh on September 5, 2006 in Chicago.

But he had to deal with injuries to key personnel, like Wood, Prior and first baseman Derek Lee. Catcher Michael Barrett served a 10-game suspension, and was then on the disabled list after sustaining a groin injury. Plus, there was the dismal 7–22 record in May when Baker was forced to rely on a rookie pitching rotation. And, he never did find a regular second baseman. So Baker had to go.

A day after the news that the Cubs would not rehire Baker, the Florida Marlins fired Joe Girardi, and the Cubs had a new name topping their wish list to replace Baker. When questioned about the Cubs, Girardi said, "They have to bring in someone who is pretty assertive. And someone has to take control of the clubhouse and just try to change the attitude of the whole organization."[4]

But someone had already taken control. The new Cubs' interim president, John McDonough, was a man on a mission. He predicted a world championship for the Cubs in 2007, and even though his statement seemed far-fetched, the firing of personnel continued. Dusty Baker's coaches were given the heave-ho.

With all this going on, Cubs fans wondered who the new take-control manager would be.

CHAPTER 24

A Winning Manager

The name of the new Cubs manager, Lou Piniella, came up on a sports Web site on October 16, 2006. In a large, bold headline, it said: "Piniella Agrees to Three-year Deal to Manage Cubs."

The deal was worth $10 million, and General Manager Jim Hendry said: "I feel terrific about Lou. I think he's a tremendous baseball man and a proven winner from the beginning of his career. I think he's absolutely the perfect choice as we move forward."[1]

Piniella had 19 years of experience managing in the big leagues with four teams — the Yankees, Mariners, Devil Rays and Reds. He managed the Cincinnati Reds between 1990 and 1992, a tenure that included winning the 1990 World Series against the heavily favored Oakland Athletics. And in 1995 and 2001 he was the American League Manager of the Year.

Known for his often aggressive and sometimes explosive behavior, Piniella is one of the most-ejected managers in major league history.[2] The Cubs hoped that he could be the spark the team lacked during the final two seasons of Dusty Baker's tenure.[3]

Jim Caple writes about Piniella in a 2002 piece titled "How to Lose Mind ... and Keep Dignity," for *ESPN Page 2*:

> There are thousands upon thousands of games each year in sports, most instantly forgettable. Too seldom do we see an athlete reach true perfection with a performance so masterful, so inspiring and so sublime that it makes men weep, poets sigh and angels sing from the heavens.
>
> Wednesday was such a night in Seattle, where Mariners manager Lou Piniella delivered the masterpiece of a long and distinguished career by calling upon his full range of talents and putting them all together on one stage. In protest of a call at first base, he charged onto the field, hurled and kicked his cap, screamed at the umpire, kicked dirt

and tossed first base into the outfield — twice — before leaving the field to deserved and thunderous applause.

"That was the best," said bench coach John McLaren, who has been witness to most of Sweet Lou's eruptions. "He had all his greatest hits in it. He had the cap, he had the base, he had yelling in the umpire's face. He had everything."

"I thought he was going to have a heart attack," said reliever Norm Charlton, who played for Piniella when he tossed his first base in 1990. "It's been awhile since I've seen him in that bad a mood...."

After further screaming, he reprised his most famous routine by reaching down and uprooting first base from its mooring, raising it aloft as if he were Rickey Henderson after breaking Lou Brock's stolen base record.[4]

After Piniella's retirement as a player from the Yankees in 1984, "Sweet Lou" stayed in the Yankees organization. First hired as a scout and batting coach, Piniella eventually became the team's manager in 1986.

George Steinbrenner opined that Lou "was my kind of player — I think he'll be my kind of manager." And Piniella indeed did lead his Yankees to a 90–72 second-place finish in his first season.

When you consider that Piniella went on to manage the Reds and in 1990, his first year in Cincinnati, the club became the first National League team to spend an entire 162-game season in first place, Cubs fans may agree with Steinbrenner. Louis Victor Piniella may be their kind of manager.

When Piniella left the Reds and returned to the AL, he took on the challenge of reviving the last-place Seattle Mariners. In his first season with the club, the Mariners finished a respectable fourth with a 82–80 record, making Piniella the third manager (after Clark Griffith and Joe McCarthy) to lead three different teams to a winning record in their first year with a club.

After the Mariners made their first post-season appearance ever in 1995, Piniella became the franchise's winningest manager with his 234th victory on May 22, 1996, against the Boston Red Sox.

Piniella seemed to be just what the Cubs desperately needed, a winning manager.

CHAPTER 25

Breaking the Curse

Bolstered by a winning manager, the Chicago Cubs should have been ready to free themselves from the curse that had kept them out of the World Series since 1945. The 2007 season was the time to arm Piniella with the very best players available.

It took money, and Jim Hendry had been given a lot of money and a mandate to spend it. So spend it he did. Free agent Alfonso Soriano and the Cubs reached an agreement on an eight-year contract worth about $136 million.

Soriano was the Cubs' new left fielder and lead-off hitter. A lot of attention was given to the 46 homers he had hit in 2006, besting his career high by seven. He was therefore expected to contribute power, over much of the life of his contract. In addition to the power he brought to the Cubs, he had also improved his ability to draw walks in 2005.[1]

In addition to Soriano, Jim Hendry signed pitcher Ted Lilly to a four-year, $40 million deal, pitcher Jason Marquis to a three-year contract for $21 million, third baseman Aramis Ramirez, to a five-year, $73 million contract, and Mark DeRosa, second baseman, to a three-year, $13 million deal.

When preparing for the new season, Hendry had to be hoping for a healthy Derrek Lee, the maturation of some young pitchers, and a few additional acquisitions in order to turn things around. He still had Catcher Michael Barrett, and also relied on Catcher Henry Bianco who had contributed more offensively than expected the previous year.

Hendry was also aware of his own two-year contract that required him to win or follow Dusty Baker out the door.[2]

With money to spend, it seemed reasonable to anticipate a powerhouse of a team with no holes left unattended. And with a tough, feisty manager like Piniella at the helm, there shouldn't have been a problem in instilling a winning attitude in the team. That's what it would take to win: a highly spirited, tough, fighting team.

Of course, a superb pitching rotation also had to be in place, along with a group of reliable closers. Prior to the start of the 2007 season, the starting five was seen as Zombrano, Lilly, Hill, Marquis, and one of a handful of other pitchers including Prior, Miller or Marshall. Prior, who was shut down toward the end of 2006 with tendonitis problems, had been working out six days a week in an attempt to strengthen his arm. A healthy Prior had the ability to get 15–20 wins and maintain an ERA below 3.00. If he could stay healthy in 2007, he would easily have been considered the number two starter behind Zombrano. As for relievers, Howry, Eyre, Wood, Wuertz, Marmol and Ohman were already in the wings.

The fat bank account was nice, but spending money guaranteed nothing. All one had to do was ask the Yankees, whose six-year drought probably felt like the 98-year drought the Cubs had endured. But the Cubs owed it to their fans to go after it, and with the aggressiveness they had shown in the off-season, it looked like they were determined to take the 2007 flag.

With a winning attitude and a highly spirited team in place, perhaps it was time for an exorcism.

Ecclesiastical exorcisms talk about "driving out demons from the possessed," and in the early years a simple and authoritative adjuration addressed to the demon in the name of Christ crucified, was the usual form of exorcism. Sometimes, in addition to words, some symbolic action was employed, such as laying hands on the subject or making the sign of the cross, the briefest and simplest way of expressing one's faith and invoking Christ's power.[3]

The sign of the cross is extolled by many fathers for its efficacy against all kinds of demoniac molestation. They further recommend that the adjuration and accompanying prayers be couched in the words of Holy Writ. The present rite of exorcism as given in the Roman Ritual fully agrees with patristic teaching and is a proof of the continuity of Catholic tradition in this manner.[4]

I discussed the idea of a Wrigley Field exorcism with Father Michael at St. Mark's church in Boynton Beach, Florida. He recommended the Rev.

Herman Jayachandra, a pastor of St. Martin de Porres parish in Boulder, Colorado, an exorcist from India. Although Father Herman is not the official exorcist of the Archdiocese of Denver, the archdiocese vouched for him as a priest in good standing.[5]

Father Herman's knowledge on exorcism can be seen in an article by Tom Hoopes, "The Dark Backward: Demons in the Real World," published in *CRISIS Magazine*, a Catholic publication examining contemporary culture. Three kinds of exorcisms are mentioned, including the solemn, public, or formal exorcism which is the one appropriate for Wrigley Field. "This ritual is only carried out with the specific authorization of a bishop. It's a serious matter, but it's a sacramental, *not* a sacrament. This means its effect is not infallible, and it may have to be repeated more than once."[6]

After receiving Fr. Michael's recommendation, I contacted Father Herman and mentioned my idea of doing an exorcism at Wrigley Field. He replied: "That would be fine. Maybe a bunch of good and holy people in the state of grace should fast a day or two and do some prayers of local exorcism in the field itself, when the players are present and remove the curse. If Cardinal approves this, you could do that with your group of good and holy people. Maybe you could, with the holy priest with you. Before you do that please say a Rosary in the field."[7]

Father Herman's advice is worth considering. Perhaps the owners of the Chicago Cubs could arrange for an exorcism at Wrigley Field.

Not everyone agrees on the use of exorcism as a means of eliminating the Curse of the Goat, however. Let me introduce you to Ali Adabieh, an automobile sales & leasing consultant in Margate, Florida.

"I am a die-hard Cubs fan, I love the Cubs," Ali says. Using his arms as he talks, he remembers the Marlins game in 2003 when Alou reaching up for that foul ball and the fan prevented Alou from catching it. "Five outs away," Ali said, "think of it, five outs away from winning the pennant and going to the World Series, and they lost. There has to be something to that curse!"

Ali talked about William Sianis buying two tickets to a World Series game in 1945, one for himself and one for the goat. Although Ali believes in the Curse, he does not believe it was Sianis who put the curse on the team, and does not believe in exorcism as a way of getting rid of it. "Wrigley put the curse on himself by rejecting Sianis and the goat," Ali said.

"The Curse is on Wrigley Field and exorcism will not work." P. K. Wrigley did Sianis wrong, Ali said. "Doing a bad thing gave Wrigley Field negative energy and you need positive energy to get rid of the Curse."

"There is only one way to get rid of the Curse," Ali said. "The Cubs must do a positive deed, something good, like giving 5,000 to 10,000 seats to sick children. Wrigley Field *must* show love."

Ali Adabieh went on to repeat the need for Cubs management to do good. He believes that this will spread positive energy over Wrigley Field, perhaps starting a legacy of love that will be enduring. He would like to see baseball become a family tradition, the way it used to be.[8]

There is scripture that supports Ali's point of view. It reveals a way in which a curse can be broken and a way in which one can be protected from it. As an Asian Internet Bible Institute article dealing with curses says, citing Malachi, Proverbs, and Romans, "Live a *righteous life* free from major sin and acts of injustice. Abide in the righteousness of Christ where no curse can penetrate."[9]

Ali's idea about positive energy suggests a final ingredient to the plan for the Cubs to win a World Series. What if a believing prayer group of all Cub fans, of all religions, all creeds, all nationalities and all faiths, would for an entire season focus on prayers asking for the team to win? Such a group would establish relationships, entanglements of the mind, and be connected through space and time as predicted by quantum theory. Albert Einstein called these connections "spooky action at a distance."

The reality suggested by the existence of such brain entanglements is so unlike the world of everyday experience that until recently many physicists believed it was interesting only for abstract theoretical reasons. But scientists are now finding that there are ways in which the effects of the brain's microscopic entanglements "scale up" into our macroscopic world. And they can persist over many miles.

There are theoretical descriptions showing how tasks can be accomplished by entangled groups without the members of the group communicating with each other in any conventional way. Some scientists suggest that this might depend in some fundamental way on quantum effects like entanglement of particles in the brain.

What if these speculations are correct? What would human experience be like in such an interconnected universe? Would such experiences evoke a feeling of awe that there's more to reality than common sense implies? Could "entangled minds" result in influencing the outcome of any kind of event, including a ballgame?

These are questions explored by Dean Radin in his book *Entangled Minds*,[10] and, in a nutshell, he found that there's substantial experimental evidence indicating that some of these experiences are genuine. Science is at the very edge of understanding entanglement, and there is much yet to learn. What we've seen so far provides a new way of thinking. We are living in an interconnected, entangled physical reality, and it is a natural phenomenon of physics.

The idea of the universe as an interconnected whole is not new. For millennia it's been one of the core assumptions of Eastern philosophies. What is new is that Western science is slowly beginning to realize that some elements of that ancient lore might be real. Of course, adopting a new ontology is not to be taken lightly. When it comes to serious topics like the nature of reality, it's sensible to adopt the conservative maxim, "If it ain't broke, don't fix it."

But in the case of the Cubs, the team is broken, so to speak. Why not try to fix it using this scientific approach? To date, nothing else has worked.

Perhaps nineteenth-century English poet Francis Thompson, said it best:

> All things by immortal power,
> Near and Far
> Hiddenly
> To each other linked are,
> That thou canst not stir a flower
> Without troubling of a star.[11]

Now all we need is an umpire who will holler "Play ball!"

CHAPTER 26

Play Ball

In 2007, Cub fans did everything they could to get rid of the dastardly Curse. One wore headphones to hear the play-by-play. Taking them off before the game was over was thought to jinx the team. Another rubbed his hands as if starting an imaginary fire when Cubs players came to the plate, a technique that "helped awaken their bats," the fan said.[1] One kept a battered blue Cubs cap hidden in a closet, to be worn only when the team reached the playoffs. Another kept the bathroom fan on during each game because the Cubs supposedly won when it was on.[2]

The home opener on April 9 introduced new Cubs manager Lou Piniella to 41,388 baseball fans. It was an overcast, forty-degree day, and the shivering crowd saw Chicago lose to Houston 5–3.

A week before, on the opening day of the season, the Tribune Company announced that the club would be sold at season's end. Perhaps this news had an adverse effect on team morale, because they didn't do too well in April and May. On May 17 in New York, the Cubs were leading the Mets 5–1 in the bottom of the ninth, but the Mets rallied for five runs and won 6–5. The Cubs lost for the sixth time in eight games, and the bullpen was 2–11 with eight blown saves.

On June 2 the Cubs lost to the Atlanta Braves 5–3, their sixth defeat in a row, putting the team next to last in their division. But the team began to win. By the end of June, the Cubs occupied second place with a 39–39 record in the NL Central Division, 7½ games behind the Brewers. Not bad for a team that had so many pitchers on the disabled list.

Pitcher	Injury	Disabled
Ryan Dempster	Strained left oblique	June 23, 2007
Angel Guzman	Strained right oblique	June 2, 2007

Pitcher	*Injury*	*Disabled*
Wade Miller	Middle back spasms	April 23, 2007
Kerry Wood	Right shoulder tendonitis	March 29, 2007
Mark Prior	Shoulder injury	March 28, 2007 (out for season)
Roberto Novoa	Right humeral head fracture	March 21, 2007

Why so many injuries? Were they in poor shape at the start of the season? Was it bad luck? The Curse? Rocky Cherry was brought up from AAA Iowa. Almost immediately, on July 1, he too was put on the disabled list. Catcher Henry Blanco had also been put on the disabled list on May 31 because of a herniated disc.[3] For decades great players had fallen victim to a quirky accident or injury — Garciaparra, Sosa, Wood, Prior, Lee and others. These injuries definitely contributed to the losing of pennants.

Frustration was evident when teammates Zambrano and Barrett exchanged punches in the dugout on June 1. And a day later when Piniella kicked dirt on third-base umpire Mark Wegner and allegedly kicked him, causing Piniella's ejection and a four-game suspension.

Maybe throwing punches in their own dugout and kicking an umpire was what the team needed to get them fired up. The Cubs soon began winning more than they lost. By July 3, the Cubs were on the upside, at 41–40, moving above .500 for the first time since they were 16–15 on May 9.

July 5 saw them 43–41, 4½ games out, and by July 7, the Cubs had won 12 of 15 and were 21–10 since June 3, the best record in the majors over that span.

On July 13, Carlos Zambrano took the mound for the Cubs against the Astros, looking fresh after a four-day All-Star break. He appeared ready to lead the Chicago club over the final 2½ months of the season. Zambrano's record against the Houston Astros was 5–0 dating back to the previous season in six starts against the Astros. True to form, he was in complete control for a 6–0 win, pushing the team up a notch, to 3½ games behind the first-place Brewers.

Fighting to stay in contention with players on the disabled list, Cubs management continuously scrambled and acquired new men. By July 21, with changes in place, they had an excellent opportunity to gain ground on the Brewers, but they lost to the Arizona Diamondbacks 3–2 before 41,632 fans at Wrigley. Just their sixth loss in twenty-five games, it kept them 2½ games out of first place in the NL Central Division.

In spite of the loss and in spite of the Cubs' ongoing injuries,

Cubs manager Lou Piniella argues with third-base umpire Mark Wegner, June 2, 2007 (AP/Worldwide Photos/Nam Y. Huh).

Chicagoans were once again dreaming of a pennant. On July 22 their hopes may have dipped a bit when the Cubs again lost to the Diamondbacks, 3–0, putting the team 3½ games behind the Brewers. The Cubs had managed only four hits in their last fifteen innings. They were in second place, though Lou Piniella had shuffled players around almost daily, using 14 different players in the seventh spot in the batting order, 12 in the eighth and 11 in the fifth.[4]

As Chicago headed to St. Louis for a key NL Central series, the Cubs starting pitchers were second in the National League in ERA (3.86) and first in strikeouts (730). Only seven starters had been used and none of them were named Wood or Prior, two pitchers who seemed destined to remain on the disabled list.

The Cubs beat the Cardinals two out of three. Then a sweep of the Reds, capped by Zambrano's 6–0 victory on July 29, had them only half a game out of the top spot. By August 1, Chicago was a percentage point ahead of Milwaukee after a 5–4 win over Philadelphia.

But the Cubs were not consistent. On August 2 they lost 10–6 to the Phils, and the next day, after Zambrano was forced to leave in the sixth inning with cramps and dehydration, the Mets beat the Cubs 6–2. Zambrano admitted he would have to change his habits going forward, especially in the heat of summer. "I'm not the type that likes to drink water," Zambrano said. "That's been a problem for me. Maybe I will force myself to drink some from now on. I was disappointed to come out of the game when the team needed me to pitch seven or eight innings."[5] That afternoon, the 6–5, 255-pound Zambrano threw just 95 pitches with the temperature in the 70s. He failed to become the first 15-game winner in the major leagues in 2007.

The next day the Cubs suffered another meltdown in the ninth inning against the Mets when Ryan Dempster allowed four runs to turn a tie game into a 6–2 loss.

After a Cubs win on August 4, they lost to the Mets 8–3 the next day and suffered an even greater loss when left fielder Alfonso Soriano strained his right quadriceps while running from first to third. Soriano was in so much pain that he hopped toward third on his left foot before being thrown out by center fielder Lastings Milledge to end the inning. It was reported that Soriano would miss at least two weeks and perhaps a month of play, something the Cubs could not afford, because he was leading the team with 18 homers and 74 runs scored.[6]

"Bats on Strike," read the *Chicago Tribune* sports page headline on August 7.

The punchless Cubs has struck out 13 times in Soriano's absence, and the *Tribune* reported, "The first day of their Alfonso-free period didn't go

Alfonso Soriano scoring against the Seattle Mariners, June 6, 2007 (AP/World-wide Photos/M. Spencer Green).

smoothly for the Cubs who failed to mount any offense Monday in a 2–1, 10-inning loss to the Astros."

A Cubs downslide had begun, but the Brewers were also doing poorly, keeping the Cubs with 1½ games of first. They'd had an opportunity to move into a first-place tie on August 8 after Milwaukee lost by 15 runs at Colorado, but Carlos Zambrano had a rough outing in an 8–2 loss to Houston, as the Cubs were swept at Minute Maid Park.

The slumping Cubs lost four straight, six of seven and 11 of 18 games, while the free-falling Brewers lost four straight and 14 of 20.

On August 9, manager Lou Piniella called a team meeting to remind his players of the tough luck they'd had, and to tell them he just wanted all of them to use their talents and go out and have fun. The team heeded their manager's advice and broke out of their offensive slump, throttling the Rockies 10–2 at Coors Field.[7]

Zambrano was still doing poorly, though. As of August 16, with three starts for the month, he was 0–2, with an earned-run average of 7.13, compared to July when he had a 1.38 ERA, earning him the National League Pitcher of the Month honors. Nevertheless, on August 18 the *Chicago Tribune* announced that the Cubs had given Zambrano 5-year, $91.5 million contract extension.

After the announcement, Carlos Zambrano was quoted as saying, "I'd like to thank God. Without him, I'm nothing, I'm screwed."[8] His humility may have had an effect on his teammates that day as they moved into first place with a half-game lead over Milwaukee when Daryle Ward hit a grand slam that beat the Cardinals 5–3.

It had been 2003 since the Cubs had sole possession of first place this late in the season. And it should have been time to break the Curse. But the Cubs were the Cubs. In two games with the Diamondbacks, on August 25 and 26, they were shut down, losing both, turning a good road trip into a 3–3 wash.

On August 28, though, Soriano was back. And it was one of those nights at Wrigley when everything fell into place at just the right time. A Jacque Jones line drive to the gap in right field rolled all the way to the wall. A Ryan Theriot chopper to the pitcher bounced out of an outstretched glove. When all was done, a raucous crowd of 40,884 had watched the Cubs beat Milwaukee 5–3, bouncing back from a three run deficit to grab the opener of their National League Central showdown.

Still in first place, not everything was peaches and cream. Carlos Zambrano was still struggling and on August 29 lost to the Brewers, giving him a 0–4 record for August and an ERA of 8.14, having given up 36 hits. When questioned, manager Lou Piniella said, "I don't know what the problem is, but he's not pitching like the guy who won nine in a row earlier in the year."[9]

Cubs relievers were doing better. On August 30 against the Brewers, and with Murton and Soriano hitting consecutive homers, closer Ryan Dempster got out of a ninth-inning jam to preserve a Cubs' 5–4 victory and the team's hold on first place, with the Brewers 2½ games back and the Cardinals in third place, three games behind.

With the Cubs in first place, Chicago fans must have been holding their breath, hoping that this would finally be their year, hoping the Curse would finally be broken.

Their hopes would have been raised a bit higher when they read an article in the *Chicago Tribune* on September 2 and headlined "Positive

Signs from a Healthy Wood." It told of Kerry Wood throwing 96 m.p.h. and fanning two batters in 2 innings of scoreless relief, a sign that his arm was returning to normal. The article pointed out that Piniella was using him mostly in non-pressure situations, hoping to gain some consistency from Wood before throwing him back into the fire.

In spite of the good news, the Cubs then lost four out of five, starting with an 11–3 loss on September 3. But on September 8, Zambrano at last found his groove, beating the Pirates 5–1, keeping the Cubs tied for first. After a 10–5 Cubs loss the next day, the National League standings in the Central Division showed the Brewers on top, the Cubs second, one game out and St. Louis third, three games behind.

The Cubs went back into a tie for first with a 12–3 win on the tenth, dropped a game back with a loss on the next day, then tied it again on Wednesday, September 12, when Ryan Dempster earned his 26th save, despite allowing a run in the ninth, by inducing a game-ending double

Carlos Zambrano finished 2007 regular season play with an 18–13 won-loss record (AP/Worldwide Photos/Jerry Lai).

play. The Brewers had lost to the Pirates 7–4 while the Cardinals had lost to the Reds 5–1. The Brewers and the Cubs were now 74–71 while the Cardinals were in third place at 69–74.

On September 14, Zambrano won again, beating St. Louis 5–3, but he lost to Cincinnati 5–2 September 18, and the Cubs were tied after having been up a game. The standings three days later were Chicago in first with 80–73, the Brewers second at 78–74, and St. Louis fading in third, 71–81, 8½ games behind.

On September 23, Zambrano was back, beating Pittsburgh 8–0. This put his record at 16–13 and his ERA at 4.20. And it put the Cubs 3½ games up with just six to play.

But the game that drove long-suffering Cubs fans into the streets around Wrigley Field, dancing, shouting and celebrating, was on September 28 when Zambrano pitched another shutout, leading the Cubs to a 6–0 win over the Cincinnati Reds, thus clinching the National League Central Division championship.

A fan Web site said, "Carlos Zambrano is the greatest man in the world." The runner-up greatest man was Alfonso Soriano who had two hits — one being a homer to deep center in the first inning, and scored two runs.

The Cubs management made a wise investment when they signed Zambrano to a 5-year $91.5 million contract extension in August and Soriano to an 8-year contract for $136 million. They were worth every penny.

Chicago finished the regular season 85–77. Milwaukee was second, two games out and St. Louis third, seven games behind. The Cubs-Diamondbacks playoff series was scheduled to begin Wednesday, October 3, in Arizona.

In Game 1, Brandon Webb took the mound for the Diamondbacks. He astounded the Cubs with his sinker, then had them swinging at air with his curves and changeups. Webb shut down the Cubs, while two of his teammates powered home runs for a 3–1 victory.

It had been a 1–1 game when Lou Piniella pulled his ace, Zambrano, after six innings and 85 pitches. Mark Reynolds proceeded to hit a tie-breaking homer off reliever Carlos Marmol, while the Diamondbacks bullpen maintained their lead.

Piniella explained his decision to remove Zambrano by saying that he planned to bring back his right-hander after three days rest in Game

4, but Piniella was being optimistic in thinking the series would last that long, and his plan may have cost the Cubs a victory.

In Game 2 the next evening, rookie Chris Young hit a three-run homer for Arizona in the second inning after the Cubs had gone up 2–0 in the top of the second. Chicago starter Ted Lilly slammed his mitt to the ground. "I've never seen a pitcher throw a glove like that," manager Lou Piniella said.[10]

The Diamondbacks kept scoring, driving Cubs starter Ted Lilly out of the game in the fourth after giving up six runs and seven hits. The final score was 8–4 Arizona and everything seemed to be going their way, with only one more win needed to take the series.

With the two losses in Phoenix, the Cubs' first four batters had gone 5 for 35 with 13 strikeouts. Alfonso Soriano was 2 for 10, Derrek Lee 2 for 8 and Aramis Ramirez 0 for 9. The trio had no RBIs. Unless the Cubs could turn it around at Wrigley on Saturday, October 6, they would make it 99 years and counting without a World Series title, and the Billy Goat Curse would still be alive.

In Game 3, on Sunday, October 7, Chris Young, Arizona's center fielder, homered on the game's first pitch. The next batter doubled and scored later in the inning, and that was all the Diamondbacks needed. They beat the Cubs 5–1 to complete a three-game sweep of their National League Division Series.

Even a return to Wrigley Field and its cheering fans couldn't get Chicago's bats out of a series-long slump. Chicago's RBI leader, Aramis Ramirez, came up twice in early innings with two runners on, but struck out and hit into a double play, illustrating the Cubs' offensive woes. He finished the series 0 for 12. Alfonso Soriano also struggled, going 2 for 14.

The Cubs best chance to win a game had been in the opening game when Piniella pulled Carlos Zambrano after six innings with the score tied 1–1 because he planned to bring Zambrano back on three days of rest. What Piniella failed to heed the old adage: Play 'em one game at a time. If the Cubs had won Game 1, they might have picked up some momentum and gone all the way.

Call it the Curse of the Goat, bad luck, or whatever. For anguished Cub fans, waiting till next year now meant 2008 — the 100-year anniversary of their last championship season.

Conclusion

As this book goes to press, the Tribune Company's sale of the Cubs had been delayed. One person interested in purchasing the team is Dallas Mavericks owner Mark Cuban. When Cuban went to Wrigley Field in 2007, he sat in the right-field bleachers. "That's the best place to watch a game," he said. "I don't do things just for the sake of doing them," Cuban asserted in December 2007, calling the potential purchase "a passion project."[1]

Back in April the Tribune Company announced a pending deal to sell the company, including the Cubs, for $8.2 billion to a media conglomerate led by real-estate magnate Sam Zell. But as of January 2008, a proposal to sell Wrigley Field had slowed progress on the Cubs' sale.[2]

In addition to Cuban and Zell, another rumor introduced the name of John Canning, chairman of private equity firm, Madison Dearborn Partners, and a longtime friend and business partner of baseball commissioner Bud Selig.[3]

While future ownership negotiations were slowly grinding away behind closed doors, the Cubs signed Kerry Woods to a one-year, $4.2 million contract. The 1998 NL Rookie of the Year will get the opportunity to be the Cubs' closer in 2008, it was said.[4]

Free-agent Jason Kendall was signed to a tentative deal by the Brewers in late 2007, and Craig Monroe was traded to the Twins for a player to be named later. And Prior, the right-handed pitcher who appeared to have a brilliant future in 2003 when he went 18–6 with an ERA of 2.43, was released in December 2007 and then signed by the Padres.

In the front office, Cubs top executive, John McDonough resigned and signed on as the new president of the Chicago Blackhawks.

Mark Prior pitching against the San Diego Padres (AP/Worldwide Photos/Rob Schumacher)

Who will be the new faces of the Cubs? Rumors in late 2007 had Japanese stars Kosuke Fukudome and Hiroki Kuroda signing with the team; in the end, the Cubs got Fukudome, but Kuroda went to the Dodgers. It is certain that there are many uncertainties.

When the Cubs reconvened at HoHokam Park in Mesa, Arizona, in February 2008, many of the uncertainties were resolved. But what about the Curse? Cub fans everywhere, let us join together and pray.

It would be a glorious day
To end the Curse
And see the Cubs
Go all the way.

Chapter Notes

Introduction

1. "Chicago Cubs, Loveable Losers," Funtrivia.com, http://www.funtrivia.com/trivia-quiz/Sports/Chicago-Cubs-Lovable-Losers-153259.html (accessed January 15, 2008).
2. "Chicago Cubs," Sportsencyclopedia.com, http://www.sportsecyclopedia.com/nl/chicubs/cubs.html (accessed January 15, 2008).
3. *Ibid.*
4. *Ibid.*
5. Bogen, Gil, *Tinker, Evers and Chance: A Triple Biography* (Jefferson, NC: McFarland, 2003), 37–38.
6. Burns, Edward, *Chicago Tribune*, November 1, 1945.
7. *Chicago Tribune*, October 6, 1945.
8. Snyder, John, *Cubs Journal* (Cincinnati: Emmis Books, 2005), 343.
9. "Curse of the Goat," Everything2, http://www.everything2.com/index.pl?node=Curse%20of%20the%20Goat (accessed January 15, 2008).
10. *Chicago Tribune*, October 7, 1945.
11. "Curse of the Goat," Everything2.

Chapter 1

1. Bogen, Gil, *Tinker, Evers and Chance*, 59–60.

2. *New York Evening World*, February 16, 1924.
3. Golenbock, Peter, *Wrigleyville: A Magical History Tour of the Chicago Cubs* (New York: St. Martin's Griffin, 1999), 103.
4. Rice, Grantland, "Tinker to Evers to Chance," *Collier's*, November 29, 1930, 11.
5. Pietrusza, David, *Baseball: The Biographical Encyclopedia* (Kingston, NY: Total/Sports Illustrated, 2000), 39.
6. "Joe Tinker and Frank Chance Get Into a Row with Spectators at Cincinnati and Are Roughly Handled." Uncredited Baseball Hall of Fame scrapbook news item, April 16, 1906.
7. "President Murphy Returns from Redville and Talks of Change," *Chicago Tribune*, April 16, 1906.
8. Chance, Frank L., "Chance and Tinker Evolved New Play." *New York Times*, March 28, 1915.
9. Golenbock, Peter, *Wrigleyville*, 108.
10. *Chicago Daily News*, October 2, 1907.
11. "Johnny Evers Speaks." Uncredited Baseball Hall of Fame scrapbook news item, December 26, 1936.
12. *Chicago Daily News*, October 5, 1907.
13. "Johnny Evers Speaks."
14. Evers, John J., and Hugh S. Fullerton, *Touching Second* (Chicago: Reilly and Britton, 1910), 91

15. *Ibid.*, pp. 91–99.
16. Honig, Donald, *The Greatest Catchers of All Time* (Dubuque, IA: Wm. C. Brown, 1991), 9.
17. Hirshberg, Al, *Baseball's Greatest Catchers* (New York: G. P. Putnam's Sons, 1966), 22.
18. Snyder, John, *Cubs Journal.* (Cincinnati: Emmis Books, 2005), 146.
19. Bogen, Gil, *Tinker, Evers and Chance*, 88–90.
20. *Ibid.*, 91–92.
21. Golenbock, Peter, *Wrigleyville*, 144.
22. Bogen, Gil, *Tinker, Evers and Chance*, 93–95.
23. Deford, Frank. "Curses: From Boston to Chicago to Japan, Baseball Teams Can't Shake Bad Luck." *SI.com*, September 24, 2003, http://sportsillus trated.cnn.com/2003/writers/frank_de ford/09/24/viewpoint/index.html (accessed January 10, 2008).
24. *Kansas City Times*, January 25, 1909, 8.
25. *Chicago Tribune*, March 20, 1909, 10.
26. *Chicago Tribune*, April 4, 1909.
27. *Chicago Tribune*, March 20, 1909, 10.
28. *Kansas City Star*, January 10, 1909, 4.
29. *Washington Post*, May 16, 1909, 54.

Chapter 2

1. Bogen, Gil, *Tinker, Evers and Chance*, 116–117.
2. 1930 United States Federal Census.
3. Kogan, Rick, *A Chicago Tavern: A Goat, a Curse, and the American Dream* (Chicago: Lake Claremont Press, 2006), 6.
4. "Record Broken Again!!!" American VULCAN Corporation, July 20, 1988, http://www.vulkanusa.com/blueri band.htm (accessed January 15, 2008).
5. "British Rower Makes Fastest Atlantic Crossing," *Evening Standard* (London), July 14, 2007.
6. Letter dated July 5, 2007, from Spiros A. Coutsoubinas.
7. Kogan, Rick, *A Chicago Tavern*, 6–7.
8. *Ibid.*, 7.
9. *Ibid.*, 10.
10. Craig, Bob, "Arts and Flowers." *Chicago Tribune*, September 30, 2007.

Chapter 3

1. Kogan, Rick, *A Chicago Tavern*, 13.
2. *Ibid.*
3. Email correspondence with Teresa Casselman.
4. Kogan, Rick, *A Chicago Tavern*, 13.
5. *Ibid.*, 14–15.
6. *Ibid.*, 15.
7. *Ibid.*, 16.
8. Snyder, John, *Cubs Journal*, 305.

Chapter 4

1. "Draft Threat Softened by McNutt Ruling," *Chicago Tribune*, March 22, 1946.
2. Billington, Charles N., *Wrigley Field's Last World Series* (Chicago: Lake Claremont Press, 2005) 111.
3. Gilbert, Bill, *They Also Served: Baseball and the Home Front* (New York: Crown, 1992), 221.
4. Nemec, David, *The Baseball Chronicle: Year by Year History of Major League Baseball* (Lincolnwood, IL: Publications International, 2002), 222.
5. Bryant, Helen, interview with Sam Sianis, *Daily Herald*, November 9, 1983.
6. Hayner, Don and Tom McNamee, *The Stadium: 1929–1994: The Official Commemorative History of the Chicago Stadium* (Chicago: Performance Media, 1993).
7. Hornsby, Rogers, "Cubs in 6— Hornsby," *Chicago Daily News*, October 1, 1945.

8. Billington, Charles N., *Wrigley Field's Last World Series*, 244–245.
9. Snyder, John, *Cubs Journal*, 341.
10. "Tigers by a Shade!" *Chicago Tribune*, October 3, 1945.
11. "A Paving Brick Helps Cubs Win," *Chicago Tribune*, October 4, 1945.
12. "In the Wake of the News," *Chicago Tribune*, October 4, 1945.
13. "Greenberg and Trucks Draw Tigers' Post-Game Applause," *Chicago Tribune*, October 5, 1945.
14. "Passeau's One Hit Shutout Stuns Detroit," *Chicago Tribune*, October 6, 1945.
15. "Bleacher Fans Keep All-Night Vigil at Gates," *Chicago Tribune*, October 6, 1945.
16. "Wrigley Shuns Series to Address Ticket Crisis." *Chicago Tribune*, October 5, 1945.
17. "Billy Sianis," Wikipedia, http:/en.wikipedia.org/wiki/Billy_Sianis (accessed January 15, 2008).
18. Peterson, Richard, "Good News for Cubs Could Dampen Angst," *Chicago Tribune*, April 15, 2007.
19. Gatto, Steve, *Da Curse of the Billy Goat* (Lansing, MI: Protar House, 2004), 3–4.
20. Billington, Charles N., *Wrigley Field's Last World Series*, 257.
21. Gatto, Steve, *Da Curse of the Billy Goat*, 5.
22. Snyder, John, *Cubs Journal*, 342.
23. Billington, Charles N. *Wrigley Field's Last World Series*, 260–261.
24. *Ibid.*, 262–265.
25. *Ibid.*, 266.
26. "7th Game Ticket Fans Besiege Cubs Park," *Chicago Tribune*, October 10, 1945.

Chapter 5

1. Kogan, Rick, *A Chicago Tavern*, 20, 22.

2. Snyder, John, *Cubs Journal*, 344–351.
3. Hayner, Don and Tom McNamee, *The Stadium*.
4. *Ibid.*
5. *Ibid.*
6. Royko, Mike, "Royko's Column," *The Intelligencer*, May 26, 1997, accessed via NewspaperArchive.com.
7. Snyder, John, *Cubs Journal*, 367.
8. "College of Coaches," Wikipedia; http://en.wikipedia.org/wiki/College_of_Coaches (accessed January 15, 2008).
9. Kogan, Rick, *A Chicago Tavern*, 32.
10. *Ibid.*
11. *Ibid.*, p. 33.
12. "Chicago Cubs," Sportsencyclopedia.com.
13. Talley, Rick, *The Cubs of '69* (Chicago: Contemporary Books, 1989), 108.
14. *Ibid.*, p. 90.
15. "The 1969 Chicago Cubs," http://www.geocities.com/colosseum/stadium/9523/1969.htm?20075 (accessed January 15, 2008).

Chapter 6

1. Langford, George, "Cardinals Will Break Cub Fans Hearts Again," *Chicago Tribune*, April 1, 1969.
2. Langford, George, "Jenkins And Phils' Short Mound Foes," *Chicago Tribune*, April 8, 1969.
3. Dozer, Richard, "Jenkins Gets Victory With 3-Hit Yield," *Chicago Tribune*, August. 17, 1969.
4. "Cubs to Print Tickets," *Chicago Tribune*, August 28, 1969.
5. Markus, Robert, "Stops Along the Sports Trail," *Chicago Tribune*, September 11, 1969.

Chapter 7

1. Snyder, John, *Cubs Journal*, 465–466.

2. *Ibid.*, p. 466.
3. Kogan, Rick, *A Chicago Tavern*, 37–38.
4. Cromie, Robert, "Billy Goat Sianis Dead at 76," *Chicago Tribune*, October 23, 1970.
5. Kogan, Rick, *A Chicago Tavern*, 17–18.
6. *Ibid.*, 17–20.
7. *Ibid.*, 49.
8. *Ibid.*, 56.

Chapter 8

1. Langford, George, "Cubs vs. Expos in Season Start," *Chicago Tribune*, April 6, 1973.
2. "Huge Crowd Watches Cubs Win Opener, 3–2," *Chicago Tribune*, April 7, 1973.
3. Langford, George, "Cubs Edge Expos 3–2 on Santo's Hit in 10th." *Chicago Tribune*, April 8, 1973.
4. Snyder, John, *Cubs Journal*, 487.
5. Langford, George, "Cubs Frolic 10–4," *Chicago Tribune*, April 30, 1973.
6. Langford, George, "Pooped Cubs Beat Mets 3–2," *Chicago Tribune*, June 26, 1973.
7. Condon, David, "If Cubs Blow It, Look for the Goat," *Chicago Tribune*, July 6, 1973.
8. Langford, George, "Phils Foil Cubs' 'Daily Miracle' 7–4," *Chicago Tribune*, July 6, 1973.
9. Logan, Bob, "Reuschel Fans 11 in 4-hitter," *Chicago Tribune Press Service*, August 4, 1973.
10. Dozer, Richard, "No Hand Fracture, but Jenkins May Miss Turn," *Chicago Tribune Press Service*, August 28, 1973.
11. "The Cubs Are on Their Way," *Chicago Tribune*, August 28, 1973.
12. *Ibid.*
13. Dozer, Richard, "Cubs Rained Out; Whitey Ponders Plans," *Chicago Tribune*, September 15, 1973.

14. Langford, George, "That's All, Folks! Mets R.I.P. Cubs," *Chicago Tribune*, October 1, 1973.

Chapter 9

1. Personal observation by author.
2. Bryant, Helen, "Bill Goat's," *Daily Herald*, November 9, 1983.

Chapter 10

1. "Jim Frey," Wikipedia, http://en.wikipedia.org/wiki/Jim_Frey (accessed January 16, 2008).
2. Colletti, Ned, *You Gotta Have Heart* (South Bend, IN: Diamond Communications, 1985), 17–20.
3. *Ibid.*, 24.
4. Mitchell, Fred, "Guess What? It's Cubs-Mets," *Chicago Tribune*, April 13, 1984.
5. "Jim Frey," Baseballlibrary.com, http://www.baseballlibrary.com/ballplayers/player.php?name=Jim_Frey_1931 (accessed January 16, 2008).
6. Lorenz, Rich, "Cubs Get Noticed Even on Capitol Hill," *Chicago Tribune*, April 27, 1984.
7. Mitchell, Fred, "Sandberg Streaks to NL Award," *Chicago Tribune*, May 15, 1984.
8. Snyder, John, *Cubs Journal*, 551.
9. *Ibid.*
10. Mitchell, Fred, "Cubs Look Bulletproof," *Chicago Tribune*, September 16, 1984.
11. Hersh, Phil, "He's a Little Big Man," *Chicago Tribune*, September 16, 1984.
12. Snyder, John, *Cubs Journal*, 552.
13. *Ibid.*, 551–552.
14. Lincicome, Bernie, "This is Sarge's Time of the Year," *Chicago Tribune*, October 3, 1984.
15. Markus, Robert, "Moreland's

Catch Slams the Door," *Chicago Tribune*, October 3, 1984.

16. Reaves, Joseph A., "Cub Fans Can't Curb Their Frenzy," *Chicago Tribune*, October 4, 1984.

17. Mitchell, Fred, "Cub Speed Kills Padres," *Chicago Tribune*, October 4, 1984.

18. Lincicome, Bernie, "Cubs Just Delayed on Way to Series," *Chicago Tribune*, October 5, 1984.

19. *Ibid.*

20. Mitchell, Fred, "Sanderson Won't Back Down," *Chicago Tribune*, October 6, 1984.

21. Mitchell, Fred, "Paradise Lost — Sutcliffe Fails to Stop Padres," *Chicago Tribune*, October 8, 1984.

22. *Ibid.*

23. Holtzman, Jerome. "Durham's Mistake Wasn't Only Cubs' Shortcoming," *Chicago Tribune*, October 8, 1984.

24. "Curse of the Billy Goat," Wikipedia, http://en.wikipedia.org/wiki/Curse_of_the_Billy_Goat (accessed January 16, 2008).

Chapter 11

1. Snyder, John, *Cubs Journal*, 577.

2. Solomon, Alan, "Fun Is New Cub Motto," *Chicago Tribune*, May 26, 1989.

3. Bagnato, Andrew, "Cubs Save Best Rally for Last," *Chicago Tribune*, August 30, 1989.

4. Bagnato, Andrew, "Dunston Keeps Cubs Rolling, Slams Pirates." *Chicago Tribune*, September 16, 1989.

5. Margolis, Jon, "Celebrate, Celebrate! Cubs Clinch Their Division," *Chicago Tribune*, September 27, 1989.

6. Verdi, Bob, "America's Team Clubbed by Clark," *Chicago Tribune*, October 5, 1989.

7. Hersh, Phil, "Sadly, Cubs Live Up to Their Old Image," *Chicago Tribune*, October 5, 1989.

8. Photograph of Florence Zangora

and Will Clark doll. *Chicago Tribune*, October 6, 1989.

9. Holtzman, Jerome, "Sutcliffe Well-armed for Game 3," *Chicago Tribune*, October 7, 1989.

10. Bagnato, Andrew, "Dawson Whiffs at his Biggest At-bat," *Chicago Tribune*, October 9, 1989.

11. Tybor, Joseph, "Cubs Done In by an Old Friend," *Chicago Tribune*, October 10, 1989.

12. "Yes, Cubs Fans, Fat Lady Does Sing," *Chicago Tribune*, October 10, 1989.

Chapter 12

1. Snyder, John, *Cubs Journal*, 607.

2. Beres, George, "Breaking the Cubs' Curse," History News Network, September 8, 2003, http://www.hnn.us/articles/1674.html (accessed January 11, 2008).

3. *Ibid.*

4. Rozner, Barry, "Pregame Goat Escapade a Giant Distraction," *Chicago Daily Herald* May 5, 1994.

5. *Ibid.*

6. Beres, George, "Breaking the Cubs' Curse."

7. Rozner, Barry. "Pregame Goat Escapade a Giant Distraction."

8. Snyder, John, *Cubs Journal*, 609.

9. Snyder, John, *Cubs Journal*, 607.

10. "Chicago Cubs," Wikipedia, http://en.wikipedia.org/wiki/Chicago_Cubs (accessed January 16, 2008.

Chapter 13

1. Granger, Bill, "This Fast Food Really Moves," *Chicago Daily Herald*, May 1, 1995.

2. Snyder, John, *Cubs Journal*, 628.

3. Sullivan, Paul, "HR in 8th Picks Up Sosa, Cubs," *Chicago Tribune*, September 2, 1998.

4. Snyder, John, *Cubs Journal*, 635.

5. *Ibid.*, 635–636.
6. *Ibid.*, 636.
7. Morrissey, Rick, "Cubs Hold Off 9th Inning Rally to Beat Giants 5–3," *Chicago Tribune*, September 29, 1998.
8. Rogers, Phil, "Braves Have Reason to Fear Cubs Matchup." *Chicago Tribune*, September 29, 1998.
9. Sullivan, Paul, "Tucker's HR All He Needs to Win Opener," *Chicago Tribune*, September 29, 1998.
10. Sullivan, Paul, "Cubs Face Maddux, Ouster," *Chicago Tribune*, October 2, 1998.
11. Sullivan, Paul, "Cubs Desperate for Wood's Work," *Chicago Tribune*, October 2, 1998.
12. DeSimone, Bonnie, "Typical Performance for Rookie," *Chicago Tribune*, October 4, 1998.

Chapter 14

1. *Chicago Tribune*, *Out of the Blue* (Chicago: Triumph Books, 2003), 6.
2. *Ibid.*, 22.
3. *Ibid.*, 29.
4. Mullin, John, "2 Weeks In, Baker Fed Up with Critics," *Chicago Tribune*, April 13, 2003.
5. *Chicago Tribune*, *Out of the Blue*, 64.
6. Sullivan, Paul, "Injury, Inconsistency Put Pitching in Bind," *Chicago Tribune*, July 26, 2003.)
7. Sullivan, Paul, "Womack Gets Crash Course in Being Cub." *Chicago Tribune*, August 24, 2003.
8. Sullivan, Paul, "Hendry Turns 95-loss Team into Contender." *Chicago Tribune*, August 26, 2003.
9. Snyder, John, *Cubs Journal*, 670.
10. Sullivan, Paul, "Ace Strikes Out 14 Pirates to Cut Gap to Half-game." *Chicago Tribune*, September 22, 2003.
11. Snyder, John, *Cubs Journal*, 671.
12. Sullivan, Paul, "Braves Favored, but Cubs Don't Fear Playoff Giant," *Chicago Tribune*, September 29, 2003.
13. Snyder, John, *Cubs Journal*, 671.
14. "Series Recap," *Chicago Tribune*, October 6, 2003.
15. Morrissey, Rick, "Unforgettable Cubs' Win," *Chicago Tribune*.
16. Jervis, Rick, "Superstitious Fans Take No Chances," *Chicago Tribune*, October 12, 2003.
17. Doshi, Supriya, "Curse Still Overshadows Cubs," *Daily Illini*, October 17, 2003.
18. Zolecki, Todd, "Curses! Chicago's Faithful Are Miserable Again," *Philadelphia Inquirer*, October 17, 2003.
19. "Curse of the Billy Goat," Wikipedia, http://en.wikipedia.org/wiki/Curse_of_the_Billy_Goat (accessed January 16, 2008).
20. "Grant DePorter," Wikipedia, http://en.wikipedia.org/wiki/Grant_DePorter (accessed January 17, 2008).
21. *Ibid.*

Chapter 15

1. Sullivan, Paul, "Maddux Prepared for That Last Dive," *Chicago Tribune*, April 2, 2004.
2. Sullivan, Paul, "Cubs Storybook Year Is Upon Us ... or Not." *Chicago Tribune* (April 4, 2004.
3. Morrissey, Rick, "Cubs Can Win without Prior, and They Better," *Chicago Tribune*, April 5, 2004.
4. Snyder, John, *Cubs Journal*, 675.
5. Morrissey, Rick, "Maddux Doesn't Seize Moment, but Just Wait," *Chicago Tribune*, April 8, 2004.
6. Sullivan, Paul. "Sosa Off to Sluggish Start," *Chicago Tribune*, April 8, 2004.
7. Snyder, John, *Cubs Journal*, 676.
8. *Ibid.*, 677.
9. Van Dyck, Dave, "Big Boppers Turning It Up a Notch," *Chicago Tribune*, August 27, 2004.

10. Snyder, John, *Cubs Journal*, 679.

11. Sullivan, Paul, "Ramirez Points the Way," *Chicago Tribune*, September 17, 2004.

12. Sullivan, Paul, "Farnsworth to Ease Back Into Bullpen," *Chicago Tribune*, September 19, 2004.

13. Sullivan, Paul, "All Systems Go for Garciaparra's Return," *Chicago Tribune*, September 22, 2004.

14. Morrissey, Rick, "Diaz Proof That Love Hurts — the Cubs," *Chicago Tribune*, September 26, 2004.

15. Van Dyck, Dave, "A Languishing Lineup," *Chicago Tribune*, October 1, 2004.

16. Van Dyck, Dave, "Cubs Find 'Choke' Tough Word to Swallow," *Chicago Tribune*, October 3, 2004.

Chapter 16

1. Snyder, John, *Cubs Journal*, 681.

Chapter 17

1. Cossette, Edward, "What Is Bambino's Curse?" http://www.bambinoscurse.com/whatis (accessed January 18, 2008).

2. *20th Century Baseball Chronicle: A Year-by-Year History of Major League Baseball* (Lincolnwood, IL: Publications International, 1992), 84.

3. "Curse of Billy Penn," Wikipedia, http://en.wikipedia.org/wiki/Curse_of_Billy_Penn (accessed January 18, 2008).

Chapter 18

1. Carroll, Robert Todd, "Curse," *The Skeptic's Dictionary*, http://skepdic.com/curse.html (accessed January 18, 2008).

2. Wolff, Alexander, "Sports Illustrated Cover Jinx: 1980s," *SI Online*, http://sportsillustrated.cnn.com/features/cover/2002/jinx/80s (accessed January 18, 2008).

3. Wolff, Alexander, "Sports Illustrated Cover Jinx: 1990s," *SI Online*, http://sportsillustrated.cnn.com/features/cover/2002/jinx/90s (accessed January 18, 2008).

4. Wolff, Alexander, "Unraveling the Jinx," *SI Online*, http://sportsillustrated.cnn.com/inside_game/alexander_wolff/news/2002/01/15/wolff_viewpoint (accessed January 18, 2008).

5. Loehr, Jim, "Mental Toughness with Dr. Jim Loehr," The K-8 Aeronautics Internet Textbook, http://wings.avkids.com/Tennis/Features/loehr-01.html (accessed January 18, 2008).

6. Wolff, Alexander, "Unraveling the Jinx."

Chapter 19

1. Stone, Larry, "The Art of Baseball: A Tradition of Superstition," *Seattle Times*, September 26, 2005.

2. *Ibid.*

3. *Ibid.*

4. *Ibid.*

5. Murdoch, Jason, "Superstitious Athletes," CBC Sports Online, May 10, 2005, http://www.cbc.ca/sports/columns/top10/superstition.html (accessed January 18).

6. Stern, Josh, "Between the Stitches," Psychology of Sports, http://www.psychologyofsports.com/guest/stitches.htm (accessed January 8, 2008).

Chapter 20

1. "Nomar Garciaparra," Wikipedia, http://en.wikipedia.org/wiki/Nomar_Garciaparra (accessed January 18, 2008).

2. Sullivan, Paul, "Putting Hendry on Spot," *Chicago Tribune*, October 7, 2006, http://www.chicagotribune.com/sports/baseball/cubs/cs-061007cubs,1,4149567.

story?coll=&ctrack=1&cset=true (accessed January 18, 2008).

3. Muskat, Carrie, "Cubs' Lee Done for Season," MLB.com, September 17, 2006, http://mlb.mlb.com/content/print er_friendly/chc/y2006/m09/d17/c166 7409.jsp (accessed January 18, 2008).

4. *Ibid.*

5. Sullivan, Paul, "Trying to Right the Cubs' Ship," *Chicago Tribune*, November 20, 2005.

6. Nightengale, Bob, "Fans Find Cubs Not So loveable," *USA Today*, August 21, 2006.

7. "More Dusty Love," June 28, 2006, *Chicago Cubs Fun*, http://cubsfun. blogspot.com/2006/06/more-dusty-love. html (accessed January 18, 2008).

8. *Ibid.*

9. *Ibid.*

10. "The Truth of It All," May 19, 2006, *Chicago Cubs Fun*, http://cubsfun. blogspot.com/2006/05/truth-of-it-all. html (accessed January 18, 2008).

11. "What Else Can Happen," May 28, 2006, *Chicago Cubs Fun*, http://cubsfun. blogspot.com/2006/05/what-else-can-happen.html (accessed January 18, 2008).

Chapter 21

1. "Our History: Birth of a Chicago Legend," Billy Goat Tavern, http://www. billygoattavern.com/history.html (accessed January 18, 2008).

2. "Curse of the Billy Goat." Wikipedia.

3. "Curse of the Goat." Everything2.

4. Personal conversations with Andy Pafko and Lenny Murello on October 7, 2006.

Chapter 22

1. Beres, George, "Breaking the Cubs' Curse."

2. "Father Guido Zamponi," Xavierian Missionaries USA, February 2, 2006, http://www.xaviermissionaries.org/M_Life /NewsArchive/AmericaNews/US_Zamponi50Priest.htm (accessed January 18, 2008).

3. "How to Deal with Curses, Hexes, and Spells," Asian Internet Bible Institute, http://aibi.gospelcom.net/articles/curses. htm (accessed January 18, 2008).

Chapter 23

1. Bogen, Gil, *Tinker, Evers and Chance*, 9–60.

2. "Macphail Resigns as President of Cubs," October 1, 2006, Chicago Cubs press release, http://chicago.cubs.mlb. com/news/press_releases/press_release. jsp?ymd=20061001&content_id=1693853 &vkey=pr_chc&fext=.jsp&c_id=chc (accessed January 18, 2008).

3. "Cubs Decline to Renew Baker's Contract," October 2, 2006, Chicago Cubs press release, http://chicago.cubs. mlb.com/content/printer_friendly/chc/ y2006/m10/d02/c1695267.jsp (accessed January 18, 2008).

4. De Luca, Chris, "Cubs' New Brass Likes Sound of Girardi," *Chicago Sun-Times*, October 6, 2006, http://www.sun times.com/sports/deluca/86264,CST-SPT-deluca06.article (accessed January 18, 2008).

Chapter 24

1. "Piniella Agrees to Three-Year Deal to Manage Cubs," ESPN.com, October 16, 2006, http://sports.espn.go.com/mlb/ news/story?id=2628162 (accessed January 187, 2008).

2. "Lou Piniella," Wikipedia, http:// en.wikipedia.org/wiki/Lou_Piniella (accessed January 18, 2008).

3. "Piniella Agrees to Three-Year Deal to Manage Cubs."

4. Caple, Jim, "How to Lose Mind ... and Keep Dignity." *ESPN Page 2*, September 20, http://espn.go.com/page2/s/caple/020920.html (accessed January 10, 2008).

Chapter 25

1. "Cubs Continue to Spend: Soriano for $136M," CubsNet.com, November 19, 2006, http://cubsnet.com/node/1566 (accessed January 2008).

2. Rogers, Phil, "No Rest for a Weary Hendry," *Chicago Tribune*, February 23, 2006.

3. Toner, P. J., "Exorcism," *The Catholic Encyclopedia*, Volume V (New York: Robert Appleton, 1909), http://www.newadvent.org/cathen/05709a.htm (accessed January 19, 2008).

4. *Ibid.*

5. E-mail correspondence with Michael Englert, December 14, 2006.

6. Hoopes, Tom, "The Dark Backward: Demons in the Real World," *CRISIS Magazine*, November 4, 2003, http://www.crisismagazine.com/november2003/hoopes.htm (accessed January 19, 2008).

7. E-mail correspondence with Fr. Herman Jayachandra, December 16, 2006.

8. Interview with Ali Adabieh, December 11, 2006.

9. "How to Deal with Curses, Hexes, and Spells."

10. Radin, Dean, *Entangled Minds* (New York: Pocket Books, 2006).

11. *Ibid.* Preface.

Chapter 26

1. Jervis, Rick, "Superstitious Fans Take No Chances," *Chicago Tribune*, October 12, 2003.

2. *Ibid.*

3. "Cubs Place Catcher Henry Blanco on the 15-day Disabled List," June 1, 2007, Chicago Cubs press release, http://chicago.cubs.mlb.com/news/press_releases/press_release.jsp?ymd=20070601&content_id=1998556&vkey=pr_chc&fext=.jsp&c_id=chc (accessed January 20, 2008).

4. Van Dyck, Dave, "Piniella Never Seems to Run out of Orders," *Chicago Tribune*, July 23, 2007.

5. "Cubs RHP Zambrano Leaves with Cramps, Dehydration." *SportsTwo*, August 3, 2007, http://sportstwo.com/MLB/Story/CHCUBS/484842 (accessed January 20, 2008).

6. Sullivan, Paul, "Cubs Suffer a Double Loss," *Chicago Tribune*, August 6, 2007.

7. Sullivan, Paul, "After Piniella Peptalk, Offense Helps Cubs Enjoy Laughter," *Chicago Tribune*, August 10, 2007.

8. Morrissey, Rick, "OK is Good Enough for Cubs in OK NL Central," *Chicago Tribune* August 19, 2007.

9. Sullivan, Paul, "Zambrano KO'd in 7th, Ace Goes 0–4 in August," *Chicago Tribune* August 30, 2007.

10. Baum, Bob, "Arizona 8, Chi Cubs 4," *Yahoo! Sports*, October 5, 2007, http://sports.yahoo.com/mlb/recap?gid=271004129 (accessed January 8, 2008).

Conclusion

1. "Cuban Says There's Little Movement on Cubs Front," *Yahoo! Sports*, December 3, 2007, http://sports.yahoo.com/mlb/news?slug=ap-cubs-cuban&prov=ap&type=lgns (accessed January 20, 2008).

2. Sullivan, Paul, "Sale Hardly Sailing Along," *Chicago Tribune*, January 20, 2008, http://www.chicagotribune.com/business/chi-080120cubs-sale-story,0,7627614.story?coll=chi_tab01_layout (accessed January 20, 2008).

3. Helyar, John, "Canning Considered

Favorite to Land Cubs," ESPN.com, September 21, 2007, http://sports.espn.go.com/mlb/news/story?id=3030144 (accessed January 20, 2008).

4. Muskrat, Carrie, "Woods to Return with Cubs in 2008," MLB.com, November 26, 2007.

Bibliography

Books

Billington, Charles N. *Wrigley Field's Last World Series.* Chicago: Lake Claremont Press, 2005.

Bogen, Gil. *Johnny Kling: A Baseball Biography.* Jefferson, NC: McFarland, 2006.

_____. *Tinker, Evers and Chance: A Triple Biography.* Jefferson, NC: McFarland, 2003.

Chadwick, Bruce, and David M. Spindel. *The Chicago Cubs.* New York: Abbeville Press, 1994.

Chicago Tribune staff. *Out of the Blue: The Amazing Story of the 2003 Chicago Cubs.* Chicago: Triumph Books, 2003.

Colletti, Ned. *You Gotta Have Heart.* South Bend, IN: Diamond Communications, 1985.

Evers, John J., and Hugh S. Fullerton. *Touching Second.* Chicago: Reilly and Britton, 1910.

Gatto, Steve. *Da Curse of the Billy Goat.* Lansing, MI: Protar House, 2004.

Gilbert, Bill. *They Also Served: Baseball and the Home Front.* New York: Crown, 1992.

Golenbock, Peter. *Wrigleyville: A Magical History Tour of the Chicago Cubs.* New York: St. Martin's Griffin Press, 1999.

Hayner, Don, and Tom McNamee. *The Stadium: 1929–1994: The Official Commemorative History of the Chicago Stadium.* Chicago: Performance Media, 1993.

Hirshberg, Al. *Baseball's Greatest Catchers.* New York: G. P. Putnam's Sons, 1966.

Honig, Donald. *The Greatest Catchers of All Time.* Dubuque, IA: Wm. C. Brown, 1991.

Kogan, Rick. *A Chicago Tavern, a Goat, a Curse, and the American Dream.* Chicago: Lake Claremont Press, 2006.

Neft, David S., and Richard M. Cohen. *The Sports Encyclopedia: Baseball.* 14th ed. New York: St. Martin's Press, 1994.

Nemec, David. *The Baseball Chronicle: A Year-By-Year History of Major League Baseball.* Lincolnwood, IL: Publications International, 2001–2005.

Pietrusza, David. *Baseball: The Biographical Encyclopedia.* Kingston, NY: Total/Sports Illustrated, 2000.

Radin, Dean. *Entangled Minds.* New York: Pocket Books, 2006.

Snyder, John. *Cubs Journal.* Cincinnati, OH: Emmis Books, 2005.

Bibliography

Talley, Rick. *The Cubs of '69*. Chicago: Contemporary Books, 1989.
20th Century Baseball Chronicle: A Year-by-Year History of Major League Baseball. Lincolnwood, IL: Publications International, 1992.

Articles

Bagnato, Andrew. "Cubs Save Best Rally for Last." *Chicago Tribune*, August 30, 1989.
_____."Dawson Whiffs at His Biggest At-bat." *Chicago Tribune*, October 9, 1989.
_____. "Dunston Keeps Cubs Rolling, Slams Pirates." *Chicago Tribune*, September 16, 1989.
Baum, Bob. "Arizona 8, Chi Cubs 4." *Yahoo! Sports*, October 5, 2007, http://sports.yahoo.com/mlb/recap?gid=271004129 (accessed January 8, 2008).
Beres, George. "Breaking the Cubs' Curse." History News Network, September 8, 2003, http://www.hnn.us/articles/1674.html (accessed January 11, 2008).
"Billy Sianis," Wikipedia, http:/en.wikipedia.org/wiki/Billy_Sianis (accessed January 15, 2008).
"Bleacher Fans Keep All-Night Vigil at Gates." *Chicago Tribune*, October 6, 1945.
Bryant, Helen. "Billy Goats." *Daily Herald* (Illinois), November 9, 1983.
Caple, Jim. "How to Lose Mind ... and Keep Dignity." *ESPN Page 2*, September 20, 2002, http://espn.go.com/page2/s/caple/020920.html (accessed January 10, 2008).
Carroll, Robert Todd. "Curse," *The Skeptic's Dictionary*, http://skepdic.com/curse.html (accessed January 18, 2008).
Chance, Frank L. "Chance and Tinker Evolved New Play." *New York Times*, March 28, 1915.
"Chicago Cubs." Sportsencyclopedia.com, http://www.sportsecyclopedia.com/nl/chicubs/cubs.html (accessed January 15, 2008).
"Chicago Cubs." Wikipedia, http://en.wikipedia.org/wiki/Chicago_Cubs (accessed January 16, 2008.
"Chicago Cubs, Loveable Losers." Funtrivia.com, http://www.funtrivia.com/triviaquiz/Sports/Chicago-Cubs-Lovable-Losers-153259.html (accessed January 15, 2008).
"College of Coaches." Wikipedia, http://en.wikipedia.org/wiki/College_of_Coaches (accessed January 15, 2008).
Condon, David. "If Cubs Blow It, Look for Goat." *Chicago Tribune*, July 6, 1973.
Craig, Bob. "Arts and Flowers." *Chicago Tribune*, September 30, 2007.
"Cuban Says There's Little Movement on Cubs Front," *Yahoo! Sports*, December 3, 2007, http://sports.yahoo.com/mlb/news?slug=ap-cubs-cuban&prov=ap&type=lgns (accessed January 20, 2008).
"The Cubs Are on Their Way." *Chicago Tribune*, August 28, 1973.
"Cubs Continue to Spend: Soriano for $136M." CubsNet.com, November 19, 2006, http://cubsnet.com/node/1566 (accessed January 2008).
"Cubs Decline to Renew Baker's Contract." October 2, 2006, Chicago Cubs press release, http://chicago.cubs.mlb.com/content/printer_friendly/chc/y2006/m10/d02/c1695267.jsp (accessed January 18, 2008).
"Cubs Place Catcher Henry Blanco on the 15-day Disabled List," June 1, 2007, Chicago Cubs press release, http://chicago.cubs.mlb.com/news/press_releases/press_

Bibliography

release.jsp?ymd=20070601&content_id=1998556&vkey=pr_chc&fext=.jsp&c_id =chc (accessed January 20, 2008).

"Cubs RHP Zambrano Leaves with Cramps, Dehydration." *SportsTwo*, August 3, 2007, http://sportstwo.com/MLB/Story/CHCUBS/484842 (accessed January 20, 2008).

"Cubs to Print Tickets." *Chicago Tribune*, August 28, 1969.

"Curse of Billy Penn." Wikipedia, http://en.wikipedia.org/wiki/Curse_of_Billy_Penn (accessed January 18, 2008).

"Curse of the Billy Goat." Wikipedia, http://en.wikipedia.org/wiki/Curse_of_the_Billy_Goat (accessed January 16, 2008).

"Curse of the Goat." Everything2, http://www.everything2.com/index.pl?node= Curse%20of%20the%20Goat (accessed January 15, 2008).

Deford, Frank. "Curses: From Boston to Chicago to Japan, Baseball Teams Can't Shake Bad Luck." *SI.com*, September 24, 2003, http://sportsillustrated.cnn.com/2003/ writers/frank_deford/09/24/viewpoint/index.html (accessed January 10, 2008).

De Luca, Chris, "Cubs' New Brass Likes Sound of Girardi," *Chicago Sun-Times*, October 6, 2006, http://www.suntimes.com/sports/deluca/86264,CST-SPT-deluca 06.article (accessed January 18, 2008).

DeSimone, Bonnie. "Typical Performance for Rookie." *Chicago Tribune*, October 4, 1998.

Doshi, Supriya. "Curse Still Overshadows Cubs." *Daily Illini*, October 17, 2003.

Dozer, Richard. "Cubs Limp Home 6 Games out of 1st after 5–3 Defeat." *Chicago Tribune*, September 7, 1973.

_____. "Cubs Rained Out; Whitey Ponders Plans." *Chicago Tribune*, September 15, 1973.

_____. "Jenkins Gets Victory with 3-Hit Yield." *Chicago Tribune*, August 17, 1969.

_____. "No Hand Fracture, but Jenkins May Miss Turn." *Chicago Tribune*, August 28, 1973.

"Draft Threat Softened by McNutt Ruling." *Chicago Tribune*, March 22, 1946.

"Father Guido Zamponi." Xavierian Missionaries USA, February 2, 2006, http:// www.xaviermissionaries.org/M_Life/NewsArchive/AmericaNews/US_Zam-poni50Priest.htm (accessed January 18, 2008).

Granger, Bill. "This Fast Food Really Moves." *Chicago Daily Herald*, May 1, 1995.

"Greenberg and Trucks Draw Tigers Post-Game Applause." *Chicago Tribune*, October 5, 1945.

Helyar, John, "Canning Considered Favorite to Land Cubs," ESPN.com, September 21, 2007, http://sports.espn.go.com/mlb/news/story?id=3030144 (accessed January 20, 2008).

Hersh, Phil. "Color Padres Red and Blue." *Chicago Tribune*, October 3, 1984.

_____. "He's a Little Big Man." *Chicago Tribune*, September 16, 1984.

_____. "Sadly, Cubs Live Up to Their Old Image." *Chicago Tribune*, October 5, 1989.

Holtzman, Jerome. "Durham's Mistake Wasn't Only Cubs Shortcoming." *Chicago Tribune*, October 8, 1984.

_____. "Sutcliffe Well-armed for Game 3." *Chicago Tribune*, October 7, 1989.

Hoopes, Tom. "The Dark Backward: Demons in the Real World," *CRISIS Magazine*, November 4, 2003, http://www.crisismagazine.com/november2003/hoopes.htm (accessed January 19, 2008).

Hornsby, Rogers. "Cubs in 6 — Hornsby." *Chicago Daily News*, October 1, 1945.

203

Bibliography

"How to Deal with Curses, Hexes, and Spells." Asian Internet Bible Institute, http://aibi.gospelcom.net/articles/curses.htm (accessed January 18, 2008).

"Huge Crowd Watches Cubs Win Opener, 3–2." *Chicago Tribune*, April 7, 1973.

"In the Wake of the News." *Chicago Tribune*, October 4, 1945.

"Jervis, Rick. "Superstitious Fans Take No Chances." *Chicago Tribune*, October 12, 2003.

"Jim Frey." Baseballlibrary.com, http://www.baseballlibrary.com/ballplayers/player.php?name=Jim_Frey_1931 (accessed January 16, 2008).

"Jim Frey." Wikipedia, http://en.wikipedia.org/wiki/Jim_Frey (accessed January 16, 2008).

"Joe Tinker and Frank Chance Get into a Row with Spectators at Cincinnati and Are Roughly Handled." Uncredited Baseball Hall of Fame scrapbook news item, April 16, 1906.

"Johnny Evers Speaks." Uncredited Baseball Hall of Fame scrapbook news item, December 26, 1936.

Langford, George. "Another Comeback for Title." *Chicago Tribune*, October 2, 1973.

_____. "Cardinals Will Break Cub Fans' Hearts Again." *Chicago Tribune*, April 1, 1969.

_____. "Cubs Edge Expos 3–2 on Santo's Hit in 10th." *Chicago Tribune*, April 8, 1973.

_____. "Cubs vs. Expos in Season Start." *Chicago Tribune*, April 6, 1973.

_____. "Jenkins and Phils' Short Mound Foes." *Chicago Tribune*, April 8, 1969.

_____. "Phils Foil Cubs' 'Daily Miracle' 7–4." *Chicago Tribune*, July 6, 1973.

_____. "Pooped Cubs Beat Mets 3–2." *Chicago Tribune*, June 26, 1973.

_____. "That's All, Folks! Mets R.I.P. Cubs." *Chicago Tribune*, October 1, 1973.

Lincicome, Bernie. "Cubs Just Delayed on Way to Series." *Chicago Tribune*, October 5, 1984.

_____. "This is Sarge's Time of the Year." *Chicago Tribune*, Octobers 3, 1984.

Logan, Bob. "Reuschel Fans 11 in 4-hitter." *Chicago Tribune*, August 4, 1973.

Lorenz, Rich. "Cubs Get Noticed Even on Capitol Hill." *Chicago Tribune*, April 27, 1984.

"Lou Piniella," Wikipedia, http://en.wikipedia.org/wiki/Lou_Piniella (accessed January 18, 2008).

Lustberg, Richard. "Superstition in Sports." *Psychology of Sports*, June 23, 2004.

"Macphail Resigns as President of Cubs." October 1, 2006, Chicago Cubs press release, http://chicago.cubs.mlb.com/news/press_releases/press_release.jsp?ymd=2006100 1&content_id=1693853&vkey=pr_chc&fext=.jsp&c_id=chc (accessed January 18, 2008).

Margolis, Jon. "Celebrate, Celebrate! Cubs Clinch Their Division." *Chicago Tribune*, September 27, 1989.

Markus, Robert. "Moreland's Catch Slams the Door." *Chicago Tribune*, October 3, 1984.

_____. "Stops Along the Sports Trail." *Chicago Tribune*, September 11, 1969.

Mitchell, Fred. "Cub Speed Kills Padres." *Chicago Tribune*, October 8, 1984.

_____. "Cubs Look Bulletproof." *Chicago Tribune*, September 16, 1984.

_____. "Guess What? It's Cubs-Mets." *Chicago Tribune*, April 13, 1984.

_____. "Paradise Lost — Sutcliffe Fails to Stop Padres." *Chicago Tribune*, October 8, 1984.

_____. "Sandberg Streaks to NL Award." *Chicago Tribune*, May 15, 1984.

_____. "Sanderson won't back down." *Chicago Tribune*, October 6, 1984.

Bibliography

"More Dusty Love," June 28, 2006, *Chicago Cubs Fun*, http://cubsfun.blogspot.com/ 2006/06/more-dusty-love.html (accessed January 18, 2008).

Morrissey, Rick. "Cubs Can Win without Prior, and They Better." *Chicago Tribune*, April 5, 2004.

_____. "Cubs Hold Off 9th Inning Rally to Beat Giants 5–3." *Chicago Tribune*, September 29, 1998.

_____. "Diaz Proof that Love Hurts — the Cubs." *Chicago Tribune*, September 26, 2004.

_____. "Maddux Doesn't Seize Moment, but Just Wait." *Chicago Tribune*, April 8, 2004.

_____. "OK is Good Enough for Cubs in OK NL Central." *Chicago Tribune*, August 19, 2007.

_____. "Unforgettable Cubs' Win." *Chicago Tribune*, October 6, 2003.

Mullin, John. "2 Weeks In, Baker Fed Up with Critics." *Chicago Tribune*, April 13, 2003.

Murdoch, Jason. "Superstitious Athletes," CBC Sports Online, May 10, 2005, http://www.cbc.ca/sports/columns/top10/superstition.html (accessed January 18).

Muskat, Carrie, "Cubs' Lee Done for Season," MLB.com, September 17, 2006, http://mlb.mlb.com/content/printer_friendly/chc/y2006/m09/d17/c1667409.jsp (accessed January 18, 2008).

Muskat, Carrie, "Woods to Return with Cubs in 2008," MLB.com, November 26, 2007, http://chicago.cubs.mlb.com/news/article.jsp?ymd=20071126&content_id=2307408&vkey=news_chc&fext=.jsp&c_id=chc (accessed January 20, 2008).

Nightengale, Bob. "Fans Find Cubs Not So Lovable." *USA TODAY*, August 21, 2006.

"The 1969 Chicago Cubs." http://www.geocities.com/colosseum/stadium/9523/1969. htm?20075 (accessed January 15, 2008).

"Our History: Birth of a Chicago Legend." Billy Goat Tavern, http://www.billygoat tavern.com/history.html (accessed January 18, 2008).

"Passeau's One Hit Shutout Stuns Detroit." *Chicago Tribune*, October 6, 1945.

"A Paving Brick Helps Cubs Win." *Chicago Tribune*, October 4, 1945.

Peterson, Richard. "Good News for Cubs Could Dampen Angst." *Chicago Tribune*, April 15, 2007.

"Piniella Agrees to Three-Year Deal to Manage Cubs," ESPN.com, October 16, 2006, http://sports.espn.go.com/mlb/news/story?id=2628162 (accessed January 187, 2008).

"President Murphy Returns from Redville and Talks of Change." *Chicago Tribune*, April 16, 1906.

Rakove, Jack. "The Curse That Won't Quit." *Chicago Tribune*, October 1, 2004.

Reaves, Joseph. "Cub Fans Can't Curb Their Frenzy." *Chicago Tribune*, October 4, 1984.

"Record Broken Again!!!" American VULCAN Corporation, July 20, 1988, http://www.vulkanusa.com/blueriband.htm (accessed January 15, 2008).

Rice, Grantland. "Tinker to Evers to Chance." *Collier's*, November 29, 1930.

Rogers, Phil. "Braves Have Reason to Fear Cubs Matchup." *Chicago Tribune*, September 29, 1998.

Rogers, Phil, "No Rest for a Weary Hendry," *Chicago Tribune*, February 23, 2006.

Rozner, Barry. "Pregame Goat Escapade a Giant Distraction." *Chicago Daily Herald* May 5, 1994.

"Series Recap." *Chicago Tribune*, October 6, 2003.

Bibliography

"7th Game Ticket Fans Besiege Cubs Park." *Chicago Tribune*, October 10, 1945.

Solomon, Alan. "Fun Is New Cub Motto." *Chicago Tribune*, May 26, 1989.

Stern, Josh. "Between the Stitches," Psychology of Sports, http://www.psychologyof-sports.com/guest/stitches.htm (accessed January 8, 2008).

Stone, Larry. "The Art of Baseball: A Tradition of Superstition." *Seattle Times*, September 26, 2005.

Sullivan, Paul. "Ace Strikes Out 14 Pirates to Cut Gap to Half-game." *Chicago Tribune* September 22, 2003.

_____. "After Piniella Pep-talk, Offense Helps Cubs Enjoy Laughter." *Chicago Tribune*, August 10, 2007.

_____. "All Systems Go for Garciaparra's Return." *Chicago Tribune*, September 22, 2004.

_____. "Baker's Team Finds September Success." *Chicago Tribune*, September 25, 2004.

_____. "Braves Favored, but Cubs Don't Fear Playoff Giant." *Chicago Tribune*, September 29, 2003.

_____. "Cubs Desperate for Wood's Work." *Chicago Tribune*, October 2, 1998.

_____. "Cubs Face Maddux, Ouster." *Chicago Tribune*, October 2, 1998.

_____. "Cubs Roster Needs Radical Surgery." *Chicago Tribune*, August 31, 2006.

_____. "Cubs Storybook Year Is Upon Us...or Not." *Chicago Tribune*, April 4, 2004.

_____. "Cubs Suffer a Double Loss." *Chicago Tribune*, August 6, 2007.

_____. "Farnsworth to Ease Back into Bullpen." *Chicago Tribune*, September 19, 2004.

_____. "HR in 8th Picks Up Sosa, Cubs." *Chicago Tribune*, September 2, 1998.

_____. "Hendry Turns 95-loss Team into Contender." *Chicago Tribune*, August 26, 2003.

_____. "Injury, Inconsistency Put Pitching in Bind," *Chicago Tribune*, July 26, 2003.

_____. "Maddux Prepared for That Last Dive." *Chicago Tribune*, April 2, 2004.

_____. "Mark Prior." *Chicago Tribune*, September 30, 2007.

_____. "Putting Hendry on Spot." *Chicago Tribune*, October 7, 2006, http://www.chicagotribune.com/sports/baseball/cubs/cs-061007cubs,1,4149567.story?coll=&ctrack=1&cset=true (accessed January 18, 2008).

_____. "Ramirez Points the Way." *Chicago Tribune*, September 17, 2004.

_____. "Sale Hardly Sailing Along," *Chicago Tribune*, January 20, 2008, http://www.chicagotribune.com/business/chi-080120cubs-sale-story,0,7627614.story?coll=chi_tab01_layout (accessed January 20, 2008).

_____. "Sosa Off to Sluggish Start." *Chicago Tribune*, April 8, 2004.

_____. "Trying to Right the Cubs' Ship." *Chicago Tribune*, November 20, 2005.

_____. "Tucker's HR All He Needs to Win Opener." *Chicago Tribune*, September 29, 1998.

_____. "Womack Gets Crash Course in Being Cub." *Chicago Tribune*, August 24, 2003.

_____. "Zambrano KO'd in 7th, Ace Goes 0-4 in August." *Chicago Tribune*, August 19, 2007.

"Tigers by a Shade!" *Chicago Tribune*, October 3, 1945.

Toner, P. J., "Exorcism," *The Catholic Encyclopedia*, Volume V (New York: Robert Appleton Company, 1909), http://www.newadvent.org/cathen/05709a.htm accessed January 19, 2008.

"The Truth of It All," May 19, 2006, *Chicago Cubs Fun*, http://cubsfun.blogspot.com/2006/05/truth-of-it-all.html (accessed January 18, 2008).

Bibliography

Tybor, Joseph. "Cubs Done In by an Old Friend." *Chicago Tribune*, October 10, 1989.

Van Dyck, Dave. "Big Boppers Turning It Up a Notch." *Chicago Tribune*, August 27, 2004.

_____. "Cubs Find 'Choke' Tough Word to Swallow." *Chicago Tribune*, October 3, 2004.

_____. "A Languishing Lineup." *Chicago Tribune*, October 1, 2004.

_____. "Piniella Never Seems to Run Out of Orders." *Chicago Tribune*, July 23, 2007.

Verdi, Bob. "America's Team Clubbed by Clark." *Chicago Tribune*, October 5, 1989.

Ward, Arch. "In the Wake of the News." *Chicago Tribune*, October 11, 1945.

"What Else Can Happen," May 28, 2006, *Chicago Cubs Fun*, http://cubsfun.blogspot.com/2006/05/what-else-can-happen.html (accessed January 18, 2008).

Wolff, Alexander. "Unraveling the Jinx," *SI Online*, http://sportsillustrated.cnn.com/inside_game/alexander_wolff/news/2002/01/15/wolff_viewpoint (accessed January 18, 2008).

"Wrigley Shuns Series to Address Ticket Crisis." *Chicago Tribune*, October 5, 1945.

"Yes, Cub Fans, Fat Lady Does Sing." *Chicago Tribune*, October 10, 1989.

Zolecki, Todd. "Curses! Chicago's Faithful Are Miserable Again." *Philadelphia Inquirer*, October 17, 2003.

Personal Communications

Ali Adabieh

Teresa Casselman

Fr. Michael Englert

Rev. Herman Jayachandra

Lenny Merullo

Andy Pafko

Index

Index

Index

Index

Index

Index

Index

Index